ST MARTIN'S

TRUE CRIME
CLASSICS

OUTSTANDING PRAISE FOR *POISON MIND*

POISON MIND

JEFFREY GOOD &
SUSAN GORECK

St. Martin's Paperbacks

Published by arrangement with William Morrow and Company, Inc.

POISON MIND

Copyright © 1995 by Jeffrey Good and Susan Goreck.

Cover photograph by Don Banks.

Library of Congress Catalog Card Number: 94-44132

ISBN: 0-312-96016-6

Printed in the United States of America

William Morrow and Company hardcover edition published in 1995
St. Martin's Paperbacks edition/November 1996

St. Martin's Paperbacks are published by St. Martin's Press, 175 Fifth Avenue, New York, NY 10010.

10   9   8   7   6

For Laura
and Gary

Authors' Note

This is a work of nonfiction. The people, places, and events are real. There are no composite characters or "imagined" conversations. Much of the dialogue—particularly between the suspect and the undercover cop—is drawn from the transcripts of police tape recordings and edited only for clarity. When conversations had to be reconstructed, we did so with the help of one or more of the people involved. Additional information came from thousands of pages of court files, voluminous police records, and hundreds of hours of interviews.

Although Susan Goreck is both a central character in this book and its co-author, she never is referred to by the personal pronoun "I," except when quoted. While Goreck's insights form the heart of this story, the reader will also hear the voices of many other people who played key roles. One of those voices is that of Goreck's alter ego, Sherry Guin. She was a character created by Susan, a woman who existed for one reason: to catch a killer.

*And I looked, and behold a pale
horse: and his name that sat on
him was Death, and Hell
followed with him.*

REVELATION 6:8

POISON
MIND

BOOK I

Why?

PROLOGUE

The voice came to him in the darkness, as in a dream. George, she said, it's time.

It was one in the morning, but George Edward Trepal didn't mind. A grin tugging at his mouth, he bundled Mabel up and helped her down the four flights of stairs from their apartment to East Forty-sixth Street. This was the hour George and his wife had prayed for, the end to seven years of trying to make a family, of visiting doctor after doctor, of watching their hopes disappear each month in the gray wash of despair. The troubles hadn't ended when Mabel got pregnant. She was carrying twins, but at three months she had suffered a miscarriage. One of the twins was lost, but the other remained in her womb and throve, cells dividing in the darkness, taking human shape. At last, on this morning, the baby would emerge. George and Mabel were to become parents.

It was bitter outside, rainy and raw, and George wasted no time getting his wife to New York Hospital. George, a blunt-nosed New York cop, had been born in the sprawling institution in 1912. His wife, Mabel, a dark-eyed beauty who traced her roots to Light-Horse Harry Lee, was forty-two, four years older than her husband, when she checked in to bear her first and only child.

They arrived at the hospital shortly after 1:00 A.M. Mabel was in labor, the doctor said, but she was not ready to deliver. While she settled in, George went home to get some sleep and wait for a phone call. It came at 10:00 A.M., while the expectant father was shaving. The hospital said, "Get down here immediately."

The doctor was waiting for him. He said, "We ran into trouble."

"What trouble?" George demanded.

"It's this," the doctor said. "It's going to either be the baby or your wife."

"I can't handle a baby by myself," George said. "I want the wife."

The doctor took him upstairs on the elevator. As they wheeled Mabel into the operating room, George leaned over and kissed her. The doors swung shut, and the doctors began the grim task of separating life from death. To save Mabel, they tried to take her baby. "They didn't measure her the right way," George later recalled. "And when Georgie was coming out, his head was just coming out. She wasn't wide enough. And his head slipped, and he went back up. He went up into her guts; he got mixed up in all the intestines. They had a hell of a time."

The doctor took a scalpel and performed an emergency Cesarean section. The operation was a surprising success. The doctor emerged to say, "We saved both of them."

The new father was thrilled. He asked, "Can I see my wife?"

"No," replied the doctor. "You come back at seven tonight, and you can see her."

George returned that evening but found his wife's bed empty. She's probably just in the nursery looking at the baby, he figured. He asked a nurse.

"Nobody's been in that room," the nurse said.

"My wife's supposed to be in there," George said.

The nurse repeated, "*Nobody's* been in there."

George's footsteps echoed down the long corridors until, a city block away, he found Mabel alone in a hallway. She lay unconscious on a gurney. Nobody could tell George how she had gotten there.

Three days later Mabel emerged from the coma to discover that she was the mother of a healthy baby boy. The parents decided to name him George James Trepal. "Georgie" came out weighing eight pounds, fourteen ounces. He was perfect, except for one thing: a deep scratch in his cheek.

Had there been some kind of struggle in the womb, two brothers fighting until, like Cain and Abel, only one survived? No, that would be too farfetched, the stuff of myth, not life. The doctors said that Georgie had probably just scratched himself with his fingernails before birth. Whenever George Trepal sees his son's face, he sees that first scar.

Chapter
ONE

Georgie Trepal grew up and asked his friends to call him George. He moved to a tiny Florida town called Alturas, to a house in the middle of an orange grove, where he didn't have to put up with the city's bleating horns and bright lights. George didn't work, not in the usual way, but his wife was a doctor, and she supported him, sometimes writing him a check for $150. That left him free to write for a computer magazine, care for a tribe of cats, and dream up puzzles for his brainy friends. When he looked out the window, he could see the orange trees and their sweet white blossoms, a lake shaped like a teardrop, and the home of his only neighbors.

In 1988, six years after George moved to Alturas, Peggy Carr and her family settled into the house next door. George and his wife, Diana, did not welcome them. Although George was home many days and could have gotten to know Peggy Carr, they remained strangers. Both sensed, correctly, that they didn't have much in common. While George had been born in the city, Peggy came from an Alabama farm town. While George socialized mostly with a small group of high-IQ friends from Mensa, Peggy loved to gab with just about anyone. While George prided himself on his lack of attachments, Peggy's greatest joy came from pouring herself a cup of coffee and sitting at the kitchen table to ask her husband and children about their days.

Before dawn on October 23, 1988, a bulb flickered on in Peggy's kitchen, throwing light through the window and into the darkened groves outside. Most of the other townspeople could sleep late this morning. After all, it was Sunday, and they had toiled all week in the groves, tending the soil and preparing for the winter harvest. But Peggy couldn't join their leisure. It was 6:00 A.M., time to strap on her apron and head to work.

Peggy's waitressing shift at Nicholas Family Restaurant didn't start until 7:00 A.M., but she wanted to get there early and have a cup of coffee with her favorite customer, Floyd Graham. As she drove south through the darkness, Peggy breathed in the morning air. It smelled good; it always did, the trees spilling their perfume into breezes blowing in from the Atlantic Ocean and Gulf of Mexico. Peggy's car joined the pickup trucks and dusty sedans rolling off Highway 17 and crunching across the diner's parking lot. The farmers and insurance salesmen and retirees began filing in with newspapers tucked under their arms. Before long the breakfast room had become a merry blend of smells, sights, and sounds: frying bacon, clattering plates, and debate over the upcoming presidential election.

Peggy found Floyd at his usual spot, at a table near the kitchen door. Floyd thought that Peggy was very pretty with her blue eyes and petite figure, "kind of daintylike." He also admired Peggy's dedication to her children; it seemed she would do anything for them. On more than one occasion Peggy had excused herself to retreat into the bathroom and mend a tear in her bra; she told Floyd she couldn't afford a new one and still keep the kids clothed and fed. A retired machinist, Floyd was happily married. But that didn't stop him from developing a close friendship with the forty-one-year-old waitress. Peggy turned to Floyd for advice so often that she began calling him "my psychiatrist."

Peggy smooched Floyd on the cheek and joined him as

he ate his standard breakfast, Polish sausage and hot cakes. She didn't eat; she just sipped her coffee and smoked filtered cigarettes. Floyd was a Pall Mall man himself, and he often teased Peggy about those filtered numbers, calling them "Tampax." That line always made Peggy giggle. But this morning Peggy wasn't in a joking mood. Clutching her hand to her chest, she said, "Floyd, I think I'm having a heart attack."

Floyd, who had been a medic in the Army, reached across the table. "Give me your hands, Peg," he said. He looked at her face, then under her fingernails. Her skin was pink, getting plenty of blood. He took her pulse; it was eighty-two, in the normal range. She was breathing twenty-two times a minute, also normal. He told her, "It can't be a heart attack. If I thought it was for a second, I'd take you to the hospital so quick—"

Peggy interrupted Floyd, taking his hand and sliding it down her blouse. He could feel her heart going thump-thump. She said, "There's where it hurts."

It got worse. For the next forty-five minutes Floyd kept checking her vital signs. Still normal. He couldn't figure it out. Rita Tacker, another waitress and Peggy's good friend, came over. "What's wrong?"

"I'm having a heart attack," Peggy said.

Floyd gently took her hand. "No, darling, you're not having a heart attack," he said. "You can't be. Look at your fingernails, nice and pink. You're getting plenty of oxygen."

When 7:00 A.M. rolled around, Peggy pulled herself to her feet and went to work. As Floyd was leaving, she walked over to him. Most times Peggy would say, "See you tomorrow, Floyd." But this day her voice came out flat, almost resigned.

"Good-bye," she said, giving him one last kiss on the cheek. "Thanks for everything."

*   *   *

It wasn't like Peggy to complain about nothing. In her four decades she had cheerfully overcome her share of adversity. She grew up in a house with a single heater, one of five children born to deaf parents. Her first two marriages had collapsed, leaving her to raise three children—Cissy, Allen, and Duane—on a waitress's wage. Recently, though, things had begun looking up: She had married a burly phosphate miner named Pye Carr. She had moved into Pye's Alturas home with her children, her granddaughter, Kacy, and Pye's children, Tammy and Travis.

Peggy's eldest child, Cissy, was also a waitress at Nicholas Family Restaurant. A small woman with blond hair and a heart-shaped mouth, Cissy shared her mother's spunk and easy smile. A few hours after Peggy complained of chest pain, Cissy showed up for the lunch shift. Seeing her mother standing by the coffeepot, Cissy called out, "Hi, Mama!" and walked over to kiss Peggy's cheek. Cissy asked Peggy if she could pick up Cissy's two-year-old daughter, Kacy, after work.

Peggy agreed, but Cissy could hear the reluctance in her voice. Peggy told Cissy she wasn't feeling well. "My hands," Peggy said, rubbing them together. "They just feel so numb." Cissy reached out and touched her mother's fingers; they were freezing. And that wasn't all, Peggy said. "My legs are just hurting so bad."

"Sit down and rest," Cissy said, pointing her mother toward a table the waitresses used for coffee breaks. As Peggy eased herself down into a chair, Cissy thought, What could be wrong with Mama? She's never sick.

She gently touched her mother's cheek. "Go home and get some rest," she said. "If you lay down, Kacy will lay down with you and take a nap."

When Peggy got home to Alturas, the house was empty. Her new husband, Pye, was still off on a weekend hunting trip. When he returned home a few hours later, Peggy greeted him weakly from the sofa. Instead of calling the doctor, Pye thought of his sister, Carolyn Dixon. A nurse with a round face and gentle hands, Carolyn doubled as her family's personal walk-in clinic. As darkness fell that Sunday afternoon, the phone rang in Carolyn's house. "Will you come over?" Pye asked. "Bring your blood pressure cuff and see what you think."

Pye's real name was Parearlyn, but Carolyn and everyone else had been calling him Pye as long as anyone could remember. Carolyn lived less than a mile away, just across the teardrop lake, and she said she'd be right over. Just as Floyd Graham had earlier, Carolyn checked Peggy's vital signs: blood pressure, pulse, respiration. Peggy's blood pressure was up a little, but nothing Carolyn thought was abnormal.

Peggy kept getting worse. When Cissy came by after work that night, around nine, she found her mother lying on her side in bed with the covers pulled up around her. The blood had drained from her face, leaving her skin chalky and cold. Her lips were parched and cracked. She couldn't open her eyes; they seemed paralyzed.

Cissy walked up to the bed. "Mama?"

Normally Peggy would have asked about Cissy's day and given her firstborn child a squeeze. But Peggy didn't seem to recognize Cissy, and her voice had shrunk to a whisper. "You don't know how bad it hurts," Peggy said. "Do you hear what I'm saying? I'm just hurting."

The bathroom was right next to the bed, but Peggy's legs had grown so weak that Cissy had to help her to the toilet. Peggy's eyes clouded with confusion. "Please, just help me get rid of the pain," she begged. Cissy helped Peggy back to bed, where she collapsed, exhausted from the journey of a few feet. Cissy walked into the kitchen, where Pye sat at the table, sipping a vodka and orange juice and paying bills.

"Pye, are you going to take her to the hospital?" Cissy demanded, her soft voice brittle with worry. "She needs to go."

Pye looked up. "No," he said. "She's just got the virus or something."

Cissy went back into the master bedroom and kissed her mother good night. Peggy's eyes remained closed, and she didn't say a word. Cissy walked back to the kitchen and repeated her plea. "I really think she needs to go to the hospital," she told Pye. "I'll take her to the hospital."

"No," Pye said, growing annoyed. "She says she doesn't want to go to the hospital."

Cissy stormed out the door and down the hill to the garage apartment, where she lived with Kacy. A half hour later, around 11:30 P.M., Pye knocked on her door. "I'm fixing to take your mom to the hospital," he said. "Do you want to go?"

It was still warm that night; winter's chill hadn't yet settled in. As Pye carried Peggy out to her truck in her nightshirt and slippers, Cissy loaded Kacy into her car. Kacy called her grandmother MeMe. Cissy told the child, "We're going to the hospital, because MeMe is sick."

The two cars set out in the night, driving toward the closest hospital, in the nearby city of Bartow. Pye carried Peggy into the emergency room, where a doctor took her pulse, listened to her breathing, and shone a light into her eyes. Peggy told him, "I feel like I'm on fire."

Three days later Peggy was still in Bartow Memorial Hospital, but the doctors couldn't offer a diagnosis. Peggy bristled when one of the physicians suggested her problem was psychosomatic. When the doctor touched her arm, arrows of pain shot from skin to bone. She said, "This is real."

But then, just as suddenly as she had fallen ill, Peggy felt better. Cissy rejoiced in the sight of her mother sitting up in bed, drinking coffee, even complaining about the hospital food. When an orderly delivered a plate holding a hamburger steak and sweet potato patty, Peggy wrinkled her nose, saying. "Ooh! What kind of *shit* is that?"

"Mama, be nice!" scolded Cissy. But she had to smile; Mama was getting back to her tart-tongued self. Maybe Pye was right; maybe it *was* just a flu bug.

The doctors sent Peggy home, but any improvement in her condition quickly vanished. As Peggy got worse, the mysterious illness began hitting other members of the family. Duane, Peggy's younger son, and Travis, Pye's son, started to complain about feeling ill. The boys, both teenagers who had recently dropped out of high school, looked healthy, their skin tanned from hours spent painting outside, their muscles chiseled from weights and shooting baskets with their friends. But they voiced the same complaints as Peggy: tingling fingers and toes, upset stomachs, and strange feelings of burning from the inside out.

The day after Peggy came home from the hospital, Carolyn brought some fried chicken for dinner. In one corner of the kitchen, sitting on the floor, she found a carton containing sixteen-ounce bottles of Coca-Cola. She opened up a bottle and poured it into glasses for Peggy, Travis, and Duane. If it was a flu bug, she reasoned, it would be important to keep the fluids coming. Some of the soda overflowed as she poured it, and Travis teased her. "Aunt Carolyn," he said, "you do that every time!"

The next morning Cissy walked into her mother's bedroom and whispered, "Mama?" Peggy's eyelids fluttered slightly, but she said nothing.

Duane and Travis weren't as sick as Peggy, but they felt pretty ragged. They figured it was just a killer hangover, a souvenir of their Friday night drinking binge by Star Lake. "Man, you got toasted!" Duane said to his stepbrother. But Travis thought it was something else, something that made his feet throb in time with his heart. As Travis complained, Duane felt his own feet begin to tingle.

I'm not going to let it affect me, Duane told himself. Thinking the problem might be "dead circulation," he pulled on his sneakers and jogged to the center of town and back. He took off his shoes and rubbed his feet. They looked normal, but they felt awful, as if a giant pair of pliers were clamped down on them, piercing his flesh with a thousand needles.

* * *

Physically Cissy felt fine. But emotionally she was crumbling. During a break at the restaurant she confided in Peggy's waitress friend Rita Tacker that she thought Pye was poisoning Peggy with his sister's help. "They're killing her," she said. "I know they are."

"God, Cissy, I don't know," Rita said. "That bastard better not be doing nothing to her." The more Rita thought about it, though, the more she came to believe that Cissy might be right about Pye. After what Peggy had been through with him, Rita wouldn't be surprised if he would try to kill his wife.

At seven-thirty that evening the restaurant phone rang. It was Pye, calling for Cissy. "They've come and got your mom in the ambulance," he said. "You need to go to the hospital."

TWO

———

"Doctor, what's wrong with me?" Peggy said. "I'm in terrible pain."

Looking up from her bed, she saw a man in a white coat with thinning hair and a dimpled chin. While other physicians had been unable to identify her ailment, Dr. T. Richard Hostler, the neurologist on call at Winter Haven Hospital that day, had a hunch.

Hostler spoke in tones that were precise and clinical but not unkind. "We're going to do something about this pain," Hostler told her. "But first I need some idea of what is making you hurt."

He held down Peggy's tongue with a wooden tongue depressor and peered into her throat. Shining a penlight into her eyes, he asked her to look from side to side. He told Peggy to try to hold her eyes closed while he tried to pry them open. Most healthy adults have no problem keeping their eyes shut; Hostler easily opened Peggy's. He asked her to wrinkle her forehead; she could not.

Hostler recorded his first impressions of Peggy in the chart: An acutely ill-appearing woman; awake, alert, able to cooperate with me but unable to maintain her eyelids open; displayed weakness in both sides of her face; ulcerations within the mouth covered by a whitish plaque; an exquisite sensitivity to touch.

Hostler, the thirty-eight-year-old father of three, specialized in disorders of the nervous system. While many medical students look at neurology as a subject to be endured and then left behind, Hostler welcomed its complex challenges. To diagnose problems in the millions of tiny branches of the human nervous system, he had to pay attention not only to scientific data but also to his instincts. He liked to say that the neurologist is the detective of the medical world.

Many of Hostler's patients were able to give him some idea what was wrong with them, but Peggy could not. "My feet feel like they're on fire," she said, her voice slurred by weakened muscles. "It feels like I walked on a bed of burning coals."

Peggy's husband, Pye Carr, took Hostler aside. "There's something I think you should know," he told the doctor. "My son and stepson are also getting sick. They're not as bad as Peggy, but they're heading that way." To Hostler, that was a "tremendous piece of information." It told him that Peggy and the boys were likely suffering from a common infection or perhaps a poison. He began peppering Pye with questions: Had the house been sprayed recently for bugs? Had anyone been sick in another way? Pye said no, at least not that he knew of.

Hostler worried that the teenagers might also need medical care, and soon. He said to Pye, "You'd better have the boys brought in today."

As Pye headed off down the hallway, Dr. Hostler went off to sit at a desk behind the nurses' station. After dictating orders for some routine tests, he pondered Peggy's condition. Peggy said it felt as if she had burned her feet on hot coals, but there was no sign of external burns. More than likely, he reasoned, she was suffering from a malady affecting the peripheral nerves. Hostler envisioned the nervous system as a tree. The spinal cord is the trunk, the arms and legs are its roots, and the peripheral nerves its branches and twigs. In Peggy's case, the "branches and twigs" scattered from her feet to her face seemed to be under attack.

But from what?

Dr. Robert VanHook, an infectious disease specialist, walked by the door. Hostler hailed him down. "Bob, come on in here," he said. "I've a patient I'd like you to look at."

After briefly summarizing the case, Hostler said he suspected that Peggy had been poisoned by some sort of heavy metal. He told VanHook he was going to have Peggy's body tested for the most common of those poisons: lead, arsenic, and mercury. Harking back to something he had read in a medical textbook, Hostler said he was also going to order an extra test, one for a rarer poison—a poison that would make a patient feel as if she were burning to death.

"I think it's thallium," Hostler said.

"Isn't that extremely unlikely?" VanHook said.

"Yes," said Hostler. "Thallium should not be on the shelf in anybody's home these days. It's very unlikely that that's what it is. But doggone it, it fits better than anything else."

As Hostler did his detective work, a phone rang in northern Alabama, where Peggy had grown up. Peggy's older sister, Shirley, answered the call. A woman with big green eyes and three earrings in each ear, Shirley was a professional truck driver who thought nothing of a long drive. After learning that her sister was in the hospital, she borrowed some traveling money from a brother and drove through the night to Florida.

The sight of Peggy stole Shirley's breath. She had never seen Peggy sick in bed with the flu, let alone like this. Always vibrant and on the go, Peggy lay tangled in a web of tubes and wires and blinking machines. Someone had tied her hands down to keep her from pulling the tubes out of her nose and throat. A nurse explained that Peggy couldn't open her eyes.

Shirley took a few moments to compose herself. She had

to see, really *see*, that this was Peggy. Struggling for control, she stepped over to her sister's side.

Her voice came out in a squeak. "Peggy?"

Peggy turned her head a little at the sound. But she couldn't speak. Shirley saw Peggy's hands flutter. She realized that Peggy was reaching back into their childhood, using her hands to replace the voice she had lost.

Peggy, Shirley, and their three brothers had grown up in an Alabama farm community called Macedonia Blackwater. Both their parents were deaf, but all five children had been blessed with hearing. Peggy's father made cedar furniture, taking home thirty-eight dollars a week. If he had business in town, he took Shirley or Peggy with him as an interpreter. Lying in that hospital bed decades later, Peggy used sign language to answer her sister's questions.

"Do you know who this is?" Shirley asked.

"Y-E-S."

Shirley rubbed her sister's cheeks, so cold they felt like they had been packed in ice.

"Peggy, how are you feeling?"

Peggy's hands moved again.

"I H-U-R-T."

Dr. VanHook looked in on Peggy and confirmed his colleague's impression that she wasn't suffering from an infection. He noticed something else: clumps of hair falling onto Peggy's pillow, a telltale sign of thallium poisoning.

The doctors knew they didn't have much time. When Hostler first examined Peggy on a Monday morning, she was in pain but otherwise stable. By evening she lay in the intensive care unit, too weak to breathe for herself. A sample of Peggy's urine was rushed to an Atlanta laboratory for testing. Soon the results came back. Hostler's hunch was right: Peggy had thallium in her system—so much poison that it ran right off the lab's scales.

"Bob, I think she was poisoned," Hostler said to his colleague. "I think it's a criminal act."

Until this point, more than a week after Peggy first told Floyd Graham that she was having a heart attack, Hostler had not considered the possibility of foul play. But now he knew the police should be involved. The more he thought about it, the more sense it made. Thallium was odorless and tasteless, and it dissolved easily in food or drink. Lethal in a dose the size of a few aspirin tablets, it wouldn't show up on the standard tests for heavy-metal poisoning. It was a perfect murder weapon.

From his studies Hostler knew thallium was a naturally occurring chemical, a member of the aluminum family, and one of the ninety-two elements found in nature. The human body can tolerate tiny amounts, and for a time the chemical was thought to have therapeutic value. After thallium was discovered in 1861, doctors used it to treat syphilis, gonorrhea, gout, dysentery, tuberculosis, even ringworm. But doctors soon learned that the metal's toxic side effects outweighed its benefits. Once inside the body, thallium masquerades as potassium, an element the body needs to turn oxygen and nutrients into energy. Potassium helps nerves and muscles to thrive; its evil twin, thallium, causes them to atrophy and die. Victims typically begin by experiencing burning sensations in their limbs, upset stomachs, and hair loss. In severe cases the symptoms progress to tremors, delirium, paralysis, coma, and death.

Word of thallium's deadly side had spread outside the scientific community. In the late 1950s thallium was the poison of choice for European murderers and was used more often than arsenic. By the 1960s, a century after its discovery, it was used mostly as a pesticide, to kill ground squirrels, prairie dogs, ants, cockroaches, and, most commonly, rats. Because of its risk to humans, the United States Environmental Protection Agency outlawed widespread use of the chemical in 1972. Its use continued in some areas—nuclear medicine, chemistry labs, and factories manufacturing camera lenses and fireworks—but only under tight restrictions. When Peggy Carr got sick in 1988, thallium poisoning was almost unheard of in the United States.

Since thallium is a naturally occurring element, Hostler knew, people who don't work with it can be expected to have a trace in their bodies. The lab tests showed Peggy's urine contained twenty thousand times that amount. Even when compared with people who work with thallium, Peggy had fifty times the maximum human exposure. Travis and Duane also tested positive for thallium, at levels as high as twenty times the maximum industrial exposure. Hostler hoped he would be able to save the boys, but he feared Peggy had consumed far more than her body would be able to flush out. He began searching the medical literature for an antidote, but he was not optimistic.

Walking into the ICU, Hostler found Pye in his usual spot, pacing outside Peggy's room. A big man with beefy hands and a bristly crew cut, Pye looked haggard and worn. He had been spending most of his time at the hospital, sitting with Peggy and the boys.

Hostler got right to the point. "Pye, my suspicions have been confirmed," the doctor said. "Your wife has been poisoned with thallium."

"You mean to imply that someone tried to kill her?" Pye said.

"It would appear from what we now know that someone tried to poison your entire family," Hostler said. "Somehow you were spared."

For several long moments, Pye said nothing. Finally he spoke. "Doctor," he said, "I don't think anyone dislikes us enough to do that."

Peggy got worse. The nausea, hair loss, and burning sensations were only the mildest symptoms. The branches of Peggy's nervous system were steadily wasting away. Already she could not open her eyes or breathe on her own; it wasn't long before she had lost nearly all muscular control.

Shortly after she arrived, Shirley communicated with her sister for the last time. As they visited that morning, Pye came in. Shirley asked if he wanted to be left alone with Peggy.

"No, it's okay," Pye told her.

Pye leaned over his wife and took her hand. He asked, "Peggy, do you know why you're in here?"

Peggy's hands moved.

"N-O."

"Peggy," Pye said. "You've been poisoned."

Peggy's fingers flew. "W-H-Y?"

"I don't know," Pye said. "But we'll get to the bottom of this."

Peggy's hand made the same sign over and over. Her fist clenched, her thumb and index finger waved back and forth in a small agony of motion.

W-H-Y?

W-H-Y?

W-H-Y?

Chapter
THREE
___

Detective Ernie Mincey looked fondly at the cigarette burning between his fingers. He raised it to his lips and drew the smoke into the deepest recesses of his lungs before turning back to the mountain of paper on his desk. There were parts of his job that he loved: learning about a mysterious death, squeezing information out of sources, bringing a killer to justice. But filling out all these damn reports . . .

"Got a phone call," said a deputy, poking his head in Ernie's door at the Polk County Sheriff's Office. Ernie looked up, but just for a moment. He said, "Give it to a supervisor."

Just like his old days in the Army, he thought, exhaling a luxurious cloud. Following the chain of command. Can't hardly take a phone message without the brass signing off. A few minutes later Ernie's boss came in with the note in his hand. A woman was in Winter Haven Hospital, deathly ill. Her teenage son and stepson were also in the hospital, getting sicker by the hour. The doctor thought they had been poisoned with some kind of rare chemical. "I don't know what it is," the captain said. "Take care of it."

For all its neon boulevards, shiny speedboats, and condo canyons, Florida remains a frontier, a place where old meets new, sometimes with violent results. Two federal highways, Interstates 75 and 95, drop into Florida like giant arteries. Each winter northerners—the locals call them snowbirds—jam the highways, moving through the state like a giant blood clot. Children frolic on sandy beaches, grandmothers stroll beneath the palms with Noxzema-spiced skin, and fathers reach into their pockets to pay for yet another inflatable alligator.

Most visitors arrive with pale faces and fat wallets, then leave, after a week or two, sunburned and spent. Some practice a more sinister tourism. After Ted Bundy had passed through, two sorority sisters and a twelve-year-old schoolgirl were dead. While Aileen Wuornos roamed the roads, middle-aged men began turning up as corpses. Before Danny Harold Rolling left Gainesville one August, five college students had started school and then lost their lives. The murders here are so plentiful, and so peculiar, that the tabloid newspapers rarely have to stray far from their Florida headquarters for a juicy headline.

Situated in the geographic heart of Florida, Polk County—"Imperial Polk," as the county fathers like to call it—seems far from all that. Although millions of tourists drive through each year, many regard it as an annoyance, an empty stare between Disney and the beach. The traveler who pulls off the highway long enough to look finds a refreshingly different side of Florida. There are no ocean beaches, but the land swells into hills braided with orange groves, cattle ranches, and wood-frame houses. Resort hotels don't illuminate the night sky, but phosphate plants do, castles of green light that tower like eerie cities of Oz. There are signs of growing prosperity: shopping malls, sprawling houses, traffic jams in the small but booming cities. But for the most part life proceeds peacefully. Unlike their Miami brethren, Polk's residents generally look upon one another as neighbors rather than as potential assailants.

But in Polk County, as elsewhere, people get to disliking one another. Dislike leads to angry words, and words to fists, knives, or gunshots. The phone starts ringing on Ernie's desk.

In appearance and manner Ernie is a sort of country Columbo. Years of staring at bodies in the blazing sun have leathered his face beyond its thirty-nine years. Thousands of cigarettes have turned his fingertips yellow. When Ernie questions suspects, the words trickle out in a gravelly drawl and a billow of smoke. Some criminals might mistake Ernie's slow ways for a slow mind, but they would be mistaken.

Three days after Dr. Hostler had first examined Peggy, Ernie walked into Winter Haven Hospital and met Dr. Hostler. The doctor told him Peggy was in intensive care and fading fast. The detective said, "I need to talk to her."

Walking into Peggy's room, Ernie saw a tiny woman surrounded by whirring machines. She lay on her back, clumps of frosted brown hair scattered on her pillow, the light bouncing off patches of bare scalp. Tubes dangled from Peggy's arms and nose, and a machine slowly breathed for her. Peggy's eyes were open, but her gaze was blank. This woman wasn't going to be talking to him, Ernie realized. But a nurse told him that Peggy had a sister who could communicate with sign language.

In the intensive care waiting room he walked up to Peggy's sister and showed her his badge. "I'd like to ask Peggy some questions," he said to Shirley. "Would you mind going in there with me to tell me what she says?"

Shirley nodded. "No, I don't mind at all."

They walked to Peggy's side, where Shirley passed along Ernie's questions.

"What happened to you?"

"Do you know how you got poisoned?"

"Do you know if anybody did this to you?"

Nothing. The only response Peggy gave was to squeeze Shirley's hand. Finally Shirley shrugged her shoulders and looked at the detective with sad eyes. "I just can't communicate with her. She's past that."

"Maybe we can try again later," Ernie said. "Let's go outside; I need to talk to you."

At this point Ernie didn't share Dr. Hostler's certainty that the poisoning was intentional. It was possible, Ernie reasoned, that some pesticide had seeped into the family's water well and poured out the tap. Environmental officials had begun testing the water and the other foods and beverages the family might have consumed. If it was a murder attempt, Ernie wanted to look first for suspects within the family. In particular he wanted to know about Pye Carr. Was it just coincidence that he was out of town when the rest of his family was poisoned?

As they talked, Shirley raised a question of her own. She asked, "What about that threatening letter?"

Ernie stared at her. "*What* threatening letter?"

Four months before the poisoning, an envelope had arrived in the mail. It was addressed to "PIE CARR, 2690 Alturas Road, Bartow, Florida." Inside was a small piece of yellow paper bearing an unsigned typed message: "YOU AND ALL YOUR SO CALLED FAMILY HAVE TWO WEEKS TO MOVE OUT OF FLORIDA FOREVER OR ELSE YOU ALL DIE. THIS IS NO JOKE."

Sitting around the table that day, the family had passed around the letter and discussed it. They knew, *everyone* knew, that Pye's name wasn't spelled P-I-E. Had the letter been sent by someone who didn't know Pye? Or was this somebody's sick idea of a joke?

After a while the kids began to think the letter really was nothing. They started laughing about it. Duane turned to his mother and said, "You'd better start packing, Mom." Peggy, usually the first to see the bright side, did not laugh. She just sat there, clutching her granddaughter in her lap. She told Duane and Travis to stop riding their motorcycles on other people's property and to watch their mouths. "I want you to stay close to the house," she said. "Be nice to people. This could be real."

After learning about the death threat, Ernie walked into room 163, looking for Travis and Duane. A big man blocked the detective's way. He introduced himself as Pye Carr. After Ernie showed his badge, Pye's face softened. "I'm glad you're here," he said. "Anything that I can do to help you, I will."

Ernie looked past Pye to see two teenage boys lying in their beds, elbows and knees poking out of hospital gowns. Ernie walked up to Travis. "What are you feeling?" Travis complained that he ached when anything, even bed sheets, touched his skin. Travis said, "My body's on fire."

Duane echoed his stepbrother's complaints, and both boys said they had no idea how they had gotten sick. One day, they said, they had been outside painting the garage. The next, they were hurting. The boys did give Ernie a lead: They remembered seeing a man on a red Massey Ferguson tractor spraying the grove west of their house. It smelled like some kind of pesticide.

As he listened to the boys talk, Ernie was struck by how unusual this case was. The only poisonings he had ever dealt with were crude suicides, some desperate soul gulping down a bottle of drain cleaner. Most of the other victims he'd seen had been subjected to obvious violence: shotgun blasts, stab wounds, crushed skulls. In all those cases the victims' lives were over. Ernie never saw them as living, breathing, laughing human beings. This case was different. Ernie could picture these boys grinning and tossing basketballs through a hoop. Thallium had reduced them to pale ghosts.

Ernie took Pye into the hallway. "Pye," he said, "did you get a threatening letter in the mail?"

"Oh," he said. "I forgot about it."

"Where is this letter?" Ernie demanded.

"I think it's at the house."

"I certainly need it."

After Pye had promised to dig up the letter, Ernie asked him for some background on the family. Pye told the detective that he and Peggy had married seven months earlier and that he had returned from a hunting trip in South Carolina to find her and the boys sick. He said he didn't know why someone would want to poison his family. The only recent trouble he could recall was the neighbor complaining that the Carr family teenagers were playing their radios too loudly.

Ernie was more interested in Pye than his neighbors. If this is a criminal act, this man probably did the crime, Ernie thought. He found Pye's demeanor "somewhat questionable." Despite Pye's offer to help, he seemed gruff and emotionally flat. And why hadn't he told police about the letter? I just can't believe that anybody could get a threatening note and not remember to tell me when his family's in the hospital, Ernie thought. There was one possibility, of course, Ernie said to himself. He might have mailed the note himself.

But then the detective thought about Pye's son, Travis. He thought about how Pye had blocked the door like a bear, protecting Travis and his stepbrother. Mincey, who had two children of his own, wondered, How could a man poison his own son?

Peggy's older son, Allen, didn't learn that his family was sick until they had been in the hospital several days. Allen was stationed at a U.S. Navy base in Tennessee, where he was learning to disable bombs, rappel from helicopters, and create electrical circuits. The last time he had heard from his mother was three weeks before she got sick, when she telephoned to say she wanted to come visit him. Peggy wouldn't say why. She would only say, "I just need to talk to you. I'm getting tied up around here, having some problems."

But Peggy never went, and Allen never got to talk to her

again. When Cissy called, Allen caught the first plane down and rushed to the hospital with his sister. She took him to see his brother first.

Allen took a deep breath, but he couldn't have prepared himself for the shock of seeing Duane. His brother had melted away, and his blond hair was falling out by the handful. Duane looked up and saw his brother standing there, all smooth creases and sharp angles. For a moment they just stared at each other, the soldier and the shadow.

Allen had promised himself to be strong, but he couldn't blink back the tears. He said, "Who did this to you?"

"I have no idea," Duane said. "I guess that death threat wasn't a joke."

A nurse came in and whispered in Cissy's ear. "We gotta go," Cissy said to Allen. "We're going up to see Mama."

As they walked down the hall, Allen's heels clicked out an anxious rhythm. "I can't believe that this all happened so fast," he said to his sister.

"This has been building for a while," Cissy told him. "Mom's been sick for a few days."

"Nobody called me," Allen said.

"Pye wouldn't let us call you," Cissy said.

The double doors swung open, and Peggy's two children walked into the ICU. Everything about the place assaulted their senses. The refrigerated air stung their skin. The beeping machines echoed in their ears. And the light. It reminded Allen, who was training to be a Navy diver, of the way light transforms things underwater, washing over the edges of familiar objects, turning them soft and blurry, suddenly foreign.

Allen felt the nurses' eyes follow him as he walked behind Cissy. Cissy pulled open the curtains, and there Peggy was. The nurses had strapped belts over his mother's waist and legs, to keep her from pulling out her tubes. But seeing that they had left her hands free, Allen went over and pressed her fingers into his.

Peggy was conscious, and her hands began to move.

"W-H-E-R-E A-M I?"

Allen knew sign language, and he tried to respond.

"I A-M H-E-R-E."

But Peggy didn't seem to understand. She kept grimacing, tossing her head back and forth, searching for comfort but finding none.

"W-H-E-R-E A-M I?"

Allen stared at his mother's face, once so beautiful; the nurses had put a bonnet over her balding scalp and smeared Vaseline around her eyes. He looked at her hands; they had turned pale and bony, stripped of the rings and bracelets that usually tinkled in time with her laughter. Beneath her white skin Allen could see the blue veins, pumping poisoned blood back to her heart.

Allen held his mother's hand to his, making one last sign.

"I L-O-V-E Y-O-U."

The next day a nurse gathered the family. They inched forward in their seats, their weary eyes a blend of hope and fear. Had Peggy sat up in her bed and demanded a cigarette? Had the doctors found an antidote for the thallium? Would they be able to take Peggy home?

"She's slipping into a mild coma," the nurse said. "We don't know how long this is going to be."

She said it was no use for the family to wait around the intensive care unit anymore. She gave them a code number to use when they called the hospital. Cissy, Allen, Shirley, and the others called again and again. Every time they got the same answer: "Nothing's changed."

Chapter
FOUR

———

Detective Mincey headed out Highway 60, turning right at the Circle K convenience store. The ribbon of asphalt unrolled under his wheels, carrying him between the lakes and orange groves, and up the hill to Alturas. As he pulled into the driveway, Pye walked up. He seemed impatient, as if he expected Ernie to have already cracked the case.

"I want to know what happened," Pye said. "I want you to find out what happened."

Good God, I don't have a crystal ball, Ernie thought. I'm as confused as this man is. But Ernie didn't tell Pye that. Instead he delivered the standard line: "We're going to do our best."

As Pye began showing him around the house, Ernie reflected on how strange it was to be conducting an investigation in Alturas. Alturas isn't a city. Technically it isn't even a town, just a sprinkling of houses built around a lake, one school, a general store, and no stoplight for miles. The same handful of farm families that settled the town in the early part of the century still make up the core of the population. Even as they heard about rising murder rates in the big cities, Alturas residents had felt comfortable leaving their doors unlocked or at least not double-bolted—until now.

Ernie knew residents were horrified by the poisoning.

Although environmental officials were still testing the water well and fields around the Carrs' home for signs of accidental poisoning, Ernie was growing more convinced that this was an attempted murder. After learning that thallium had been banned since 1972, he decided the odds were slim that it would just turn up in a water well or orange grove. The odds were even slimmer that the Carrs would be the only family poisoned. The people living right next door, George Trepal and his wife, Diana Carr (no relation to Peggy and Pye), had been drinking water from the same well yet showed no signs of illness.

Pye showed him the kitchen where Peggy had brewed her last pot of coffee, the bedroom where she had lain ill, the doors through which an intruder might have entered. Ernie didn't see any obvious evidence: There was no screwdriver mark on the doorframe, no forgotten bottle of poison, no muddy footprint. But the detective wasn't there just to look for physical evidence. Ernie also needed to understand the *psychology* of the act. He wanted to get inside the poisoner's head, to walk where the poisoner had walked.

The investigation moved into its second week, and Peggy showed no sign of emerging from her coma. Ernie got some help from another homicide detective, Paul Schaill. While Ernie was slight of build, Schaill was a broad-shouldered former high school football star. While Ernie tended to dress like an unmade bed, Schaill wore spiffy clothes and a gold watch. Despite their different appearances, the two men worked well together. They had to; at that time, they were the department's only two homicide detectives.

As Schaill was familiarizing himself with the case, Ernie called with a tip. He heard that right before the poisoning, Peggy Carr had spent the night in the Tropical Motel, a squat one-story place not far from Alturas. Schaill said he'd find out why. Walking into the motel office, Schaill saw the manager watching TV in back and tucking away a chicken dinner. Schaill rang the bell, identified himself as a homicide detective, and asked if Peggy Carr had been a guest.

Yes, the manager said, Peggy and her children had stayed in a room for one night. The manager remembered something odd about Peggy. She had paid for her room with one-dollar bills.

That detail struck Schaill. Why was Peggy so desperate to take her kids and stay in a cheap motel a few miles from home? Maybe, Schaill thought, it was because she could no longer bear to be with her husband, Pye.

Schaill's hunch about the trouble between Peggy and Pye was confirmed by a note that Ernie came across on a visit to the house. Peggy had written it right before checking into the Tropical Motel.

DEAR PYE,

I do love you very very much. Right now I'm at the point that I don't really know how you feel. I told you I could handle anything as long as I had you! Now I'm not sure!

I'm going to give you some time to think about us . . . I can't live like we have been. No respect from the kids, not talking, not caring.

I love you & want to be your wife. Key word is wife!

I don't know if this is right or not, what I'm doing, but I don't know what else to do!

I can't imagine living without you but I can if you don't want me!

There's no question in my mind whether or not I want you & love you! Is there a question in your mind?

I'll be OK if anyone is interested.

I love you with All My Heart!

PEGGY

Schaill and Ernie went to the cafeteria at Winter Haven Hospital, looking for Peggy's daughter, Cissy, and her waitress friend Rita Tacker. The two women were sitting at a table, drinking coffee. They confirmed that Pye and Peggy had been having some trouble; the tensions had come to a head right before Peggy and the boys got sick. Cissy said, "She was telling me how she thought that she needed to get away because she wasn't sure if her and Pye was going to make it."

In their talk with detectives and in later interviews for this book, Cissy and Rita recalled that Pye and Peggy had started out very much in love. When they joined hands, Peggy and Pye had also joined families, each bringing teenage children to the home. Before long the kids were acting like brothers and sisters, splashing in the pool, riding motorcycles in the grove, and washing their cars in the driveway. At first Pye and Peggy seemed like teenagers themselves, moon-eyed with their new love. But six months into the marriage things had begun to sour.

Cissy remembered the night Pye had called from the mine to say he would be late. It wasn't the first time. Peggy and Pye had planned to have dinner that night with Pye's sister, Carolyn, and her husband. But Pye hadn't given a good reason for canceling, just "I have to work late." Cissy suggested driving out to Pye's mine, and her mother agreed. Rounding the corner in Cissy's black Mustang, they saw Pye's office nestled in among the huge phosphate machines. If Pye was really working late, they expected to see workers scurrying back and forth amid the clack and hum of machinery. But the mine was quiet and dark, and there was only one other car parked beside Pye's. Peggy told her daughter, "Well, I guess I know what's going on now."

Then the kids began fighting. Pye's daughter, Tammy, accused Duane of stealing a friend's stereo speakers. Once Peggy had built a fragile truce, she collapsed into a chair and began sobbing. She said to Cissy, "I don't know if I can handle it anymore."

"Mama, why don't you go off for a couple of days?" Cissy said. So Peggy did; that was when she took Duane and Cissy and Kacy to the Tropical Motel. But a few days later Peggy and Pye reconciled. Peggy moved back home, and the sparkle returned to her eyes. Peggy went to work and told Rita, "My sweetie's gone. He went hunting."

That weekend she was poisoned.

After talking to Cissy and Rita, Schaill and Ernie visited the hospital room where Duane and Travis lay with baseball caps on their balding heads. As they were questioning the boys, Larry Dubberly walked in. Larry, Duane's father and Peggy's ex-husband, told the police that he suspected Pye.

"I believe that he and his sister, Carolyn, have something to do with this," Larry told the detectives. Just the other day, Larry said, Pye was "trembling all over" after Ernie had questioned him about the poisoning. "Yes, sir," Larry said. "He was so nervous he couldn't even talk."

There was something else, Larry said. The other night he had heard a commotion in the boys' hospital room. He ran in and saw that Pye and Carolyn were visiting. But instead of welcoming his father and aunt, Travis was screaming hysterically.

"Larry, help me. They're trying to kill me!" Larry recalled Travis's shouting. "And Carolyn told him, she said, 'Son, we're not trying to do a thing in the world but help you.' "

Larry said he worried about the food Carolyn and other family members had been bringing into the hospital for the boys. "If someone has done something like this, I'm afraid they'll get back in that room and do it again," he said. "Finish what they started."

Larry said, "Peggy told me that Pye had insurance on her, Duane, and Travis."

"Did she tell you how much?" Ernie asked.

"Eighty thousand dollars on her and sixty thousand dollars apiece on the boys," Larry replied.

The other day, Larry continued, family members had been discussing the poison thallium. When someone said it might come from phosphate mines, Pye's ex-wife, Margaret, turned to Pye and said, "You've been working at Silver City Mines all these years. They've got two chemist labs out there. Do y'all have any of that shit out there? Do you know anything about this?"

According to Larry, Pye turned toward his ex-wife and said, "You shut your goddamn mouth."

Some of what the detectives learned seemed to support the suspicions about Pye. A health department official called to say that thallium, packaged in small tins as rat poison, was still used in Germany. Meanwhile, a worker at Pye's mine had come across some mysterious pesticide in a tin covered with German letters and adorned with a skull and crossbones. Schaill sent the tin off for analysis. If it contained thallium, it could explain where Pye would have obtained a poison banned for nearly two decades.

Then a woman called police with a tip. According to her, Pye had once dated a junior high school teacher. Barely a month after he married Peggy, Pye had called the teacher to say that "he had made a bad mistake" and wanted to start seeing her again.

Not everyone was convinced of Pye's guilt.

The Reverend Bob Grant, the minister who had married Pye and Peggy, never considered Pye a suspect. Neither did Dr. Hostler. Both men were at the hospital almost every day. And almost every day they saw Pye sitting at Peggy's side, holding her hand, talking to his comatose wife. "You never know," Pye told Reverend Grant. "Maybe she can hear."

The weeks went by. Hostler told family members he couldn't do much for Peggy except see if she came out of the coma on her own. While Duane seemed to be improving, Travis was getting worse, losing control of his muscles and needing a respirator to breathe. Despite an intensive search of the medical literature, Hostler had found no antidote for thallium. The boys would just have to wait until the poison had run its course.

The doctors' pessimism weighed heavily on the entire family, including Pye. But that didn't keep Cissy from hammering at him. Grant saw Cissy standing in the hospital waiting room, right outside the ward where her mother lay, pointing at Pye. Grant heard her tell one relative, "He just wants to hurry up and kill her."

Grant's heart ached for Pye. He took Cissy aside. "Cissy," he said, "you know better than that deep down, don't you?" But she wouldn't respond; she didn't seem to want to hear anything good about Pye. Like many victims of crime, she was frustrated and angry. She needed someone to blame.

Later Pye took the minister aside. Pye said police had just told him that he was the prime suspect. Although the news surprised him, Grant tried to downplay it. "Isn't that normal?" he asked Pye. "Anytime that something happens to one, the first one they think of is the mate."

"Yeah," Pye said. "I guess so."

But Grant could see Pye's shoulders sag. Pye wasn't the type to feel sorry for himself, but Grant could see that the accusations had doubled Pye's load of hurt. Grant leaned up against the hospital wall and looked his friend in the eye. "You know, Pye, I don't believe it," he said. "Nothing would make me believe it. If you told me right here today that you had done it, I wouldn't believe you."

The strongest argument for Pye's innocence came from the laboratory. Because Pye had been out of town and seemed healthy, the detectives had assumed that he hadn't consumed any of the thallium. But then Schaill got a call from the state health lab. Tests on urine samples collected from the family showed that Peggy, Duane, and Travis weren't the only ones with thallium in their systems. Cissy and two-year-old Kacy also had been poisoned. Although neither mother nor daughter had displayed signs of sickness, the tests showed the baby had toxic levels of the poison in her system.

The tests showed that one other family member had ingested the poison: Pye. He had enough in his system to make a smaller man very sick, although in Pye's large frame it had produced only some minor aches. The only family member who didn't have any thallium in her system was Pye's daughter, Tammy.

Schaill took off his glasses and chewed on them. What does this mean? he wondered. Is Pye off the hook since he somehow consumed thallium? Or could he have absorbed it through his skin while he was poisoning the family? And what about Pye's daughter, Tammy? Why didn't she have any thallium in her system? She could have poisoned her family—but why?

If this wasn't the perfect crime, it came close. Police had found no bottle of poison, no telltale fingerprints, no real clues. As November wore on, Peggy and her sons remained hospitalized, and the police were left with no solid suspects. They didn't even know where the thallium had come from.

With every new lab report, the list of potential thallium sources grew shorter. Tests showed the poison hadn't come from the water supply, from the tractor Travis and Duane had seen, or from the tin of rat poison found at Pye's mine.

Schaill met Pye at his house to make one more sweep for possible evidence. Seeing some broken glass on the kitchen floor, Schaill crouched down and looked under the counter. There, behind the trash can, he saw the carton of Cokes Carolyn had found when Peggy and the boys first got sick. Some of the bottles were empty, others full, and one bottle had been broken at the neck. Schaill grabbed the empty bottles, leaving the unopened ones behind. Time for one last shipment to the lab.

FIVE

"POISONING LEAVES PAIR CRITICALLY ILL."

For the first few weeks of the investigation the detectives had worked without the press looking over their shoulders. But they knew a case like this wouldn't go unnoticed for long. Nearly a month after Peggy first got ill, the Tampa *Tribune* alerted its readers:

> Health officials are tracking a month-old trail to discover how three members of an Alturas family were poisoned.
>
> A mother and her stepson were in critical condition Monday night in Winter Haven Hospital, said Tony Edwards, spokesman for the state Department of Health and Rehabilitative Services.
>
> Investigators have determined the pair and one other family member were poisoned by thallium sulfate, but they have not determined how the family came in contact with the chemical, which is clear, odorless and tasteless, said Lynne Breidenbach, Polk County Sheriff's Office spokeswoman.
>
> Peggy Carr, 41, and her stepson, Travis Carr, 16, were on respirators at the Winter Haven Hospital intensive care unit Monday.... Carr's son, Duane Dubberly, 17, also was hospitalized.

George Trepal, who lives next door to the family, said he and his wife had been using water from the Carrs' well to wash with for several days because their water pump was broken. Trepal said he and his wife were drinking bottled water, however, because HRS had told them not to drink the water from the Carrs' well.

"Nobody knows how they got sick, so it's kind of hard to take precautions when you don't know what it is," said Trepal's wife, Diana.

As the investigation moved into its fourth week, Ernie lost his partner. Officials at the sheriff's office learned that Schaill's ex-wife, Wilma, had once had a date with Pye Carr. While Schaill said the date was "no big deal," his supervisors worried that Schaill's personal connection might compromise the investigation. They pulled him off the case.

Ernie did not share Schaill's strong suspicions about Pye. Now that he was working solo, Ernie decided to investigate some others who had surfaced as possible suspects: Carolyn Dixon, a nurse who some said was jealous of her brother's affection for Peggy; Pye's daughter, Tammy, who had been the only family member not to ingest thallium; and the next-door neighbors, George Trepal and Diana Carr. Just before the poisoning Peggy and Diana had gotten into a fight over the Carr teenagers' playing their radios too loudly. Rita Tacker said that "the neighbor lady" had "threatened to whip the shit" out of Peggy.

Loud radios didn't sound like much of a motive for murder, but Ernie knew he needed to explore it. As leads in this case went, it was about as good as any other. Diana was an orthopedic surgeon; Ernie knew that thallium was sometimes used in hospital tests.

Ernie had a hard time reaching the neighbors. George never seemed to be home, and Ernie didn't know where he worked. Ernie found Diana at her office. As she discussed the poisoning of her neighbors, her voice was bright, even cheerful. She said she never socialized with the neighbors, that they were not "her type of people." She acknowledged arguing with Peggy about the Carr boys' playing their radios loudly but said the fight didn't amount to much more than a neighborly spat. She said she never used thallium in her orthopedic practice, although she had read about the chemical in an Agatha Christie mystery, *The Pale Horse.*

Months after his first meeting with Diana, Ernie realized that her words should have left more of an impression. But he still wasn't prepared to see loud radios as a motive for trying to kill an entire family. His talk with Diana, Ernie thought at the time, was a "nothing interview."

Ernie drove back to his office, which was, by any standard, a dump. Outside, a few bolts held together sheets of blue corrugated steel. Inside, the detectives labored amid fake wood paneling, cheap gray carpet, and two air conditioners that seldom won their battle against the Florida heat. Ernie and his colleagues dubbed their quarters the lawn mower shed.

After interviewing Diana, Ernie settled at a desk decorated with an overflowing ashtray and a picture of his wife, Patty. Someone told him Carolyn Dixon was in the lobby. Dressed in a white nurse's uniform, Carolyn walked in with eyes swollen and red from crying. She was clutching her purse as if it were a life preserver.

They had barely sat down when Carolyn blurted out: "Am I the suspect?"

Ernie kept his voice neutral. He asked, "Why do you think that?"

Carolyn told him that Cissy was telling people she suspected Carolyn and Pye of poisoning her mother.

"Yes," Ernie said gently. "She told me the same thing."

Ernie hadn't ruled out Carolyn as a suspect; at this point he couldn't afford to rule out anyone completely. But he told Carolyn that he wasn't jumping to the same conclusion as Cissy. He told her, "I need your help to find out what's going on."

Carolyn loosened the grip on her purse and recalled how she had cared for Peggy and the boys when they got sick. Thinking it was some sort of bug, she said, she had rubbed their aching feet and given them Cokes to replenish their fluids. She said that Pye and Peggy had been having some trouble before the poisoning, but "the problems were of the normal type caused by the marriage of two single parents who have teenage children." Although Peggy had left Pye for a few days "to get her thoughts together," Carolyn said the two were very much in love.

Ernie wasn't just gathering information; he was watching for signs of a guilty conscience. As Carolyn told the story of Peggy's last hours at home, she pulled a tissue out of her purse and dabbed at her eyes. Her reactions seemed appropriate: sorrow, anger, and bewilderment.

Carolyn seemed more hurt than angry by Cissy's suspicions about her. By the end of his meeting with Carolyn, Ernie had moved her to the bottom of his ever-shortening list of suspects. Carolyn didn't seem to have the guile to plan a sinister poisoning and then sit by her victims' side, pouring them Cokes. It just didn't fit.

The next day Ernie's K-car bumped down the road to Pye's office at the Silver City Mine.

One thing still weighed against Pye: two-hundred-thousand-dollar life insurance policies he supposedly had taken out on Peggy and the boys. In Ernie's view, that would be "more than enough motive to kill somebody." It might even persuade someone to swallow a little thallium himself. And what if Peggy had been right about Pye's seeing another woman? What if he had wanted to kill his wife, collect the cash, and run off with his mistress? Maybe he had messed up, poisoning the rest of the family by accident.

So far background checks hadn't turned up any evidence

of the rumored insurance policies. But Ernie wanted to confront Pye on the issue, to see if he would confess to having them hidden somewhere.

Pye invited Ernie into his office, closing his door to shut out the phosphate dust and the rattle of machinery. When Ernie asked about the insurance, Pye didn't blink. He told Ernie that he had a fifty-thousand-dollar policy on himself and one thousand dollars for Travis and Tammy.

"Did you take out two hundred thousand dollars on Peggy and her kids?" Ernie asked.

Pye looked the detective in the eye. No, Pye said, he hadn't taken any policies. Not for two hundred thousand dollars, not for two dollars.

Chapter
SIX

"Call Dr. Coppenger ASAP."

Ernie looked at the note handed to him by a secretary. George W. Coppenger was the head chemist at the state lab checking for the source of thallium in the Carr family home. The lab had tested more than four hundred items—from rat poison to ice cubes to homemade pickles—but had so far not discovered the poison source.

Ernie picked up the phone and dialed the lab. "Dr. Coppenger," he said, "I hope you've got good news for me."

"I've got great news for you," Coppenger said. "We found the thallium." He explained that lab technicians had detected the poison in a thin layer of sludge at the bottom of each of the four Coke bottles police had found under the kitchen sink. If the same concentration of thallium had been found throughout the soda when the bottles were full, Coppenger said, the amount of poison "would easily be staggering."

Ernie's mind raced. Five weeks after Peggy and her sons had been admitted to the hospital, Ernie finally knew where the poison had come from. But the more daunting task—discovering who had tainted the Cokes—remained. The detective made a mental checklist: He needed to secure those bottles, check them for fingerprints, and make sure someone didn't break one. And he seemed to remember there were some other Cokes, unopened ones, back in the kitchen. He would need to get those, too. Ernie thanked Coppenger and hung up. There was no longer any doubt: The thallium had not got in those bottles by accident. Ernie was investigating a murder plot.

Ernie learned about the thallium at 4:45 P.M. on December 2, the night of the annual sheriff's Christmas party. Everyone was leaving early to go home and get dressed for the event. Ernie had tickets, and he and his wife had been looking forward to it. But they wouldn't be going now. Ernie walked across the hall to the office of his sergeant, Roy McGuirt. Ernie said, "We've got a break."

After briefing his boss, Ernie went back to his office to try to reach Pye. He found him just before 6:00 P.M. in a familiar spot, the hospital waiting room. He told Pye the news and asked about the bottles of Coke left in the kitchen.

"They're still there," Pye said, "as far as I know."

Ernie said, "I need you to meet me at the house immediately."

Winter was coming, and as Ernie stood in the driveway, waiting for Pye to open the door, his breath came out in impatient swirls of steam.

"How could this thallium get in these four bottles?" Pye asked Ernie as he unlocked the door. "I don't understand it."

Ernie didn't have time for a discussion just then. Striding into the house, he said, "Where are these other bottles?"

Pye led him into the kitchen and pointed to a corner where two cabinets met. A garbage can sat beneath them. Pye said, "They're behind this garbage."

Ernie peered into the darkness under the cabinets and saw the Coke carton with three full bottles. "Fine," Ernie said. "We're going to wait until our crime scene technician gets here." Before moving the bottles, Ernie wanted to get photos of where they had been left. Laurie Ward, the crime scene technician, arrived with a camera and clear plastic evidence bags to hold the bottles. Ward was seven months pregnant, and Ernie warned her that the Cokes might contain a deadly poison that could seep through her skin. That was all she needed to hear. "There's no way in this world I'm collecting those bottles," she said. "No way I'm touching that carton."

"Okay," Ernie said with a gentle laugh. "You don't have to do it. Just take some photographs." He held out his hand. "But you're going to have to give me some gloves so I can collect these bottles. Give me at least two for each hand."

After depositing the bottles in bags, Ernie turned to Pye. "Do you know where these Cokes came from?"

Pye said he did not, although he did remember seeing the eight-pack. When Peggy first got sick, he had mixed himself a whiskey and Coke. Pye said it was Peggy who bought most of the family's groceries, including soft drinks. He said she normally shopped at the Family Market grocery store, sometimes stopping at the Alturas Circle K convenience store for small items.

Then Pye handed Ernie a document containing a list of thallium suppliers. What was Pye doing with this? Ernie wondered. Since being banned, thallium was used in only a handful of American industries; Pye's industry, phosphate mining, wasn't one of them. Pye explained that he hadn't been getting enough information about the poison from police or health officials. So, he said, he had done some research of his own.

"You don't seem to know anything about it," Pye told Ernie. "I'll give you this copy if you want it."

"Sure, let me have it," Ernie said. Once again Pye had raised suspicion about himself. As police officers moved through Pye's house, collecting evidence in the soft evening light, Ernie watched Pye closely. Would he fidget when police gathered the bottles? Would anxiety creep into his voice as Ernie asked him questions?

The answer, at least from Ernie's perspective, was no. As police worked, Pye stood to the side, arms folded across his chest, face blank. The same old gruff, inscrutable Pye Carr.

Ernie drove back to headquarters, where he and his boss started working the phones. They had a deputy drive by Coca-Cola's local bottling plant, now closed for the night, to get the emergency phone number listed on the door. If the Carr family had purchased poisoned Cokes, perhaps other customers had, too. Somewhere there might be other families suffering from strange burnings in their feet, fretting over the clumps of hair falling from their heads, wondering why their doctors, couldn't identify the problem. Ernie thought of the 1982 Tylenol poisoning case in Chicago.

I don't want people dying, Ernie thought. What if some mad person at the bottler decided to throw this stuff in a vat of Cokes? You'd have mass murder.

As the night wore on, the brass poured in, most dressed in their party best. Lieutenant Juanita Crawford arrived in high heels, Captain Ray Church in suit and tie. Ernie, still dressed in the work outfit he had been wearing for sixteen hours, lit another cigarette and briefed them.

Ernie telephoned the FBI lab in Washington, D.C., to see if he could ship the full Coke bottles there for analysis. The FBI said it could accept the bottles the next morning. Ernie looked at his watch. It was midnight, and he wouldn't be going home anytime soon.

All night Ernie and his colleagues studied the familiar Coke bottles for a clue to the deadly secret they might contain. But they saw nothing unusual: no scratch marks on a bottle cap, no fingerprints on the glass, no swirls of sinister color in the beverage itself. Ernie loaded the bottles into cartons, cradling them in popcorn packing material for the trip north. Ernie was treating the bottles as if they were bombs. He thought, If these break, I die.

Early Saturday morning Ernie carried the Cokes onto a jet and took off for Washington, D.C. He had never been to the FBI lab before, but he figured it was always open, staffed by experts in white lab coats who toiled around the clock to solve tough cases. He anticipated being greeted at the door by a chemist eager to examine the bottles and share his insight.

A taxi took Ernie to the J. Edgar Hoover Building on Pennsylvania Avenue, just down from the White House. The guards were expecting Ernie, and they waved him through. Once Ernie was inside, though, he found no chemists working in lab coats. There was just a lone agent sitting at a desk, watching a football game.

The agent said he could accept the bottles, but nothing more. "There's nobody here to do what you need," he said. "It'll be Monday."

"Wait a minute," Ernie said, his voice rising. "I want to make sure you understand how serious a problem I've got here. We could have mass deaths over this stuff. Do you have somebody that you could please call for me?"

The agent said he'd see what he could do.

Ernie flew home. The next day, Sunday, the Tampa *Tribune* reported that Duane Dubberly had gotten out of the hospital: "Duane Dubberly, 17, who had been moved two weeks ago from the intensive care unit to a regular room, was discharged Friday, a nursing supervisor said Saturday. She said Dubberly's mother, Peggy Carr, 41, remained in the intensive care unit in critical condition. Carr's stepson, Travis Carr, 16, was in guarded condition Saturday in intensive care."

Ernie went into the office. At 11:00 A.M., FBI Agent Tom Forgas called him from Washington. Forgas had good news: The lab had begun analyzing the Coke bottles.

All day a Coca-Cola executive named Frank Hynes kept

leaving messages for Ernie. The detective wadded the message slips and threw them in the trash. He had more important things to worry about than Coke's corporate headquarters. Night fell, and the switchboard operator called Ernie.

"He's called again," the operator said. "Can we patch him through so we can get rid of him? He's calling here every ten minutes."

"I've had enough of this shit," Ernie muttered. "This guy must have an ego bigger than God. Patch him through."

The voice came over the phone. "This is Frank Hynes. I'm director of security of Coca-Cola. We're getting reports that one of our products was used, or empty bottles were used, in a thallium poisoning case."

"That's correct," Ernie said.

"What can you tell me about it?" Hynes said.

Ernie wasn't about to start spilling his case to a voice on the phone. What if Hynes wasn't who he said he was? What if he leaked vital information to the press? What if Coke had something to hide? His voice frosty, Ernie refused to discuss the case.

"Detective," Hynes said, "we're not intending to interfere with your investigation whatsoever. We're coming down tomorrow morning, two of us. We'd like to offer our assistance."

"I can't tell you, Frank, not to come down," Ernie said. "But I want to tell you right now, if you do come down, you'd better be awfully certain that you do not interfere with my investigation. Because I will put you in jail."

Hynes, still polite, thanked Ernie for his time and repeated his pledge to stay out of the way. When Ernie hung up, he didn't expect to see Hynes or anyone else from Coke the next morning. If he hadn't alienated Hynes, it wasn't for lack of trying.

The next morning, promptly at eight-thirty, Hynes and

another Coke official, L. G. Cunningham, walked through Ernie's door.

The news of the poisoned Cokes spread quickly.

"Polk County detectives are one step closer now to solving the mysterious poisoning of forty-one-year-old Peggy Carr and two others in her family," the TV anchors reported. "Our top story tonight: The bizarre thallium poisoning case turns its attention to eight bottles of Coca-Cola. Investigators discovered traces of the highly toxic chemical in bottles at the Carr family home."

Polk County Sheriff's Office spokeswoman Lynne Breidenbach appeared on the screen. "We don't know if it was put into the bottles of soft drink during processing or after processing," she said. "So that is an important question."

A reporter continued. "A question that may be answered tomorrow, when the investigation moves to the Coca-Cola bottling plant in Tampa. Using lot numbers, Coke executives traced the tainted bottles to this plant. The Coke was bottled here more than six weeks ago. Already a Coke spokesman from Atlanta is telling consumers to remain calm, saying your Coke at home is safe to drink."

Five days after the Cokes had been identified as the poison source, Ernie and a team of other officials visited the Tampa bottling plant. So far there had been no reports of anyone besides the Carr family getting sick. But if officials found evidence of contamination at the plant, they would consider a recall of all the sixteen-ounce Cokes sold in Florida.

The poison Cokes had come from a batch of 262,000 bottles. Ernie and health officials watched the bottling process: Empty bottles came off trucks and dropped onto a conveyer belt. They were washed, filled with Coke, and capped. The entire process was done by machine, with human hands standing by only to fix problems in the mechanical assembly line.

Ernie paid particular attention to what happened to the bottles after they were filled. Once each bottle was capped, it joined a jiggling river of bottles, each constantly changing position, playing tag. Ernie and other officials concluded that short of a massive conspiracy, it would have been impossible to send eight tainted bottles onto that assembly line and direct them all into the same carton.

"Two hundred sixty-two thousand [bottles of Coke]. And only eight of them have thallium in them?" Ernie said. "I wouldn't play that on the lottery."

The next day's newspaper headline reported: COKE PLANT UNLIKELY POISON SITE—POLK, FEDERAL INVESTIGATORS FIND TAMPERING MUST HAVE OCCURRED AFTERWARD.

Two days later, on December 9, FBI lab technicians reported that each of the full bottles of Coke contained "significant levels of thallium"—between one-half and one gram. One gram, a dose the size of four aspirin, can kill a full-size adult. Children and smaller adults, such as the 105-pound Peggy Carr, could succumb to a smaller amount.

FBI chemist James Gerhart told Ernie that further testing would be needed to identify the precise form of thallium used in the Cokes. Gerhart said that chemists would start by testing for thallium sulfate. Since that form had been used as a pesticide, it would be the most common type. If that test was negative, chemists would check for other, more exotic forms.

FBI experts had found signs of tampering on the bottles. While the Coke inside didn't seem discolored, testing showed it had lost some of its carbonation. And when lab workers put the bottle caps under a powerful microscope, they found tiny diagonal scratch marks. FBI Agent James Cadigan, a specialist in criminal tools, said the poisoner could have used any of a number of tools: a pocket can opener, a home bottling machine, even a screwdriver. Cadigan told Ernie that the tampering was impossible to see with the naked eye. The poisoner had worked with a steady hand and great care, Cadigan said. This was no amateur.

Chapter
SEVEN

Here we go again, Ernie thought. Another FBI agent who thinks he knows it all.

Like many local detectives, Ernie didn't have much use for federal agents, their starched shirts, advanced degrees, and high tech investigative methods. Although Polk County was a mostly rural place, its sheriff's office was large and modern, with three hundred deputies working around the clock. Ernie was one of the best of them, and he didn't want outside help. But in this case Ernie didn't have much choice. With the discovery of thallium in the Coke bottles, the poisoning might involve violations of federal product tampering law. As the federal police force the FBI automatically got involved.

Ernie's new partner was Brad Brekke, a lanky thirty-two-year-old who had recently joined the FBI after getting a master's degree in church history and graduating from law school. Brad enjoyed studying the criminal mind, and he had followed the Alturas poisoning with fascination. Whoever had targeted the Carr family had been clever enough to pick a poison, thallium, that wouldn't change the color or taste of Coke; sophisticated enough to know that thallium doesn't show up on normal lab tests; skilled enough to pry the caps off sixteen-ounce bottles and replace them without leaving obvious clues.

That technical skill paled beside the coldness of heart that would lead someone to poison a mother, her sons, even her two-year-old granddaughter. You have to be almost emotionless to poison a family, Brad thought. He wondered, Was the poisoner so angry that he needed to see a family die? Or was the poisoner even more frightening: someone who plotted painful deaths for the pure thrill, a modern-day Mengele?

It didn't take Brad long to win over Mincey. The young G-man listened carefully, didn't interrupt with silly notions, and came up with solid ideas. The two made a curiously well-matched team. Mincey, grizzled and slow-talking, played the country cop. Lighting one cigarette after another, he'd ask most of the questions when they interviewed a witness or potential suspect. Brad, whose Nordic features and dry humor reminded some of the actor Kevin Bacon, would hang back as Ernie got things started, then watch for nonverbal clues, the glance or twitch that signals guilty knowledge. Brad paid especially close attention to the feet. While many guilty people make a conscious effort to control their hands and facial expressions during an interrogation, Brad knew, most didn't think to stop their feet from shifting anxiously beneath the table.

Ernie told Brad that he had pretty much ruled out family members as suspects. But he began introducing Brad to them to see if he had a different impression. Pye Carr stopped by the office one day to answer a few questions and, unbeknownst to Pye, gave Brad a chance to size him up.

Emotionally he's pretty flat, the FBI agent thought. But Brad didn't hold that against Pye. In his experience people who had been through severe traumas often seemed drained and numb. Also, holding his feelings close might simply be Pye's way. With his slow voice and sun-leathered skin, Pye reminded Brad of his grandfather, a Minnesota farmer who had rarely shown emotion. Brad watched Pye light a cigarette. Watching Pye's thick fingers work, Brad found it hard to imagine them delicately prying off a bottle cap and injecting poison inside.

Two days later Brad and Ernie interviewed Pye Carr's daughter, Tammy. As the only family member without thallium in her system, Tammy was a logical suspect. There was just one problem: She had no motive.

A teenager with bleached hair and thick makeup, trying to look older than her eighteen years, Tammy walked into Ernie's office. She didn't hesitate when asked why she hadn't drunk any of the thallium-laced Coke. "I had started a very strict diet," she said. "I was drinking mainly Diet Pepsi and unsweet tea." Listening to her, Brad heard no trace of deceit. Watching her, he saw no guilty movements. Her feet stayed perfectly still.

In mid-December Peggy Carr was still in a coma and the investigation stalled. Having ruled out family members, Ernie and his new partner knew they had to focus on outsiders who would have had the motive, opportunity, and skill to kill the Carr family. Trouble was, they had no idea who they might be. At Brad's suggestion, they sought the help of another FBI agent, Bill Hagmaier.

Hagmaier worked in the FBI's Behavioral Science Unit, a group made famous by the book and movie *The Silence of the Lambs*. In their efforts to solve some of the world's most violent crimes, Hagmaier and his colleagues tried to comprehend the incomprehensible. They tried to see through a killer's eyes.

When Brad called, Hagmaier was sitting at a desk piled high with paper and anchored by a jar of Atomic Fireballs. His eyes swam with fatigue. He needed a vacation, but there was no time. Ted Bundy was about to be executed in Florida's electric chair, and Hagmaier was using the final days to squeeze out as much information as he could from the serial killer. Authorities still weren't sure how many women Bundy had murdered; Hagmaier was working to extract a confession before Bundy met his end. Hagmaier was based at the FBI Academy in Virginia, but he was scheduled to leave soon for a marathon session of interviews at Florida State Prison.

"Bill, this is Brad down in Florida," said the voice on the phone. "I was wondering if you might be able to help us out on a case."

Hagmaier didn't really have enough time for this. But then he could never bring himself to say no. Leaning back in his chair, he said, "Tell me about your case."

As Brad recapped the investigation, Hagmaier felt a rush of curiosity. Of the roughly eight thousand cases he and his colleagues had studied, only eight had involved poisoning. Most poisonings, Hagmaier knew, were either suicides or crude murders by family members. It was rare for a sophisticated killer to choose poison as a weapon. And he had never come across a case where the killer had chosen a poison as unusual as thallium.

Hagmaier began by making sure the Florida investigators hadn't overlooked the obvious suspects, the ones close to home. He asked Brad about domestic tensions, jealousies within the house, insurance policies. Brad told him that none of those angles had panned out. And while some family members had reason for resentment, Brad said, none of them had the technical skill needed for this crime.

There was something else unique about the case, Brad said. The poisoner had targeted not only adults but also children, including a two-year-old girl. To Hagmaier that was a key point. Even the most violent criminals—be they murderous family members, serial killers, or Mafia hit men—spare the children. Whoever had poisoned the Carrs must have been extraordinarily angry, he said, or extraordinarily cold. Few killers are so indiscriminate.

That was the problem, Brad said; police hadn't found any reason to justify that kind of hatred toward Peggy or her family. Pye and Peggy had been having a fight. Two of their children had been through divorces. Peggy and a

neighbor had gotten into an argument over the teenagers'
loud radios. But those were ordinary tensions, the stuff of
everyday life. And they had the predictable results: harsh
words, some hard feelings. But they just didn't seem to
provide a motive for murder, particularly one this carefully
planned, this diabolical.

This poisoner may not fit the ordinary molds, Hagmaier
said. Psychopaths rarely do.

The FBI Academy rises from the rural landscape of Quantico, Virginia, like a mountain range of brown brick and
tinted glass. With its busy classrooms, vast lobbies, and
lawns shaded by lush oaks and shimmering magnolias, the
academy could be a college campus. In a way it is. By
offering lessons in the latest law enforcement techniques to
crime fighters from around the world, Quantico has become
the police officers' Harvard.

Six stories below the ground, working in a web of windowless offices, are the men and women of Behavioral Science. Police agencies from around the world bring them
their toughest cases, cruel crimes without obvious suspects.
By sifting through the available evidence, the experts provide a profile that describes—often with uncanny accu-
racy—a suspect's likely age, race, sex, personality,
lifestyle, behavior before and after the crime, even taste in
cars. Once the suspect has been identified, the unit can then
help police build their case.

When Peggy Carr was poisoned, Bill Hagmaier was one
of the unit's young stars. The oldest of six children, Hagmaier grew up in a blue-collar Pittsburgh neighborhood,
where he learned to use his fists early. After watching
friends and relatives get into serious trouble, though, Hagmaier decided he wanted something different. He served as
an MP in the Army, got a psychology degree at Slippery
Rock University, and put his name on the FBI's waiting
list. At last he got the job.

With a fresh face and gentle voice, Hagmaier could pass

for the high school guidance counselor he once was. But his eyes tell the truth; they are dark and knowing, drained of innocence. His knowledge didn't come just from reading books and case files. Under the direction of the unit chief, Roger Depue, Hagmaier and his colleagues pioneered a system for identifying the common features of the world's ghastliest crimes. The profilers logged hundreds of hours inside prison walls, listening to criminals tell why they committed their heinous crimes—and how they almost got away with them.

The walls of Hagmaier's office were lined with mementos from his biggest cases: cracking the largest cash robbery in U.S. history, hunting a judge-stalking bomber, and, most memorable, getting Ted Bundy to share his secrets. Not long after Brad's phone call, Hagmaier was to add a new photo to his collection, one showing Hagmaier and Bundy sitting together in a guarded room, looking up like two old friends caught in the middle of a reunion. The caption: "Final confession—Theodore Robert Bundy."

Hagmaier's career was filled with successes. But another wall of his office held his "Reality Board," a bulletin board stocked with the debris of disappointment: a poster offering seventy-five thousand dollars for the return of a missing coed, photos of still-missing children, cases Hagmaier had sweated over but never solved. As he worked on perfecting his skills, those young faces reminded him how much there was to learn.

The most important item in Hagmaier's office had nothing to do with murder, and everything to do with life. It was a drawing of a garden made by Hagmaier's children, Colt and Ashley. Just as the unrelenting bleakness of his caseload seemed to be closing in, Hagmaier would look at his family's garden, at the tomatoes and flowers growing in the sun and rain, and feel restored. On the drawing, in a child's script, his son Colt had written a passage entitled, "Why My Dad's the Best."

*He is very nice to everyone. That's why he has so manny
freinds. He is my Dad and I love him. And he doesn't wont
us to get hert.*

With Brad scribbling notes at the other end of the telephone, Hagmaier began building his profile of the person
who had poisoned Peggy Carr and her children.

Hagmaier told Brad they were dealing with a formidable
person. Not a stupid person. Not a naive person. Not a
person who simply uncorked a bottle and poured in some
Drāno. More than likely, he told Brad, the Carr family's
attacker shared the characteristics of other poisoners the
FBI had studied: an intelligent, educated white man in his
mid-thirties who liked to resolve conflicts without direct
confrontation.

Poisoning is considered a "feminine" crime, Hagmaier
said. Historically, he explained, poisoners have been
women or men with personalities that are, at least out-
wardly, passive. Like people who plant bombs and then
flee, they take pleasure in watching death from a distance.
It's so much cleaner, so much *smarter* than firing a gun or
raising a knife. "Most of your bombers and most of your
poisoners perceive themselves to be intellectual giants because their method of approach, their method of killing, is
very difficult to detect or trace," he said.

The suspect chose a murder weapon that was hard to
identify, slow-acting, and hideously deadly—a chemical
time bomb. The poisoner probably thought, These people
are going to kill themselves, and they are going to get rid
of the evidence for me, Hagmaier said. Because thallium
acts so slowly, the family could well have drunk the Cokes
and then thrown away the bottles and caps before they got
sick. It was only luck that some of the bottles remained in
the kitchen for the police to find.

Coke was the perfect vehicle for carrying poison, Hagmaier said. "Nobody tied anybody up and forced it down
their throat. It's not like there was a bottle of champagne

put on their front door with a ribbon around it saying 'Welcome to the neighborhood.' '' What could be more ordinary, more *American,* than a bottle of Coke? Most families have it in their homes, he said, and few would suspect foul play if an extra carton showed up in the kitchen.

It was also significant that the poisoner chose an *eight-pack* of Coke, Hagmaier said. That showed he or she was looking not only for revenge but also for an intellectual thrill. It would have been so much easier to poison one of the two-liter plastic bottles Peggy generally bought for her family—just unscrew the plastic cap and pour in the thallium—but the eight-pack was a greater challenge because each bottle had its own cap made of precisely crimped metal. With eight caps, there were eight chances to leave a scratch or dent that could arouse suspicion.

The Carr family poisoner was likely what profilers call "organized," Hagmaier said. Like Bundy, he or she had probably read about murder, watched violent films, then fantasized about committing a murder. When it came time to turn fantasy into reality, the poisoner carefully and methodically carried out his plan, patiently experimenting to find the type of thallium that wouldn't alter the taste and look of Coke, studying the victims' house to find an opportune time, carefully removing and replacing the bottle caps, wiping away fingerprints and other evidence, and finally delighting in the sight of police officers locked in a fruitless search for clues.

However, Hagmaier said, there was one key difference between the Carr family poisoner and most organized killers: cowardice. Serial murderers see the consequences of their actions, Hagmaier explained. Bundy killed pretty young women with his hands and then dumped their bodies in the woods. He listened to their cries, saw them gasp for breath, felt their bodies go still in his hands. A poisoner would never get so close.

"Poisoners are unique," Hagmaier said. "It's an extremely nonconfrontational crime. If I want to poison you, okay, I can do it and I don't even have to be there when you die. I can achieve my purpose without watching you suffer. My intestinal fortitude may be not that I can come up and beat you up, or shoot you, or cut your throat, okay? But I want to eliminate you, and I don't care who else dies. It's a very cowardly act," he said. "It's passive assassination."

But don't get the idea that catching a poisoner will be easy, Hagmaier warned. Part of the assailant's planning most likely included a careful study of police investigative techniques. That works against police because the obvious clues have been wiped away. But one characteristic may work in your favor, Hagmaier told Brad. Poisoners often leave a trail of threats.

"Were there any anonymous phone calls, any written warnings, anything like that?" As a matter of fact, Brad said, the family had received a letter four months before the poisoning. Hagmaier urged him to look closely at that note, to try to find its author.

One more thing, Hagmaier said: Look hard at the neighbors. Whoever poisoned the Carrs knew enough about the family's comings and goings to plant the poison Cokes and then leave without being seen. Other than family members, there wouldn't be many people who fitted that description. "What does the neighborhood look like?" Hagmaier asked. "Who can see the house?"

EIGHT

On December 22, two months after Peggy got sick, Ernie and Brad drove to Alturas. The road rose through the lakes and orange groves, carrying the investigators around a bend to a place where the hill falls away from the sky. A place where Peggy Carr lived and was happy. A place where someone had decided she should die.

The detectives had scheduled an interview with Cissy's ex-husband, and they decided to drive by the Carr house en route. They knew nobody would be home. Pye had changed the locks and moved in with his sister; Peggy's children were staying with other relatives; Peggy and Travis still lay hospitalized. But Ernie and Brad wanted to drive by just the same. "It's a cop thing," they said later, an impulse to return again and again to the scene until the crime is solved.

As they pulled up, they saw Diana Carr's husband standing outside his garage, holding a piece of freshly sawed wood.

"Hey," Ernie said to Brad, "there's George."

Hagmaier, the FBI profiler, had asked about the neighbors. Outside of family members, Ernie and Brad knew, George Trepal and Diana Carr would have had the best opportunity to poison Peggy and her family. But the detectives still didn't consider them strong suspects. Neither met the most important test: *motive*. Who would kill over loud radios?

As the investigation wore on, more and more people wanted to talk about that last fight between Peggy and Diana. It had happened a day or two before Peggy first got sick, while Pye was off on his hunting trip. Duane was helping Travis wash his red Ford Ranger truck. The boys had driven through muddy fields the day before and were scraping off the grime and polishing the truck in anticipation of a big night out with their buddies.

It was a sunny day, really hot. The boys had parked the truck under a big shade tree and turned on the hose. Both were bare-chested, wearing only baggy shorts and sunglasses. They turned on the truck stereo, and music boomed out the windows, the bass notes shaking the ground beneath them. Peggy was in the kitchen, washing dishes. She kept lifting the kitchen window, sticking her head out, and shouting, "Turn that down!" So they did—until Peggy shut the window again. Then the boys smiled at each other and reached for the volume. *Pump it up.*

After a while Duane saw Diana Carr heading their way. She had always seemed pleasant, if somewhat aloof, but this time Duane thought she looked "hateful." She was waving her finger and yelling, "Turn that damn music down!"

Duane tried to head off disaster. "I'm sorry," he said. "Please don't go tell Mom. We'll turn it down."

"No." Diana said. "I want to speak to your mother, right now."

Peggy emerged from the house, wiping her hands on an apron and forcing a smile. But Diana was not in the mood for pleasantries. She said, "You need to tell these damn kids of yours to turn their music down!"

"Well, I told them one time," Peggy said. She smiled again, adding with a shrug, "Kids will be kids."

"I don't give a damn," Diana replied. "I'm going to call the law."

Diana was waving her finger at Peggy now, pressing her face close. Menacing. Peggy's smile faded, and she finally lost her cool. She yelled, "You leave my kids alone! They're teenage boys. Boys will be boys. I've told them to turn it down. You just get the hell out of my yard before *I* call the police."

"Well, I'm going to call the police on *you*," Diana replied. "I don't like some of the stuff going on around here."

Duane and Travis were sitting on the truck's tailgate, eating it up. They laughed and cheered Peggy on. Peggy turned to them and yelled, "Y'all shut the hell up!" Although Peggy did her best to act angry, Duane could see the smile playing at the corners of her mouth, as if to say, "Can you believe this?"

But then Peggy turned a serious face back to Diana. She had heard enough. She yelled, "Shut up and get out of my yard!"

Storming off, Diana called out, "You aren't going to get away with it!"

Brad hadn't had a chance to meet Diana yet, but Ernie didn't consider her a strong suspect. After all, the FBI profiler had said that poisoners shy from direct confrontation. That description certainly didn't seem to fit Diana. Ernie knew less about George. He was a white man and looked to be in his late thirties; that much fitted the FBI profile. But neither Brad nor Ernie could imagine a motive; they hadn't heard about any trouble between him and the Carr family. Then again, they hadn't had a chance to talk to him; every time the investigators were in Alturas, it seemed, George was somewhere else.

Today was different. Brad pulled into the driveway of the home George and Diana shared. It was an old wood-frame place, perched on the hillside next to Peggy's place.

In fact, it was the only other house in sight; beyond their yards the groves spread out in all directions. As he got closer, Brad could see the white paint peeling from the clapboards, the yard overgrown with weeds, and a few brave flowers straggling up from the parched soil. When he saw the strangers pulling in, George stood motionless, a small man with a faded T-shirt stretched across his belly, plaid cutoffs, and sandals with black socks. A bramble of whiskers ran down his face, and he tipped his head back to look at the detectives through his thick eyeglasses. George had apparently been doing some woodwork; sawdust coated his arms and legs. He reminded Brad of "a hippie from days gone by."

It was 3:00 P.M. on a weekday; the detectives figured they had caught George on an odd day off work. Brad introduced himself, flashing his badge.

"Can we talk to you a few minutes about the neighbors, the poisoning?" Brad asked.

"Okay," George said. "Do you want to come in the house?"

"Sure," Brad said. "No sense standing outside."

George shuffled toward the back door, leading the way. Off to the side the detectives noticed a small ramp and door leading inside, apparently for some kind of pet. As they walked inside, they saw bowls scattered across the floor, and cats prowling every which way. On the wall a computer printout reminded: "George, feed the cats."

George led them into the kitchen, inviting them to sit at a round table covered with an orange cloth. A large flashlight sat on a cabinet nearby. In a library just beyond, shelves held what looked to be hundreds of books. Brad glanced at George's hand; it still held the board that he had been cutting outside. Seeing Brad's gaze, George laughed nervously. "Oh," he said, "guess I don't need this."

The detectives pulled out notebooks and began asking George some background questions. George's voice came out hesitantly, almost breathlessly, as he explained that he programmed computers and wrote articles for technical magazines. He said that he worked out of his wife's medical office and was generally gone from sunup until after dark.

George said he didn't know his neighbors well. Their contact was limited to an occasional wave and a "hello" tossed over the fence. They never had parties together, or cookouts, or even chats in the yard. The only evidence of neighborly goodwill came when one family's well pump broke down and the other shared its water.

Echoing his wife's remarks, George said he didn't mind the limited contact. "Everyone in that house owns a pickup truck," George told the detectives, disdain creeping into his voice. "They're not really our kind of people."

Brad played his usual role, sitting back, listening, and watching while Ernie got the conversation started. Brad noticed that as George spoke, his mouth made a dry, clucking sound. Most people are edgy when they talk to police, but George seemed extraordinarily tense. Brad wondered, Why is this guy so nervous?

"Have you had any problems with your neighbors?" Ernie asked.

In that instant George's demeanor changed. His brown eyes flashed, and his voice deepened. He no longer seemed nervous, just angry. It was as if he had waited years to tell someone this story. George said the trouble began when Diana and he first moved in. Pye was forever building things and trying to sell them to George and Diana, apparently assuming that the couple had money to spare. First it was a barbecue pit built out of a fifty gallon drum; Pye wanted a hundred dollars for the device, but George wasn't interested. Then, one day, Pye offered to sell George his workshop for ten thousand dollars. This time George agreed—but only to yank Pye around. He knew Pye would later regret having made the offer and would ask George to forget it.

As George told his story, Brad noticed that his jaw had

tightened. George was leaning toward the detectives, looking for sympathy, for a sign that they could relate to the frustration of living next door to a bunch of rubes. Picking up on George's signals, Brad leaned toward him and nodded. *Tell me all about it.*

Although he was feigning sympathy, Brad felt only wonder. How strange, he thought. After the next-door neighbors have been poisoned, how many people are going to talk bitterly about ancient, petty disputes? Particularly to a couple of police officers who are gathering evidence, looking for a suspect? Even if they were still angry, most people would downplay the conflict, say something like "We had a couple of run-ins, no big deal." Brad glanced under the table at George's feet. They were sliding back and forth across the floor.

Brad didn't look at Ernie, but he could tell Ernie's mind was running in the same direction. Both men felt a rush of adrenaline. They weren't just banging off another interview; they were on to something.

"What do you know about thallium?" Brad asked.

"Only what I learned from Channel Ten news," George said.

Then Ernie dropped the big question, the one they had asked every potential suspect. He said, "Why would somebody want to poison the Carr family?"

"To get them to move," George said, turning and nodding toward Pye's house. His voice dropping almost to a whisper, he added, "Like they did."

Brad and Ernie couldn't believe it. It was almost too strange to believe, something out of a B-grade detective movie. They didn't have to look at each other to know they were thinking the same thing: George had virtually recited the death threat that Pye and Peggy had received in June. "YOU AND ALL YOUR SO CALLED FAMILY HAVE TWO WEEKS TO MOVE OUT OF FLORIDA FOREVER OR ELSE YOU ALL DIE. THIS IS NO JOKE."

The detectives had guarded that note carefully, making

sure its contents didn't slip out into the newspapers or the Alturas grapevine. Although some people knew the family had received a threat, few knew what it said. Only the family—and the poisoner.

Brad and Ernie had asked dozens of people for their views on why someone would have poisoned the Carr family. None, even those who knew about the note, had answered as George had. Most had said, "I have no idea" or "That's a sick thing," or "Somebody must have really hated them." But not George.

To get them to move, George said. *Like they did.*

Was it possible that George hated his neighbors so much that he had sent the death threat and then followed through on it? Had Diana come home complaining about loud radios, demanding that George do something about those obnoxious neighbors? Those questions lingering in their minds, Brad and Ernie thanked George for his time and walked out the door.

As the detectives walked away, George couldn't stop talking. As he followed them, his words cascaded out. "This is kind of strange for Alturas," George said. "Usually they just shoot or stab each other."

"It is kind of different," Brad replied, walking toward the car, his voice carefully neutral.

George asked, "How long do you think the investigation will take?"

"It's a federal case, and the federal government's slow," Brad said, sliding into his seat and putting on a pair of sunglasses. "This thing could go on for years."

As soon as they had driven around the bend, Ernie and Brad, who hours earlier had despaired about their lack of progress, exchanged jubilant high fives.

"He did it," Brad said to his partner. "Now all we have to do is prove it."

Chapter
NINE

As Ernie and Brad drove out of Alturas, Cissy planned another trip to the hospital. En route she allowed herself a daydream: She would arrive to find her mother sitting up in her hospital bed, one eyebrow arched in mock outrage, a cigarette burning between her fingers. As her daughter walked in, Peggy would exclaim: "Where the hell have *you* been?"

But when Cissy got off the elevator in the ICU, she saw that nothing had changed. Her mother still lay motionless in her bed, her eyes not only closed but sewn shut. Because the thallium had paralyzed Peggy's muscles, she could not even blink her eyes. To keep ulcers from forming on her dried-out corneas, the doctor had sewn her eyelids together. The only sign that Peggy was still alive was her heartbeat, recorded by a machine on an endless sheet of paper.

Cissy walked to her mother's side. "Hi," she said softly, taking Peggy's hand. "I miss you. I want you to get well soon."

Peggy did not respond. Cissy had come hoping to hear her mother's Alabama twang and bright laughter, but she heard only the respirator's rhythmic sighs and the nurses' whispers. Cissy touched her mother's cheek and breathed deeply. She wished she could smell Peggy's favorite perfume on her skin. But instead of White Shoulders, there was rubbing alcohol.

"Mama," she said, "your granddaughter misses you. She wants to know where her MeMe is. You need to get better so you can come see her." Cissy didn't know if her mother could hear her, but she told her the news anyway: Cissy had gotten a new, better-paying job as a secretary at a citrus company. Kacy had fallen off her Big Wheel and scraped herself. Allen was working hard in the Navy, hoping to become an underwater demolition expert.

Then Cissy ran out of things to say, and the silence closed in.

Back at the office Ernie and Brad mapped out their plan to find out more about their new prime suspect: criminal records checks, scans of George's legal and financial records, letters to thallium suppliers to see if any listed George as a customer, and a fresh round of interviews.

The day after talking to Trepal, Brad went to the FBI office and talked to Sharon Burns, who ran the FBI's national crime computer in Tampa. "Sharon, we just talked to this guy," he said. "Find anything you can on him."

In just ten minutes Sharon called back. She had a hit: *George J. Trepal. Charged in 1975 with operating a meth-amphetamine lab in North Carolina. Arrested on federal charges. Sentenced to prison. More details to come.*

Brad called Mincey. He said, "This guy is a *chemist*!"

After Christmas the two detectives paid another visit to Pye Carr. They saw Pye no longer as a strong suspect but as a source. They had a long list of questions: If George had poisoned the Cokes, how did he get them into the neighbors' house? Could he have broken in or slipped inside while the family was away? Had Pye noticed anything strange?

Pye met them at the house. He leaned against a kitchen counter, lit a cigarette, and, for what seemed the hundredth time, told the story of his family getting sick. Peggy, Travis, and Duane had drunk glasses of Coke, Pye recalled. "We were trying to get fluids in 'em," Pye said. "All the doctors always tell you to keep, you know, keep eating and keep drinking."

"Did you have an occasion to drink any of this Coca-Cola?" Ernie asked.

"Yes. I specifically remember drinking two drinks mixed with Jim Beam and Coke."

Ernie asked him about the threatening note. "Do you have any idea who might've written that note to you?"

"I really don't. Peggy and I didn't think too much of it at the time, but for some reason or another, she said, 'I'm gonna put it up and keep it.' "

"During this period of time," Ernie was asking, "did you have any problems with family members or neighbors?"

Pye puffed on the cigarette, the smoke rolling luxuriously into his lungs. With a shrug he said, "Just the problems with George and Diana about the boys playing their music. That was in October, just prior to them getting sick."

"Okay," said Mincey. "Were there any other conversations about loud music other than in October?"

Yes, Pye said. One rainy day he, Travis, and some friends went into the garage to put a bumper on Travis's truck. They had a party tape, so they plugged it in. George came over to complain, saying, "The tape is a little loud. Would you turn it down?" Pye agreed, but his neighbor came over twice more to ask them to lower the volume. Finally Pye lost patience. "George," he said, "we done turned the tape down twice. The tape is not bothering anybody. We want to listen to it. Why don't you just go on back to the house and mind your business, and I'll mind mine."

Early in the week before Peggy and Diana fought, Pye recalled another confrontation. He had been helping Travis work on the speaker system in his truck when George came over to gripe about the noise. At that time, Pye explained, he and his family were getting their water from George's well. Pye recalled, "Travis come out and told me that George has disconnected the water, and I said, 'Well, I'll see what his problem is.' So I went over there and George said, 'The music's too loud,' and I hooked the hose back up and I said, 'George, all the boy wants to do is listen to the music. It's not bothering you. I'm right here in the shop, and I didn't pay any attention to it.'"

Ernie asked, "How did he react?"

"He said, 'Well, you know, we don't listen to that kind of music, and I don't wanna listen to it.'"

The last fight, the one between Peggy and Diana, had occurred while Pye was in South Carolina hunting. Pye said the fight had left Peggy "extremely upset."

Pye said George and Diana had lived next door for about six years; they were also Pye's neighbors during his previous marriage. "During that period of time," Ernie asked, "have they ever been inside of your home?"

George had come over once to see how Pye was building the family room, Pye said. "To my knowledge, that's the only time."

"What has your relationship been?" Ernie asked. "Have you been on a real friendly basis with 'em or just—"

"No," Pye said. "They pretty well stay to their selves, and so did we. You know, they went their way, and we went ours."

Brad jumped in, raising the issue that had so angered George. "Did you ever offer to sell your tool shop?"

"He offered to buy it one time," Pye said. "I told him I wouldn't sell it. . . . But he offered, seems like it was twenty-five thousand dollars. Then he offered me fifty-eight or fifty-five thousand or something for all of it, and I said, 'There ain't no way.' I didn't know whether he was just joking."

The detectives turned their questions from the past to the poisoning. Once again Ernie asked Pye if there had been any strange happenings around the time his family got sick. As the detectives had learned with the death threat, Pye didn't always pass along important information the first time he was asked.

There was one thing, Pye said. "I found the house open after they went in the hospital."

"After they went in the hospital?"

"Yeah. I found the back door—the back door being the door leading out of the family room onto the pool deck— I found that open two or three times," Pye said.

Ernie tested the door Pye was talking about. He took a credit card from his wallet, slipped it under the lock, and easily popped it open.

"Have you had difficulties with that door locking?" Brad said.

Yes, said Pye. Before the poisoning the teenagers often left it unsecured. "I caught it opened several times," he said. He regularly chewed them out, Pye said, "but a young un will be a young un."

"Could it appear to be locked and not be locked?" Ernie asked.

"Correct," Pye said.

"Was there a period of time," Ernie said, "that nobody was here at the property?"

Pye said there was, just two days before Peggy got sick. "Peggy went to Fort Myers on Friday after work to pay a traffic ticket for Duane, and when Peggy got home, the boys had already left."

Brad asked, "Would you know why somebody would want to hurt Peggy or you or your family?"

"No," Pye said, "I really don't."

While the detectives were talking to Pye, Allen and Duane arrived to pick up some things. They were able to fill out Pye's recollections. In the two days before Peggy got sick, Duane said, he and Travis had left the house on two occasions: one day for two hours; the next day for at least three. Duane said he wasn't sure whether they had locked the doors. But Duane did remember one thing: He and Travis got thirsty from painting outside and went looking for an eight-pack of Coke they had seen under the kitchen counter. The Cokes had disappeared. The boys searched everywhere, in the kitchen, in the utility room, but found no sign of the eight-pack.

That was on the Thursday before Peggy got sick, Duane said. A short while later the eight-pack had found its way back to that spot under the counter. Duane wasn't sure how.

As 1988 drew to a close, Ernie began summoning Peggy's family and friends into his office for another round of interviews. Some of them, especially Cissy, still wanted to blame Pye. Mincey's patience with Cissy was running out. As much as he might have liked to set her straight, though, Ernie held his tongue. If he told Cissy that Pye was no longer the prime suspect, he feared what the public—and George Trepal—would see on the evening news: Cissy, standing before the camera and saying, ''Pye Carr didn't do it. And they won't tell me who did.''

Besides, the police still had a lot of work to do before they could completely write off Pye as a suspect. They were still gathering Pye's bank records and legal documents— quietly, so that he wouldn't know about it. If that search turned up a hidden insurance policy, Pye would leap back to the top of the list; after all, he had been fighting with Peggy and talking with an ex-girl friend. That, combined with a fat insurance check, could provide an obvious motive.

That was the problem with Trepal: motive. What would drive him to poison a mother, her sons, her two-year-old granddaughter? Resentment over selling some used property? A fight over loud radios? It just didn't add up.

A week after the interview with George, Ernie tracked down Pye's former son-in-law, Mark Connelly. Earlier in the investigation Mark had seemed like a potential suspect:

He and Pye didn't get along, and the young man might have wanted to settle scores. But Ernie no longer had reason to believe Mark might be the poisoner. Now Ernie was most interested in Mark's impressions of the neighbors.

Mark said he didn't know George Trepal or his wife. But he remembered something odd. "When me and Tammy was dating, Tammy used to get obscene phone calls all the time," he said. "They knew what she was wearing. They knew when she was by herself. They knew when I was there."

"She could put her bathing suit on, go out, and wash the car," he continued. "They'd call her and you know, 'You sure do look good in your bathing suit.' "

Ernie asked, "Did she ever suspect who was making them?"

"No, she didn't," Mark said. "It had to be somebody in the area." He speculated that it might have been somebody driving by or hiding in the orange groves.

"Or in the house next door?" Ernie said.

"Yeah," Mark said. "She said it sounded like an older man."

As the investigation moved into its third month, more information about George Trepal's past trickled in. On January 3, 1989, Ernie reached Richard Broughton, an agent with the federal Drug Enforcement Administration who had arrested Trepal in 1975.

Broughton had been a drug enforcement agent for two decades, had worked dozens of big cases, but he didn't have any trouble recalling George.

"This guy is a chemist," Broughton said. "Probably the smartest chemist that I've ever known." Broughton recalled George as a brilliant and strange man who had led one of the biggest drug rings in the eastern United States during the 1970s. The ring peddled methamphetamine, an illegal drug known on the street as crank. After checking a DEA computer file, Broughton told Ernie that in making crank,

Trepal used a chemical called phenyl-2-propanone, or P-2-P.

P-2-P could be purchased legally, Broughton said. But because federal drug agents knew the chemical was an ingredient in illicit drug labs, they kept records on everyone who purchased it. Drug runners like George knew that, Broughton said, and those with enough chemistry expertise sometimes blended their own P-2-P. He said some home-brewed P-2-P was made with thallium.

As Broughton relayed this information, Ernie smiled and scribbled notes. Brekke, who by this time had come to Mincey's office, read over his shoulder. He, too, began to smile. George had told them he didn't know anything about thallium. But now Broughton was saying that Trepal was *the* chemist in one of the largest illegal drug labs around, a lab that might have used thallium. And even if the lab had not used thallium, its chief chemist would surely know what the chemical was.

Tammy Carr, Pye's eighteen-year-old daughter, walked into Mincey's office. Ernie asked her to sit down.

"Mark Connelly came in and talked to me Friday afternoon, and he brought up some things you probably forgot about," Ernie said. "He was telling me that you received, while at the house, some unusual phone calls from an anonymous person. Do you remember these phone calls?"

"Yes, sir," Tammy whispered. "I do."

"Okay," Ernie said gently, pointing to the tape recorder on the desk. "Speak up for this thing. Let's talk about the phone calls."

Tammy said the calls had begun when she was living in the Alturas house with Margaret Carr, her mother and Pye's first wife. "I started getting them right after my mom and dad split up. Me and mom were living there by ourselves, and they would start as soon as my mom walked out to go to work or as soon as she left to go somewhere. He would know when she left. He would know what I had on. He would talk obscene things to me.''

She went on, ''After I moved back into the house with Mark, which was a couple of months later, they started when Mark would leave and go to work. And he works shift work, so sometimes it would be during the day or at night.''

''Would he describe what you were wearing?'' Ernie asked.

''Yes,'' Tammy said, shifting uneasily in her chair. ''If I had to take Mark to work late at night on midnight shift, I'd just be in a nightgown and, you know, a housecoat over, and he would describe exactly what I had on. Or if I had been out in the yard like in my bathing suit or something, he would know that.''

Tammy said the caller sounded like a white man, older, ''very educated.''

The calls came in the 1980s, long before most people toted around cellular phones. ''Where's the nearest pay phone from your house?''

''The Circle K.''

''Which is approximately how many miles from the family house?''

''Mile, mile and a half.''

''Around your house,'' Ernie said, ''are there other houses that can see your house?''

''The only house that can see the house is Dr. Carr and her husband.''

''Did you hang up on him, or did you listen?''

''I would listen to him until I couldn't take it anymore 'cause sometimes he would get really disgusting,'' she said. ''One time he told me he was ejaculating and what he wanted to do to me and what he wanted me to do to him.''

Tammy said she didn't recognize the man's voice. Ernie asked, ''Have you ever spoken to the doctor or her husband, George, who lives next door?''

''Well, I'd talked to Dr. Carr,'' Tammy said. ''She put

my knee or my leg in a cast. But I've never spoken to her husband."

"So you don't know what his voice sounds like?"

"I would have no idea."

The next morning Ernie and Brad tracked down Bill Pittman, a handyman who had worked for George and his wife. Taking a break from some carpentry, Pittman said he had known George and his wife since 1982. He had helped remodel their house and for the past six years had tended their lawn and the landscape at Dr. Carr's office.

Pittman gave the detectives a description of the couple's house, which Ernie noted in a case report: "The bottom floor consists of a utility-type room, kitchen, dining room and living room. The second floor of the house consists of one large bedroom, closets and one large window which looks towards the Pye Carr residence."

Although George had told the detectives that he worked out of his wife's office, Pittman said George had no office space there. Pittman said he got along fine with George, whom he described as "an eccentric person" who talked mostly about computers.

Did he ever talk about the neighbors?

He sure did, Pittman said. George had complained that he spent a lot of money hauling in sand for a beach on the lake beside his home, only to watch Travis Carr tear up the beach with a three-wheel motorcycle. When George told Pye what had happened, Pye simply told him, "Kids will be kids."

Pittman said the incident left George "extremely upset."

Piece by piece, George's original statement to police was collapsing beneath the weight of inconsistencies and contradictions. George told them he was earning a living as a writer and computer specialist, but federal officials could find no activity for the last ten years on his Social Security number. The detectives knew that meant Trepal had been not working, not paying taxes on his legitimate wages, or making money through some illegal activity. For instance, making illegal drugs with thallium.

Brad and Ernie had scheduled a meeting with Diana Carr for January 6. They had made the appointment in mid-December, with one simple goal: to introduce Brad to one in the long list of people involved in the case. It was supposed to be a brief meeting. Routine.

That was before they had talked to Diana's husband. Now the detectives found themselves in a dilemma. If they canceled the meeting, would Diana and George get suspicious? If they did show up, how hard should they push for information? Ernie said, "Let's go over, bullshit her, and leave."

The meeting was set for 8:15 A.M. Diana arrived on time, wearing a white lab coat over a pink sweater. Ernie had warned his partner to expect a woman who was "harsh, difficult, arrogant." But Diana struck Brad as cordial and direct, if a little short on time.

As they walked into her office, Brad looked around. He saw wood trim, blue carpet, and shelves lined with books, a window looking out past an oak tree and into the parking lot, plenty of light. Brad noticed that there were no personal touches, not even a picture of her husband. The office was as polished, and impersonal, as a page out of an office furniture catalog. In most other offices Brad had been in, visitors are invited to sit near their host's desk. Diana, by contrast, showed Brad and Ernie to seats ten feet across the room. The message was clear, Brad thought. She was in charge.

Diana said she and her husband had moved in next door to Pye in 1982. She knew the neighbors only to wave at them and call out a "Hi, how are you?" Pye's kids sometimes played their music too loudly, she said, but otherwise there had been no problems. Diana answered the detectives' questions in a cool, dispassionate voice. She didn't avoid discussing the conflicts with Peggy's family, nor did she stress them the way her husband had. At the end she bade them farewell with a smile, saying, "I hope I've been of help."

In the car Ernie turned to Brekke. "So, what did you think?"

"Well," Brad said, "she didn't give anything away. That's for sure."

As they drove away, the men considered the possibilities: George might have planned and executed the poisoning on his own, without his wife's knowledge or help. George and Diana could have planned the poisoning together but decided that George would do the job. Or George and Diana could have committed the crime together, and she was simply the better actor.

Even if it was George who put the thallium into the Cokes, both Brad and Ernie tended to favor the view that Diana had played some role in encouraging him, even if she was not aware of it. Their research suggested that she was the dominant partner in their marriage; bank records showed George didn't have any obvious source of legal income besides the $150 checks his wife wrote him from time to time, apparently as an allowance. While he appeared shy and reclusive, she was a doctor who moved forcefully through the world. The detectives wondered, In what other ways did Diana dominate George? Would he kill someone to please her?

"We're getting motive now," Ernie said. "But it's bizarre motive." Ernie proposed this scenario: Diana and George were annoyed with the neighbors' country ways, their barking dogs, their loud music. George mailed them the death threat, hoping they would take it seriously and move out. When they didn't, he began thinking about ways to kill them. George wasn't the type to take a gun and shoot someone, but his knowledge of chemistry gave him another set of weapons. Knowing that thallium would be toxic in small doses, he experimented with various forms of it until

he got just the right blend for dissolving in a bottle of Coke.
Those experiments might have taken months.

The Cokes were bottled in Tampa on October 7, 1988,
and shipped to stores. Two weeks later Peggy and Diana
fought over the loud radios. According to Mincey's scenario, Diana came home and complained, ''I'm tired of
these people.''

The detectives drove to Alturas and stopped at the lakeside
church where Peggy and Pye had married just nine months
earlier. Reverend Grant invited them into his downstairs
office.

Grant didn't have much new information. He did say,
however, that the detectives might want to talk with a fellow named Ted Serdynski. It seemed that Serdynski had
told some other church members that thallium sulfate was
not the poison used in the Coke bottles. While Grant said
he did not suspect Serdynski, that was striking information.
Most people believed the press accounts stating that Peggy
and her family had been poisoned with thallium sulfate, the
most common form of thallium. They asked Reverend
Grant where they could find Serdynski.

Ted's Auto Parts, said Grant. Serdynski owned it.

Brad and Ernie walked into the parts store to find Serdynski standing behind the counter, leafing through a parts
catalog with dusty fingers. Serdynski greeted them warmly.
But when they told him why they had come, he became
visibly nervous. His hands began shaking, and he asked,
''Can we do this outside?''

Once they were outside, Serdynski's reason for anxiety
became clear. It wasn't that he had guilty knowledge of the
thallium poisoning. Just the opposite: He didn't know much
at all about the crime, and he didn't want his customers to
hear him acknowledge that to the police. All that ''inside
knowledge'' Reverend Grant had heard about was just Serdynski's repeating rumors and adding a little spice of his
own. The detectives didn't give him a hard time. He cer-

tainly wasn't the only one spreading rumors. They asked, Is there anything else you can tell us?

There is one thing, Serdynski said. Four or five years ago he had given Pye a dog, a Rhodesian ridgeback. Pye later told Serdynski that the dog had died suddenly. Pye thought it might have been poisoned.

Now *that* is interesting information, Ernie thought. If you'll poison your neighbors, you'll damn sure poison your neighbors' dog.

Ernie couldn't figure it out. The earlier poisoning could be hugely important to the case, particularly if the dog had died from thallium. Why hadn't Pye told them about it? Didn't he make the connection between one poisoning and the other? Ernie called him on the phone. "We need to talk to you."

Pye lumbered in after work, wearing boots coated with mine dust. He sat down, folded his arms across his chest, and looked at Ernie through hard eyes. Ernie glared right back.

"So," Ernie said, "tell us about the dogs."

"What dogs?" Pye replied.

Ernie told him what Serdynski had said, about the Rhodesian ridgeback that had suddenly perished. With a shrug he said, "Oh, yeah." Pye said that he got the dog in 1984 or 1985. It used to jump over the fence and roam the neighborhood, often pausing to chase George's cats. The dog was peppy and strong, with a ridge of bristly hair running along its spine. But one day it came home, lost a great deal of weight, and died. Just like that. Pye suspected that someone had poisoned the dog, but he didn't know who.

Ernie lost his cool. "Why can't you remember this important stuff?" he demanded. "We've been doing this for months. Why is this stuff not important enough to you to pass on to us?"

Pye shrugged. "I didn't remember," he said in that familiar, flat tone. "I didn't think it was important."

After showing Pye out, the detectives looked at each

other and laughed. Brad shook his head, sank into his chair, and tossed his notepad on the desk. The two men didn't even have to say what they both were thinking: What *else* has he forgotten to tell us?

Brad shared Mincey's exasperation with Pye. But once he cooled down a little, he also understood. Pye was a country man, just like Brekke's grandfather. In the country dogs get into things they shouldn't, and they die. An unhappy fact, but a fact nonetheless.

To Brekke, Pye's absentmindedness provided further proof of his innocence. If Pye was guilty, he would have seized this chance to incriminate somebody else. "Yeah," he might have said, "whoever poisoned my dogs poisoned my family." But Pye said nothing of the sort. He just promised to try to remember where he had buried the dead dog.

More evidence of George's disdain for Pye and his family came from the Polk County building and zoning department. There they found zoning document No. 47944, a "request for investigative services." It stated that George James Trepal of 2650 Alturas Road had complained on March 15, 1988, that Pye Carr was constructing an apartment building behind his house without the proper permit.

A code inspector investigated and concluded that Trepal was right. He cited Pye for a code violation on March 24, 1988, roughly three months before the family received the death threat in their mail.

Inside a conference room at Winter Haven Hospital, white cups half filled with cold coffee lined the table where Margaret Carr sat talking with the police. Margaret, Pye's ex-wife, had come to see her son, Travis. Ernie and Brad asked if they could speak to her in private. She agreed, and they retreated to the little room near the nurse's station. A gracious woman whose fair skin was set off by waves of brown hair, she answered their questions in a soft, polite voice.

Ernie turned on the tape recorder. "Margaret, could you raise your right hand for me please?" he said. "Do you swear this statement you are about to give will be true and correct, so help you God?"

"I swear," she said.

"You need to speak up for this thing," Ernie said, pointing at the tape recorder. Her voice stronger, Margaret told the investigators that she and Pye had been married from 1967 until 1986 and that she had lived in the house for a while after their divorce. During those years, Ernie asked, was there a time when someone was watching her?

Yes, she said. "It was a neighbor."

"Do you know who the neighbor was?"

"George Trepal, I think, is his name," Margaret said. "He was just watching us with binoculars from inside the house, from their house."

Like her daughter, Margaret recalled the strange phone calls. After one of them somebody broke into the house. "Nothing was taken out. It just looked like someone wanted us to know the house was broken into."

Ernie asked what parts of the house had been burglarized. "Both bedrooms, mine and Tammy's," Margaret said. "They dumped out all the jewelry. It was just costume jewelry; it was nothing. And they had unplugged the VCR from the TV, and it was sitting out under the carport."

Ernie asked if the intruder had gone through their underwear. "I can't remember," she said. "It was just so upsetting."

Ernie moved on. "During the time that you and Pye were married, did y'all own any dogs?" he asked. "Did anything odd happen to any of these dogs?"

"Yeah," Margaret said. "We had one that just died, just shriveled up and died."

"Which dog was that?"

"The ridgeback."

Until then Margaret had been answering questions cheerfully. But as Margaret recalled the dog coming home, its fur falling out, and the flesh melting from its bones, Ernie saw her eyes darken with alarm. Her son was just down the hall, a few strands of hair on his head, his lungs unable to draw breaths without the help of a machine. Was he going to die, like that dog?

Regaining her composure, Margaret told the detectives that the ridgeback was a friendly dog. "It would smile; it would kind of wrinkle its nose up at you," she said. "But you could probably stomp your foot, and he'd run."

The dog did get rambunctious at times, Margaret said. "It would chase cats, the neighbors' cats." She explained that the dog had learned to lift up the latch on the gate with its nose, then push through to freedom. Even when they tried putting a pin in the latch, the dog learned to get out by taking the pin in its teeth and giving a yank.

That upset Diana's husband, George. "He never said anything directly to us," Margaret recalled. "We'd just see him throwing sticks at the dog or running the dog out of the yard."

Turning to the poisoning of the family, Ernie asked, "Do you particularly suspect anybody?"

"I've always suspected the neighbors," Margaret said.

"Why is that?" Ernie asked.

"Well, from what I can gather it has to be somebody that knows about this drug," Margaret said. She said Pye wouldn't have that knowledge, but George's wife would. Diana could have read about it in medical textbooks.

Margaret said she couldn't imagine anyone in Alturas doing this except George and his wife. "They're not our type of people. They were never friendly. They just wanted to keep to themselves. They were just weird."

By mid-January Mincey's initial disdain for Coca-Cola officials had vanished in the warmth of their cooperation. After the thallium had been discovered in the Cokes, the company jet shuttled Ernie between Florida and the FBI lab, serving him finger sandwiches en route. After the bottling plant had been cleared of any role in the poisoning, Coke officials continued to help detectives find the poisoner and clear their company's name. Ernie grew especially fond of L. G. Cunningham, the Coca-Cola vice president who headed the company's crisis management team. Cunningham was a smart and powerful man, but he didn't condescend to the country cop.

More important, the chemists who worked for Cunningham were coming up with answers about the Carr family poisoning. Their experiments reinforced the idea that the poisoner had worked with great precision and expertise.

Before the FBI had determined which type of thallium was used to poison the soft drinks, Coke chemist Mary Ruth Walters McDonald tried placing various types of the chemical—thallium sulfate, thallium formate, and thallium malonate—into bottles of Coke. The idea was to re-create the poisoning of the Carr family's Cokes, to discover how the poisoner had spiked the beverages without changing their appearance. The first experiments failed, because the Coke foamed and gushed out of the bottles when thallium was spooned in.

Then the FBI lab determined that the Cokes had been tainted with thallium nitrate, a chemical used as a reagent in university and industrial research labs. There are different types of thallium nitrate, including thallium I nitrate and thallium III nitrate. Recalling that thallium III nitrate could be used in drug labs such as the one George had run, Ernie asked the Coke lab to add some to a sixteen-ounce bottle of Coke. McDonald added one gram—a fatal dose—to a sixteen-ounce bottle of Coke. Once again the beverage foamed. The chemist also noted that the thallium dramatically changed the Coke's appearance, creating a layer of dark sediment on the bottom of the bottle and turning the beverage above a light amber. Cunningham delivered the disappointing news to Mincey: Thallium III nitrate did not appear capable of poisoning Coke without dramatically altering its appearance.

Then Cunningham called back to say that company and FBI chemists had consulted and come up with a possible answer. Thallium III nitrate decomposes to thallium I nitrate when oxidized, Cunningham said. When the Coke chemist tried adding the thallium I nitrate to Coke, the result was a beverage that looked no different from the bottles sold in stores every day.

Ernie shook his head in wonderment. It had taken a team of expert chemists more than a month of experiments to figure out which type of thallium would dissolve into Coke. Whoever poisoned the Carr family either was incredibly lucky or had a unique combination of criminal tools: extensive knowledge of chemistry, access to thallium nitrate, and a lot of time to experiment.

Pye finally remembered where he had buried the Rhodesian ridgeback. The next day a group of cops in blue jeans and T-shirts began digging in the spot he had pointed out. The FBI's lab experts had told the detectives that animal corpses could still contain thallium. The officers dug and dug for evidence, unearthing rotten oranges, colonies of angry red ants, and enough sand to build a beach. By day's end, though, they had nothing more to show for their efforts than sore backs and blistered hands.

As the poison attacked Peggy's body, it also withered the spirit of her older son. Sometimes when Allen was driving down a road or walking through a store, he would look into the faces of strangers. Who could have done this thing? he wondered. What does a killer look like?

Allen had received permission to take emergency leave from his Navy assignment, and he used the time to care for his brother. After tucking Duane in bed one night, Allen walked into the living room and said to his father, "I can't believe somebody took Duane from me and gave me *that*. You can't imagine what I would give up to have the person who did this."

Larry told him that whoever had done it would be judged in heaven. But that didn't satisfy Allen. A black belt in kung fu, he began fantasizing about delivering his own brand of retribution: *The guards lead the poisoner into the courtroom. The criminal looks over to see the victims and their family. Allen gets up from his seat, as if ready to leave. But suddenly Allen sprints toward the poisoner, dives over the rail, and grabs him. Before the guards can react, Allen spins the poisoner around, grabs him under the chin with his left hand, then strikes him across the neck with his right hand. His windpipe crushed, the poisoner gasps for air and dies.*

In early January Allen had to return to the Navy to complete his training. Back at the Tennessee base he felt the anger and sorrow swell inside him, like a black cloud, rising from his gut to fill the hollow space the crime had made.

Allen didn't know that Ernie and Brad had just developed a major break in their case. Allen just knew that he couldn't take it anymore. He gulped down three bottles of Tylenol.

Chapter

TEN

___

Now that they had a good suspect, Ernie and Brad could not carry the case alone. Ernie went to his bosses at the sheriff's department, asking for help in surveilling George and investigating his background. They gave the assignment to Special Agent Susan Goreck.

Susan was thirty-three, a mother of two, and one of the department's most promising undercover officers. With a slight drawl and a round, merry face, she seemed more like a PTA president than a plainclothes cop. Susan's ability to blend in, her everydayness, was her great strength. Whether pursuing a pimp, a drug pusher, or a bookie, Susan struck suspects as nonthreatening, even naive. Only her eyes betrayed her: They were deep green and exceedingly watchful.

Since childhood Susan had lived two lives: one in the mainstream, the other at the edge. Growing up in the quiet town of Lake Wales, Florida, she made good grades, then came home to read books about Buddhism and correspond with pen pals in Iran, India, and Japan. She married young and started a family, then landed a job as the first woman deputy in a rural Florida county. Although she was then twenty-five years old, she had to wait to be sworn in; her boss had demanded that her husband, Gary, come and personally give his consent.

A year later, in 1982, Susan landed a job closer to home, in Polk County. She began the usual way, wearing a green uniform and patrolling the roads in a marked car. After showing a talent for working the shadows, she was promoted to vice. While she made her share of drug buys and porn cases, Susan found herself drawn to more complicated investigations into gambling rings and racketeering enterprises. While many cops like cracking heads, Susan loved the paper chase, patiently using canceled checks, bank records, and telephone calls to build cases against bookies and white-collar criminals.

Before she was assigned to assist Brad and Ernie in December 1988, Susan had read the newspaper stories about the mysterious poisoning in Alturas. But she knew little else; the investigators had kept a tight lid on information, dispensing it only on a need-to-know basis.

A few days after Ernie and Brad had interviewed George, Susan was in her office doing some paperwork. Her boss, Sergeant Rick Sloan, walked in. "We're going to start doing surveillance on a guy," Sloan said. "You need to meet me at sunup." Susan knew better than to press for details. She simply went home, set her alarm for five, and tried to sleep. The next morning she pulled on a pair of jeans, ran a comb through her hair, and drove her white Cougar through the morning darkness.

Susan pulled into the parking lot of the Circle K store just outside Alturas, wheeled around some semis, and backed into the space beside Sloan's red Camaro. As she rolled down her window, the winter air swirled in, smelling of diesel smoke and freshly brewed coffee.

"Keep an eye on this road," said Sloan. "He's going to be in a little blue or silver station wagon."

"Okay," Susan said. "Do you have a description?"

"Yeah," said Sloan. "He's supposed to have thick glasses. And one other thing: He's got a photographic memory, so be careful he doesn't see you."

As light began to drift up in the eastern sky, a small

Honda puttered by, driven by a scrawny man with a beard and thick eyeglasses. She looked at her watch—it showed a few minutes after seven—and picked up her radio handset.

"I just saw the car," she said.

Susan trailed George for several weeks, catching him in his first lie. George had told the police he worked in his wife's office, but she discovered that he actually worked out of his own office in a Winter Haven office complex. Late one night Susan and some other officers sneaked up to George's house, crawled under his car, and attached a "bird dog" to the underside of his car. A battery-operated tracking device, the bird dog barked out a radio signal that allowed Susan and her colleagues to follow George without riding in his rearview mirror. What had begun as a temporary assignment was turning into a full-time job, and Susan felt her curiosity stir. I'm devoting my life to this guy, she thought, and I don't even know why.

After the New Year Ernie and Brad walked into the office to pick up the results of some auto tag searches Susan had been asked to do. Susan remembered Brad well and with fondness. The year before, when Brad had just arrived in Polk County on his first posting with the FBI, he and Susan had raided the headquarters of a prostitution ring run by two brothers. These guys were picking up runaway girls, shipping them out of state to turn tricks, and promising them, "If you make lots of money, you can come back and we'll get married." When the girls returned, the brothers grabbed the money, beat the girls, and went out to find fresh meat. Susan had found her partner to be smart and helpful, if a little wide-eyed at his first close look at Florida sleaze. Working together, Brad and Susan had shut the operation down.

When Susan saw the FBI man walk down the hallway, she knew it must be something big. She smiled at him, calling out, "Hey, Brad."

"Hey," Brad said, returning the smile and coming into her office.

"Is this your case we're working on?" Susan asked, holding up the paperwork. She began plumbing him for details. "It really looks like something you could get your teeth into," she said.

By this time Ernie had come in. He and Brad exchanged a coy look. "Well," Brad said, "I'm glad you think it's interesting."

Next thing Susan knew, Sergeant Sloan had called her into his office. He told her she was going to be the undercover unit's lead investigator on the Alturas poisoning.

Some glamour assignment, Susan thought. It was a sunny Sunday afternoon, but instead of hanging out by the pool at home, she was standing outside a green Dumpster behind George's office. This was just the first of many Dumpster runs Susan was to conduct in hopes of finding something—used chemistry equipment, a receipt for thallium, a letter to a friend exulting in the poisoning of his obnoxious neighbors—that could tie George to the crime.

It was a hot day, and the Dumpster didn't smell sweet. Wearing tennis shoes, jeans, and a pair of gloves, Brad was inside the giant garbage can, sifting through the mountain of Styrofoam coffee cups, used envelopes, and cigarette butts. Susan stood outside, sorting through the loot and keeping an eye out. What they were doing was legal—once George threw something away, it was public property—but they didn't want him to find them there.

Deep inside the can, Brad stooped over to scoop another handful. He heard Susan's voice, urgently whispering, "Brad? Brad!" He stood up and saw a beefy guy standing there, looking serious.

"What are you doing in there?" barked the man.

Deadpan, Brad replied, "Digging through the trash."

The man stormed off, yelling, "I'm calling the cops!"

Brad and Susan didn't bother to tell him that the cops

were already there. They stuffed their trash in a box and
scurried away like two mice caught in the light.

While Ernie and Brad interviewed people about their new
suspect, Susan quietly followed the paper trail, gathering
financial records, writing thallium suppliers to see if George
was a customer, and tracking down George's former associates.

Trepal had told the detectives a month earlier that he
knew nothing more about thallium than what he had seen
on the TV news. But after learning that George had been
convicted of running an underground drug lab, they ordered
his federal prison file. The first document was a 1975 background report by a federal probation officer, L. Tony
Brown.

OFFENSE:
Official Version. The defendant was indicted by the
Grand Jury in Charlotte on 9-15-75 for conspiracy to
manufacture amphetamines for the purpose of sale
and distribution.

He was arrested on 9-16-75 and appeared before US. Magistrate Cruciani and requested court-
appointed counsel. He was found ineligible and was
released on $5,000 personal bond pending trial in US.
District Court.

DEFENDANT'S VERSION OF OFFENSE:
No statement.

PRIOR RECORD:
None.

FAMILY HISTORY:
Defendant. George James Trepal was born 1-23-49 in
New York, NY. (verified), the only child of George
Edward and Mabel Robeson Trepal. He was reared

in Florence, SC. He claims a normal childhood, and that his parents supported him adequately.
Father. George Edward Trepal.
Mother. Mabel Robeson Trepal.

MARITAL HISTORY:
Single.

HOME AND NEIGHBORHOOD:
Trepal resides alone in a lower-middle-class apartment that rents for $125 per month in Charlotte. He has lived in the Charlotte area since 1972.

EDUCATION:
He graduated from McClenaghan High School in Florence, SC., on 6-1-66 ranking 106 in a class of 284. In 1959 an IQ test score was 130 (verified). In the fall of 1966 he entered Clemson University and dropped out in August, 1968, with grades below the minimum requirements to continue (verified).

In 1969 he entered the University of South Carolina and graduated on 5-13-72 with a Bachelor of Science Degree with a major in Psychology (verified).

RELIGION:
None.

EMPLOYMENT:
The defendant claims he has been self-employed as an exterminator since 1973 earning approximately $45 per week. He also reports he is involved in kinetic sculpture art, which involves using junk parts to create sculpture figures. He advises he has not sold any of his work.

Defendant has no verifiable employment since graduating from college.

MILITARY SERVICE:
None.

FINANCIAL CONDITION:
No significant assets or obligations.

EVALUATIVE SUMMARY:
He has above average intelligence and has had ade-
quate opportunities made available to him. For a college graduate, he has not applied his talents in the
proper manner that could offer him a rewarding future.

Turning the pages, Susan saw that after receiving the
initial negative review, George went on to impress prison
officials with his intelligence and good attitude. A parole
progress report filed ten months after his incarceration
noted:

Trepal has maintained an above-average institutional
adjustment and has responded well to programs . . .
has taught a chemistry course and has worked on a
mural for the Education Department, is in the process
of making video tapes for that Department, has prepared a variety of posters and information for inmates
that relate to using mathematics in the community. . . . In addition to the above activities, he has
completed a vocational training course that led to the
securing of his FCC license. Also, he is active in the
Yoga program. . . . He offers the following release
plans: residence with parents, Mabel and George Trepal . . . Employment: Pro Film Service (guaranteed),
Columbia, South Carolina.

George had been sentenced to three years, but officials
at the North Carolina federal prison where he was being
held recommended parole.

Trepal has been in custody approximately ten months and has maintained an above-average adjustment. He has been quite active in the education process as well as being an instructor. It appears that he has gained some respect for the laws of society in that the fact of incarceration has had a significant impact on his life. Upon his release, he will have the support of his family as well as the guaranteed offer of employment. We feel these factors will contribute to his being a successful member of the community. Based on the above, we recommend that he be granted parole at this time.

Prison officials made their recommendation in August 1977, but he was not released until more than a year later. The gravity of George's offense apparently weighed against him. In a letter to United States District Judge Woodrow W. Jones, federal prosecutors made sure that the judge knew George and codefendant Michael Dwight Kitchens had been big-time narcotics dealers.

DEAR JUDGE JONES:

The conviction of George James Trepal and his associate, Michael Dwight Kitchens, was the result of six years of investigation by the Drug Enforcement Administration. . . . This clandestine drug laboratory is the largest single primary source of illicit amphetamines ever discovered on the eastern coast of the United States. Their investigation revealed that enough chemicals were purchased by Trepal, Kitchens or their close associates to make approximately 64 kilograms of the Schedule II controlled substance amphetamine. . . . This amount would convert to over 2.5 million dosages units and would have a street value of over $7.5 million dollars.

As Susan read through the file, she learned that George's attitude had taken a dramatic shift in November 1977. That month he learned that his parole had been denied, and he fired off an angry memo about his neighbors in the Virginia Living Unit of the Butner, North Carolina, federal prison. Susan read George's typewritten complaint:

A memo written by R. D. Brewere, Executive Assistant on May 26, 1976 concerning loud radios remains on some bulletin boards but is not enforced by custody or team members. The memo states: Radios may be played in individual rooms at a reasonable sound level (Reasonable level will be determined by a staff member.) It is expected that each individual choosing to play a radio will exercise good judgment and will consider others when selecting appropriate sound level. Violations will result in consideration of disciplinary action.

The former Unit Manager, Mr. Sheply, wrote several memos during the past 6 months on the noise situation stating offenders with loud radios (A radio that is played so it can be heard in another person's room or hallway) would lose their radio for an unspecified time period.

The present Unit Manager, Mr. Barncastle, wrote a memo on 10-14-77 and stated, Radios are not to be played so they can be heard outside the rooms. To date no change has taken place, no radios have been taken away, and no disciplinary action has taken place. . . .

A number of months ago I talked to several inmates about their radios and discovered that talking to noisy radio offenders in a civil manner does no good.

As far as I am concerned the necessary paper work concerning the excessive noise has been prepared but the Correctional Officers and Team Members have no intention of seeing that the rules and regulations in the memos are enforced. To date, no radios have ever been taken. (ARE THE STAFF MEMBERS AFRAID OF THE INMATES IF THEY ENFORCE THEIR MEMOS AND RULES?) . . .

According to the POB Policy Statement 7400.5c dated 10-4-74:

RIGHTS	RESPONSIBILITIES
1. You have the right to expect that as a human being you will be treated respectfully, impartially, and fairly by all personnel.	1. You have the responsibility to treat others, both employees and inmates, in the same manner.
2. You have the right to be informed of the rules, procedures, and schedules concerning the operation of the institution.	2. You have the responsibility to know and abide by them.

So if one looks at your policy statement, it can be seen that no effort is being put forth with the noise offenders to teach them responsibility or consideration for other inmates. This is one of the main reasons for inmates being locked up—lack of handling responsibility and inconsideration for others. . . .

IN SUMMARY: I want something done! I don't want another memo—I want action! As I write this three radios are going on different stations. I don't know whether the custody people are lazy or just simply terrified of inmates. I do know that they don't earn their pay. . . .

Come on fellows. I'm playing by your rules. I teach three classes a day in education, have no discipline reports, have a unanimous team recommendation for parole, and have been put in for a Section

9 monetary award. I need a lot of quiet time for study and class preparation. When are you going to play by your own rules? All I've seen so far is mostly typed memos and a lot of empty promises. How about some action?

Susan smiled. Apparently Pye Carr's kids weren't the first neighbors to have played their radios too loudly. They were, however, the first to try it when a set of bars didn't separate George from the object of his wrath.

Chapter
ELEVEN

———

Five months had passed since Peggy got sick, and three since the investigators had zeroed in on George Trepal. To the victims the investigation had become an abstraction, a dull ache in the backs of their minds. For all they knew, the police had given up, leaving them to deal with the lingering effects of the crime. Travis was still struggling to recover from the poisoning, able to breathe on his own but capable of moving only six feet with the help of a walker. Allen had survived his suicide attempt, but then the Navy insisted on discharging him, ending his dream of becoming a Navy SEAL. Peggy remained in a coma, condition unchanged.

After long months of recuperation Duane finally felt well enough to accompany a group of friends to Coquina Beach on Florida's east coast. It was a sunny March day, and the Atlantic was still frothing from a storm a few days before. Duane's friends carried him to the beach, but he wanted to try walking on his own. He took a few steps, picking a foot up and then deliberately putting it back down, as if he were wearing flippers. After he got used to it, though, Duane found that the wet sand helped, supporting his scrawny legs like a giant pair of high-top sneakers. Before long he felt the urge to run.

"Oh, my God!" Duane exclaimed as he lurched forward. "I'm running! I'm running!"

His friends began running beside him, cheering him on. Duane knew that he looked strange, stumbling along with just a few hairs sprouting out of his head. He saw strangers staring, but he didn't care.

"Come on, man," a friend yelled. "You can do it!"

Duane fell. He threw his head back in the sand, feeling its warmth against his skin, the grains streaming across his scalp. "Are you all right?" his friends asked, but Duane couldn't answer. He just laughed and laughed and laughed. For the first time in months he felt alive.

On March 3, 1989, Duane, Cissy, and Allen were summoned to Winter Haven Hospital. Magazines lay scattered on the table of the conference room where they waited, but they felt no urge to read. Machines offered sodas and snacks, but they had no appetite. They sat in silence until Pye walked in, accompanied by Dr. Hostler.

The physician delivered the news they had been dreading: Peggy would never regain consciousness. Duane looked at Pye, who sat with his hands clasped together, his eyes cast downward. Duane still suspected Pye, but he said nothing. The doctor asked if they would sign a document permitting him to disconnect their mother's life-support machines. Cissy and Duane began sobbing, while Allen sat stone-faced, staring at the wall. Seeing that Pye had already signed the paper, each picked up the pen.

Dr. Hostler asked if they would like to pay one last visit to their mother before he turned off the machinery. She wasn't suffering, Hostler told them, and she wouldn't suffer when the life support ended. Her soul would simply leave the prison her body had become.

Pye called Reverend Grant and asked him to come to the hospital. Grant had just returned from three weeks of studying in Israel, and he was exhausted. But he didn't tell Pye that. He knew that it had been weeks since the doctors had detected a brain wave response in Peggy. He knew that the family had been grasping at every hope, every twitch of Peggy's hand, every quiver of her eyelids. Now that they were ready to face the inevitable, he would stand by them.

The family filed through the double doors for the last time. Pye took his wife's hand, and Cissy gently rubbed her head. "I love you, Mama," she said. "I'm sorry."

Hostler turned the switch, and the machine fell silent. All except the heart monitor; its green line, which once chronicled the peaks of Peggy's pulsing heart, shot in a smooth, perfectly straight line across the black screen. As Grant put his arm around Pye's shoulder, Peggy died.

Duane, who had been supporting himself on Peggy's bedrails, swung around and punched the medicine cabinet. His voice filled the quiet ward.

"No!"

Word of Peggy's death spread quickly. "Sad news about the bay area woman who drank Coca-Cola laced with rat poison four months ago," the announcer reported on the six o'clock news. "After lingering in a coma since October 31, Peggy Carr died Friday night at a Winter Haven hospital. Investigators are still baffled as to how the outlawed thallium poison got in the soft drink. Carr's death turns into a murder investigation."

When Peggy first fell ill, Cissy had nightmares about seeing her mother lying in a casket. Now it was really happening. Before putting Peggy to her final rest, the funeral director asked if the family wanted to pick out her dress, put on her makeup, fix her hair. Cissy had always helped her mother with her face and hair, and she decided that this time should be no different. She volunteered for the job.

The next day Cissy stopped at the Whidden-McLean Funeral Home, carrying her mother's makeup kit. Funeral home workers led her down the hall. There her mother lay on a metal table, covered with a white sheet. Workers scurried back and forth as if Cissy weren't there. The smell of formaldehyde hung heavily in her nostrils. The telephone rang and rang and rang. Cissy wondered why someone didn't just pick it up. Cissy stood beside her mother's body. She kept telling herself, You can do it. Her hands would not move.

Her aunt Sandra had come along to help. She asked Cissy, "Are you okay?"

"Yeah," Cissy said. But she knew it was a lie. Her strength crumbling, she began to sob. "I can't do it."

The funeral brought a huge crowd of mourners and so many bouquets of flowers that they all wouldn't fit inside the chapel. A wall separated family members from visitors, and it was just as well. On the family side of the wall the gulf between Pye and Peggy's children was widening.

Cissy, Allen, and Duane had arrived at the chapel before the other relatives and took seats in the first row, in front of their mother's casket. Peggy lay in the pale pink gown she had worn to her wedding, just eleven months earlier. Gazing at her for the last time, Cissy couldn't get used to the idea that this was really her mother in there. Even dressed in the familiar gown, she didn't look like Mama.

Cissy turned to see Travis hobbling up the aisle on crutches; he was doing better but would have to undergo months of therapy to regain use of muscles paralyzed by thallium. Pye walked behind him, with a group of other relatives. He asked Peggy's children to move back one row.

"What are you talking about?" Cissy said, her mouth tightening in disbelief. "This is for the family. We can all sit here."

"No," Pye replied. "Carolyn's going to sit up here with us. Tammy's going to sit up here with us. Tammy's husband's going to sit up here with us. Travis is going to sit up here. I'm going to sit up here."

Furious, Cissy and her brothers moved. Cissy looked at Allen, who sat frozen, arms folded across his chest and staring at the casket through dry eyes. Her gaze moved to Duane, who had buried his face in his hands and begun to cry. Although the police no longer suspected Pye, Cissy did. She trembled, speechless with fury.

In the back of the chapel Brad and Ernie sat with hands folded in their laps. Since they had taken the investigation, the detectives had been able to maintain the proper emotional distance. They came to the funeral chapel for professional reasons: to pay respect but also to see who attended and to watch for suspicious behavior. They cared about the case, but that was what it was to them: *a case*.

At Peggy's funeral that changed.

Standing by Peggy's casket, Reverend Grant began his eulogy. He recalled his first impression of Peggy. Pye had been a member of Grant's congregation for years. When Pye asked Peggy to marry him, he brought his fiancée to meet the minister.

"I said, 'Well, Peggy, if you and Pye get married, will you come to church here?'

"She looked at me, didn't hesitate, and said, 'Well, that depends on what you preach,' " Grant recalled. " 'If you preach the Word, I'll be here. If you're not going to, I'll go somewhere else.' "

Grant said that was Peggy: a woman who believed in God, believed in herself, and didn't hesitate to speak her mind.

His talk punctuated by the muffled sobs of the mourners, Grant recalled how Peggy couldn't understand why she had gotten sick and how angry she became when a doctor suspected she might be imagining her ailments. "I know it's not in my head," the minister recalled her saying. "This is real."

Sadly, Grant said, she was right. "She fought in every way that she could for life, but there was no way she could overcome."

But heaven is a happy place, Grant knew. He told the mourners that Peggy was smiling down on them. "If there's a coffeepot in heaven,'' he said, ''Peggy's going to be happy.''

Sitting in the back, Brad and Ernie found themselves touched. Brad reflected that in a way he knew Peggy very well. He had never spoken to her, but he knew that she preferred Pepsi to Coke. He had never seen her and Pye together, but he knew the highs and lows of their marriage. He hadn't been there, but he knew how Peggy had spent nearly every moment of the days before she was poisoned. As an FBI agent Brad didn't get many murder cases; the ones he did work were usually mob hits. This was different. Here was a woman who hadn't robbed a bank, rigged a bid, or double-crossed a mafioso. This was a woman whose greatest crime, apparently, was letting her teenagers play their radios.

Brad thought of George Trepal, sitting in his kitchen with that piece of wood, grousing about the people next door, how much of a nuisance they were, how *inconvenient*.

The funeral procession seemed to go on forever, a line of black cars and flower trucks inching toward Peggy's grave. It was spring, and the hills of Polk County bloomed with new life. Azalea bushes burst into pink flowers, magnolia trees unfolded their white petals, and the orange groves filled the air with an impossible perfume. Lawn mower engines roared for the first time in months, mixing with the gossip of migrating birds.

Soon enough summer would arrive like a blowtorch, scorching the landscape and sending animals and humans alike scurrying for cover. But for now the light fell softly. Then the rain came, and the sky deepened in color, heartbreak blue.

Peggy hadn't wanted to be buried. She used to tell her sister that if she died, she didn't want to be put underground with ''those crawly things.'' Apparently Peggy had also shared her fears with Pye because at the cemetery he walked over, tapped Shirley on the shoulder, and asked her to follow him. Pye led her to a mausoleum, where he pointed up at a place high on the wall. "I'm going to put her right up there," he said, "so she can hear the raindrops."

Chapter
TWELVE

For all their resolve to lock him away, Brad and Ernie had developed a grudging respect for their adversary. They had to hand it to George; he was smart, very smart. He may have revealed himself during their first encounter, but he hadn't left much else in the way of useful evidence.

The detectives' interviews had turned up witnesses who told of George's hatred toward the Carr family, but nobody who saw him plant the poison Cokes in their home. They had uncovered George's background in chemistry, but no proof that he had purchased thallium. The laboratory found a potentially fatal dose in each bottle of Coke, but no fingerprints linking George to the poison inside.

Susan had discovered that George was active in Mensa, an international organization that claims its members have IQs in the top 2 percent of the population. She reported that George and his wife were leaders in the Polk County chapter and frequently hosted Mensa gatherings, including Mensa Murder Mystery parties, where other brainy guests were asked to solve make-believe murders.

The investigators were starting to wonder whether, in George's mind, the Carr family poisoning was part of some sinister game. Maybe George hadn't just blurted out a clue when they stopped by his house. Maybe he'd known exactly what he was doing: taunting the police with words that echoed the Carr family's death threat, confident in the knowledge that he had wiped away all other useful evidence. It made sense. Bill Hagmaier at the FBI's Behavioral Science Unit had told them the poisoner was most likely an intelligent man who would take pleasure not only in killing people but also in escaping detection.

If any evidence remained—a vial of thallium or some chemistry equipment—it was probably hidden inside George's house, away from the eyes of visiting investigators. They didn't have enough proof to obtain a search warrant, so they needed to find another way inside.

Ernie suggested a confrontation. Bring George in, hammer him with their suspicions, and hope for an incriminating slip. But Hagmaier advised against that approach, reminding them that poisoners tend to flee from direct conflict. George would probably say, "I want an attorney," and then where would they be? George would know they suspected him, but they would not have enough evidence for an arrest. If they wanted to make a case against George, Hagmaier said, they needed to tailor their investigation to his indirect personality. Talking to Brad on the telephone, Hagmaier suggested, "Why not send someone in undercover?"

"We need to know everything about this man," he said. "What his strengths are, what his weaknesses are, what his likes and dislikes are, where he's been, what he's done, what's important to him, where he fits into life, his neighborhood and his family. Whom he confides in. What he's afraid of; what he's proud of."

An undercover agent could do that, Hagmaier said. But he warned his colleagues that it wouldn't be like the movies. If George was a typical poisoner, he would be too cautious to come right out and admit the crime, even to a "friend." His intelligence would further complicate the mission. Whoever went undercover would have to work slowly, winning George's confidence and chipping away at his defenses.

"When you start thinking about the geniuses in history, what has been their downfall?" Hagmaier asked. "It's usually been one of two things: their ego or their sex drive. Those are going to be the two levers that we need to look at."

And what better way to attack both weaknesses, Hagmaier said, than with a woman detective? "Someone whom he would perceive as nonthreatening," he said. "She plays to his ego."

Brad immediately embraced the idea, but Ernie had reservations. He liked the traditional approach: One interview leads to another interview. One piece of evidence leads to another. Before long you get what you need: a fingerprint, a witness, an arrest. But nearly five months after Peggy first got sick, Ernie had realized that the traditional techniques weren't enough. He agreed to talk to his bosses about the undercover idea.

Mincey's top boss was Polk County Sheriff Lawrence W. Crow, Jr. By the time of Peggy's death Crow was a frustrated man. He was getting a lot of pressure to solve this case, from the press, from Coca-Cola, and most of all, from himself. Crow presided over thousands of criminal investigations each year, and he left most of the details to trusted deputies. But Crow couldn't help taking this case personally. It was such a cold crime, so senseless. And if this was part of some elaborate game by an evil genius, he was determined not to file it away as unsolved.

After hearing of Peggy's death, the sheriff went home, kissed his wife, and disappeared into his favorite room, filled with memorabilia from the 1950s, including an old jukebox right off the set of *Happy Days*. When he was a young police officer, he had served as a one-man security force for singer Roy Orbison. He chose the song "Only the Lonely" and gazed across the room. Long before he had heard of George Trepal, Crow had turned a corner of this room into a shrine to that quintessentially American drink

Coca-Cola. Crow had a Vendo 44 machine filled with 6.5-ounce bottles, a red sign saying DRINK COCA-COLA—SIGN OF GOOD TASTE, and a rack for empty bottles advertising "Coke adds life." To Crow, Coke was a piece of Americana, a souvenir of a more innocent time. To see it used as a murder weapon was incomprehensible.

Crow wanted badly to put George Trepal away, but he knew the investigation was stalling. The rainbow lights on his Seeburg Select-O-Matic jukebox danced in time with Orbison's warbly tenor. Although Ernie had resisted the undercover idea, Crow warmed to it. It would be simpler to have fingerprints or DNA test results to link George Trepal with the poisoned bottles, but Crow welcomed the chance to build the case without high-tech proof. Either George would outsmart the cops, or they would outsmart him. They would solve the crime the way police did in the fifties, with their heads.

The sheriff knew it wouldn't be simple. First there was the problem of introducing a stranger into George's life; surveillance had shown that he spent most of his time at his computer or in his garage woodshop. When he did socialize, it was almost exclusively with his brainy friends from Mensa. Unlike other Alturas residents, George didn't stop in at the post office to chat. He didn't hang out at a local diner. There didn't seem to be any opportunities for a friendly stranger to drop into his life.

Even if the opportunity arose to meet Trepal, Crow realized that not just any detective would do. Male detectives were out; he agreed with the FBI profiler that a man might intimidate George. There was a handful of women detectives, but most seemed either too young or too roughhewn to strike up a natural relationship with their suspect, who had recently turned forty. Hagmaier had said the woman detective needed to be easygoing, someone who wouldn't scare George into his shell. The undercover officer couldn't just be nice; she also needed to be clever enough to keep pace with George's mind. It wasn't just a matter of winning

George over; it was also a matter of survival. A detective who let her guard down could find herself lying in the ICU.

At the office Crow and his aides chewed over a list of candidates for the undercover job. For a while they considered going outside the department, finding a lawyer or scholar who would be willing to match wits with George. But they quickly dismissed that idea; whoever pursued this suspect needed to be able to defend herself. She needed to be a cop. Then it occurred to them: The perfect person was already working on the case.

Wayne Cross, captain of the Special Investigations Section, called Susan in and laid out the plan. According to a notice in the newspaper, George and Diana were planning to host another of their Mensa Murder Mystery weekends the next month at a Winter Haven motel. He wanted her to attend, pose as a Mensa prospect, and get close to George.

At first Susan resisted the idea, saying she was afraid George might have seen her during one of the surveillance runs. And while she had done undercover work on vice cases, she confessed that she was nervous about taking on a homicide. "I don't want to mess up," she told Cross. "Isn't there somebody else you can send?"

Cross told her that if she was going to work undercover, she needed to expand her base of experience. This assignment would last just a weekend, and another officer would come along as backup. He said, "This would be a good one for you."

Susan agreed. The more she thought about it, the more excited she became. By now Susan had begun to feel a responsibility to Peggy and her family. Whoever had done this needed to be put away.

The undercover assignment appealed to her on another level. Like Brad, Susan was fascinated by the ways criminals think, how they cross over to a place where human decency no longer matters. She was curious to know why someone like George, who had the intellectual gifts to make a good life for himself and others, had chosen evil instead. People said George was a genius. This could be Susan's chance to look inside a poison mind.

BOOK II

Murder, He Wrote

THIRTEEN

———

Shortly after Peggy Carr's funeral Susan Goreck fed a sheet of white paper into her typewriter and began to write.

DEAR GEORGE,

This letter is to request further information on the upcoming Mensa Murder Weekend.

As I am considering moving my home to this quiescent county, I am compelled to find some type of stimulating entertainment. Although I am acquainted with the renowned Mensa organization, never before have I been involved in a lifestyle that would permit such endeavors. My background consists of years of dedicated service to my perfidious mate, who took his thriving career and moved upwards and onwards alone.

A weekend filled with intrigue and intellect could be "just what the doctor ordered."

Sincerely,
Sharon "Sherry" Guin

Susan mailed the letter to the address she had seen listed in a newspaper ad for the event. Although Mensa is an exclusive club, the weekend's organizers apparently weren't checking membership cards. Within a few days George Trepal had mailed back a registration form. Susan saw that she—or, rather, "Sherry"—had three choices for the weekend: to be a murderer, a victim, or an innocent bystander. She chose the role of bystander. She had to chuckle at one sentence on the registration brochure. "Of course," it said, "everybody will be a detective."

The weekend was scheduled at the Winter Haven Holiday Inn on April 14, 1989, just five weeks after Peggy's death. Susan knew the motel. A mustard-colored building on a busy road, the place looked as unwashed and weary as the travelers it lured with a promise of cool sheets and a clean ice bucket.

Susan walked through the lobby, where a hostess directed her through the courtyard and toward the Mensa registration room. In contrast with the grit outside the motel, the courtyard was an oasis, a constellation of air-conditioned rooms, rustling palm trees, and guests splashing in blue water. Beyond the pool Susan saw the Mensa weekenders milling around in front of a hospitality suite in shorts and T-shirts, laughing and making small talk.

Every inch of Susan's body seemed to throb. But she tried not to let her nerves get the best of her. She wanted to make this assignment work. She was chasing a killer so cold that he had poisoned an entire family. Susan couldn't help thinking of her own family. She could see her husband, Gary, coming home from work and filling a glass with Coke. She could see her twelve-year-old son, Greg, pushing the lawn mower through the hot afternoon and then calling out, "Hey, Mom, can I get a cold drink?" She could see Steven, just two, wanting to drink from the bottle just like his big brother. And then . . . well, she couldn't bear to think of what would come next.

Even as murder plots went, this crime held a special horror. None of the usual motives seemed to apply. Peggy Carr hadn't surprised a burglar and taken a bullet in the head.

She hadn't been caught in a violent family fight. She hadn't been caught in a drug deal gone bad. She had simply been the mother of teenagers who liked to play their radios loud.

Then there was the choice of murder weapon. If the killer had worked with a shotgun, or a hunting knife, or even a bottle of Drāno, people could have shaken their heads, bemoaned the senselessness of it all, maybe put extra locks on their doors—and then gone back about their business. Such crimes, whatever their terror, happen to *other* people, not *us*. But who hasn't uncapped a Coke? And who, as long as this poisoner was loose, might not die?

Walking into the Mensa suite, Susan recognized George. He was standing behind the registration table, a small man, thinning on top and spreading at the middle, with brown whiskers framing a full, almost feminine mouth. She looked for a sign of sinister character, a deadness behind the eyes. But there was nothing so obvious. Magnified by thick glasses, George's eyes seemed unnaturally wide but warm enough. He looked up at Susan and smiled. "Next?"

For an instant the words stuck in Susan's throat. Lying didn't come easily to her. "Hi," Susan said. "I'm Sherry Guin. Do you have our registration?"

"Oh, yes," George replied, handing her a manila envelope. "I've got it right here."

Susan watched George closely for his reaction. As he looked at her, she wondered, whom did he see? A potential Mensa member or a cop masquerading as one? She looked for the shock of recognition, and she feared it. This guy wasn't her usual suspect, a two-bit dope dealer or the projectionist at the local porno theater. George was a member of Mensa; he could be brilliant, and he could already be wise to her. Hell, she had followed his car to work. She had poked through his trash. She had talked to dozens of chemical companies, asking if they sold the kind of poison used on the Carr family. What if some chemical salesman had not told her about George's purchases but thought George should know about the questions?

"George, the strangest thing," the salesman might say. "This lady cop from Polk County has been asking about that thallium you wanted. . . ."

As Susan reached for the envelope, she gauged his reaction. His voice was wispy and pleasant. His gaze seemed friendly, not suspicious. She allowed herself to relax a little, but not too much. If he was really smooth, she knew, he might play the game as well as she did. If not better.

"At your leisure, read this. There's some background information," George was saying.

Susan collected her name tag, an information packet, and a T-shirt depicting the weekend's logo: a woman with long legs and Barbie doll breasts, dressed in a negligee and spiked heels. She was sultry, dangerous, a bad boy's dream.

"Thank you," Susan said to George. "It was nice to meet you."

As George busied himself with the next guest, Susan glanced at the papers inside her envelope. She saw that George had assigned her the role of Roberta Putnam, a wealthy socialite from San Cristobal who is bored with life and dabbles in voodoo. She would be joining the likes of Mama Marie, voodoo practitioner; Rodrigo Castellan, arms dealer, mercenary, and spy; and Honey Divine, hooker and CIA informant.

The instruction packet laid out the ground rules for the weekend's mayhem:

> You may do ANYTHING that you think is in character EXCEPT murder unscheduled victims. . . .
> Please do not tickle, manhandle, undress or otherwise abuse corpses. . . .
> If you have received an anonymous letter, after you announce it, please post it in the hospitality suite or give it to Diana Carr or George Trepal for posting. . . .
> You may question anyone you think is suspicious. . . .

Susan was one of the only newcomers at the event. As she wandered around, she could see she had joined a group of old friends. At the center of the crowd, scurrying around to meet everyone's needs, was George. He seemed the perfect host, the all-around nice guy. But as Susan watched him, her initial fear gave way to a surprising feeling: pity. George's friends treated him like a servant.

"George, we need ice!"

"George, can you do something about the air conditioning?"

"George? George!"

Another guest walked up to George and asked about his wife. "Where's Diana?"

"She's here, but she's locked herself in the room next door," George replied. "She's doing all the cooking for the weekend."

Oh, great, Susan thought. We're supposed to eat food cooked by George's wife? She thought back to headquarters, where everyone sent her off to the murder weekend with the advice "Don't drink any Coca-Cola."

Well, Susan told herself, I'm definitely dieting this weekend.

She watched as George walked to the room where his wife was cooking. He knocked softly on the door and said in a singsong voice, "Diana. Open up. It's me-ee."

Susan had to stifle a laugh. This is so strange, she thought. She had never seen a man act like that. It was as if George were afraid of upsetting Diana, afraid that she would fling open the door and scold him. George Trepal, master chemist, ex-convict, and suspected murderer, cowered like a little boy. Susan wondered why.

Although Susan was taking up the investigation where Ernie and Brad had left off, she did not yet share their conviction that George was the killer. She had read the reports. She knew that George was the most likely suspect. But until Susan had done more of her own research, she wasn't going to close her mind. She had seen how a wrongful arrest could shatter a good man's life. Once a relative of hers was arrested after a dispute. He was fingerprinted, searched, put in the cage for a few hours, only to be released when police acknowledged they had the wrong man. By that time, though, word of the arrest had gotten around town, and for months, even years, he felt as if people didn't look at him the same way. Susan knew the power of her badge, and she didn't want to abuse it.

George wasn't the only one who could have poisoned the Cokes. What about Pye Carr, conveniently out of town when his family fell ill? Maybe that insurance policy really *was* out there, hidden in a box. But to Susan the most intriguing alternative suspect was George's wife, Diana. Before going to medical school, Diana had gotten a master's degree in chemistry. As a doctor she had access to unusual chemicals. As a neighbor she had been the one to confront Peggy Carr about her boys' loud radios.

Before the murder weekend Brekke had put Susan in touch with Bill Hagmaier at the FBI Behavioral Science Unit. Hagmaier had coached her for the weekend, telling her that if George was a poisoner, he would probably seem the submissive partner in his marriage. That fits with the "feminine" character of most poisoners, Hagmaier told her. It doesn't mean he's homosexual; it simply means he might have the passive personality traits traditionally ascribed to women. In addition to resolving conflicts indirectly, Hagmaier said, George might prefer to let his wife make the important decisions, bring home the paycheck, structure his life.

Hagmaier wasn't sure how that relationship might have figured in driving George to poison the neighbors. Once Diana got fed up with Peggy and her kids, had George taken it upon himself to eliminate Diana's problem without involving her? Or had Diana played a more active role, even ordering their extermination?

"George," she might have said, "it's time."

Whatever George's motivation, Hagmaier told Susan to remember another side of the poisoner's personality: pride. If he was indeed guilty, George had come close to committing the perfect crime. He had selected a poison with no antidote. He had left no fingerprints or other evidence. And while he was Peggy Carr's only neighbor, the police hadn't gotten wise to him. (At least he thought they hadn't.) George would be terribly proud of his accomplishment, Hagmaier told Susan. He'd already managed to get through five months without being caught. The more time that passed, Hagmaier said, the more George might want to brag—to someone who would not turn him in. Hagmaier urged Susan to give George the kind of admiration he craved, without seeming too knowledgeable. If he doesn't feel threatened, Hagmaier said, he might open up.

At last George swung open the door to the room where Diana had been cooking. Susan beheld a room full of food: platters of tacos and burritos, stacks of sliced ham and cheese, bowls of potato chips and carrot sticks. In the corner she could see a large woman with a round face and pink arms who was busy opening a can of crunchy onion rings. Her preparations complete, Diana swept across the room, gathering compliments on her buffet and talking in a voice that boomed off the walls. Everything about her was strong and self-assured, even intimidating. If George was the church mouse, Susan thought, Diana was the podium-thumping minister.

The guests began heaping food onto paper plates. At first Susan held back, taking a couple of potato chips and onion rings, items she had seen poured from factory-sealed containers. After seeing the others eat, though, Susan reasoned that George and Diana were not going to poison their own friends. She made a turkey sandwich on white bread and walked into the bathroom, where the tub was filled with ice cubes and cans of beer and soft drinks, including Coke. Susan took a Diet Sprite.

No "murders," just social events, had been scheduled for this first night. After dinner Susan joined the crowd in a windowless motel conference room with an old dropped ceiling and soft lights illuminating a small stage. It would be the scene of the weekend's first formal event: a "joke-off."

The Mensa members took turns onstage, telling jokes that ranged from goofy to obscene. George played the emcee. He didn't wear a tuxedo, just a Sherlock Holmes T-shirt, shorts, and flip-flops. Although she hadn't talked to George since registration, Susan had been chatting with some of his friends. As they watched George, one of them told her that he rarely wore long pants or regular shoes. The joke about his wedding, apparently, was that Diana's father had had to hold George down, yank off his sandals, and force on a pair of formal shoes.

George began telling some jokes of his own. His favorite topic seemed to be lawyers.

"Why does New Jersey have lots of toxic waste and Florida have lots of lawyers?" George said. "New Jersey got first choice."

People leaned back in chairs and roared their approval. As soon as the laughter died, George launched into another joke.

"A patient asks, 'Can you get pregnant from anal sex?' " George said. "The doctor replies, 'Yes. Where do you think lawyers come from?' "

More laughter, and George was on a roll, reeling off jokes effortlessly, even mechanically. It's almost like he's a computer, Susan thought, pulling jokes out of his memory banks. She wondered where his hatred of lawyers came from. Perhaps from their failure to clear him of the 1970s drug charges?

"What's the difference between a lawyer and a bucket of shit?" George said. "The bucket."

After the joke-off Susan settled into a chair in the lobby. A pretty young woman with a severe mouth and brown hair pulled into a knot sat next to her. Although Susan had come to observe George and Diana, she also wanted to learn what she could about their friends. Perhaps some of them had played a role in the killings or heard George say something incriminating.

"Hi," Susan said to her companion. "How are you?"

"Fine," the woman said, not bothering to return Susan's smile.

"Have you been to a lot of these?" Susan asked.

"Well, yes." The woman sniffed. "What's your name?"

Susan smiled, pointing to her name tag and chirping, "Roberta Putnam!"

The woman frowned, then said in a cool voice, "No, your *real* name."

"Oh," Susan said with a laugh she hoped didn't sound as forced as it felt. "Sherry Guin."

Around 10:00 P.M. people started heading off to their rooms for the night. Susan saw that George was still there, leaning against a table and talking to a Mensa friend, Stewart Prince. Stewart seemed much like George, bespectacled and intense. George and Stewart were talking loudly, entertaining a small crowd with their repartee. George pulled himself onto the table and folded his legs into the lotus position. Susan joined the small audience, settling into a chair across from George, who had begun talking about his mother.

"She was a schoolteacher," he said, "one of the tough ones. The kids hated her, but their parents fought to have them in her class because she forced them to learn." George began boasting about how he had carried his mother's lessons into the computer age, developing software to teach children how to read. Susan remembered Hagmaier's advice: "Let him impress you. George may enjoy having a reversed role, where instead of his wife dominating him, he can be the superior one." Seeing that Diana was nowhere in sight, Susan leaned forward, the wide-eyed pupil.

"Wow," she said. "You can teach reading on a computer?"

"Oh, yes," George said, smacking his lips with pleasure. "It's really very simple. . . . " And he was off, hands fluttering with excitement, voice ringing with self-satisfaction. Before long George had bounced between an amazing variety of subjects: from literacy programs to testing kinetic energy theories on hamsters and back to computers. "Someday," he said, "implants will allow human brains to access their electronic counterpart automatically."

"Oh, my!" Susan gushed.

As midnight approached, the crowd thinned out, and Susan had George mostly to herself. He was talking about how he had earned degrees in both psychology and chemistry. Susan knew that was a lie; she had seen his college transcripts. George had earned a psychology degree from the University of South Carolina, but Susan knew that most of his chemistry training had come in an illegal drug lab. But she didn't let on.

"I enjoy chemistry," George was saying. "But strict scientists have no idea of why people act the way they do. That's why I also studied psychology." He looked at Susan. "Let me give you an example," he said. "I can tell when people are lying simply by examining the muscles in their jaws and necks."

Susan became suddenly aware of the tension in her neck, her muscles straining like piano wire against her skin. She gulped.

"Oh," she managed to say, "isn't that interesting?"

The next day dawned warm and breezy, the clouds drifting by like puffs of cream. The Mensa weekenders wandered out of their rooms, spooned sugar into cups of steaming black coffee, and prepared to assume their assigned roles.

The make-believe murders organized by George and Diana were to begin this morning, and Susan was anxious to see whether they would mirror elements of the Carr family poisoning. Hagmaier had told her that poisoners enjoy fantasizing about their crime long after the act itself. In that way, he said, they are like serial killers, who often return to the crime scene to relive the act. But unlike serial murderers, who might leave with a piece of a victim's clothing, a clump of hair, a nipple sliced from a still-warm body, the poisoner would not fuel his fantasy with a *physical* souvenir. Instead, because he was not on the scene at the time of death, the poisoner would have a mental keepsake. In this case perhaps George savored the memory of sending a threatening note, of poisoning the Cokes with an exotic chemical, of watching detectives desperately scour Peggy Carr's house for evidence that did not exist. If George couldn't boast directly about his crime, perhaps he would weave threads of it into the weekend's fictional murders.

Susan heard a splash in the motel pool, followed by a scream. She raced over to the pool with the rest of the crowd. With delighted laughs, the weekend sleuths wielded pens and notebooks, ready to gather evidence on the weekend's first casualty. There, drifting in the water, was a fully clothed man whom Susan recognized as one of the Mensa guests.

"He's been poisoned!" someone cried out.

As one of the guests pulled the victim out of the pool, Susan walked around with a 35 mm camera, snapping pictures of George and his friends. A woman approached her and demanded, "Why are you doing that?"

Susan thought quickly. Earlier she had overheard a participant talking about blackmail. In addition to scoring points by solving murders, some guests were blackmailing each other to accumulate the play money circulating at the event. Susan pointed to two guests who were masquerading as a missionary and a voodoo priestess. They stood close together, whispering. "I'm taking pictures to use against them," Susan said. "I know she shouldn't be with him. This way I can blackmail them."

The woman brightened. She said, "That's a really good idea!"

More screams. The patter of guilty footsteps. The weekend detectives rushed into the next room, where they saw a body on the floor, a bearded man who Susan thought looked like a drug runner off *Miami Vice*. He turned out to be Chuck Allen, a friend of George's who was playing an arms dealer at the murder weekend. One of the "detectives" placed his hand on Chuck's chest and said, "This man's dead."

A woman yelled, "Don't disturb the evidence!"

Peering past shoulders and elbows, Susan saw a gun lying beside the body. Two bullet casings lay on the carpet nearby, but the body didn't show any signs of gunshot wounds. Susan also saw a book near the corpse. Leafing through it, Susan saw that the book described killing people with datura, a plant with trumpet-shaped flowers, prickly fruit, and a toxic core.

A man in a blue shirt, who was playing the coroner, began reading an official-sounding report. "The victim," he announced, "began to behave peculiarly shortly before he died. He appeared to be hallucinating. He appeared to be warm and was clutching his stomach as though he were having abdominal cramping. Shortly before he died, it was noticed that he had convulsions.

"There appears to be unusual flushing of the skin," he said. "Toxic screens are still pending."

Someone cried out, "Where's the note?"

What note? Susan wondered. Following the crowd, she ran into the Mensa hospitality suite. There, tacked to the bulletin board, was a threatening note the victim had received before his demise. A crazy quilt of letters cut from magazines, the note sounded a dire warning: "Pay off now. Or wait till death does its part."

As the morning unfolded, George was still running around, dressed in a tie-dyed T-shirt and shorts. Seeing him toting a bucket of ice near the pool, Susan raised her camera and called out, "George, smile pretty!"

George obliged her, then scurried off without a word. Susan saw his friend Stewart Prince standing nearby. While most of the guests were starting to treat her as one of them, Stewart seemed leery. Was he being protective of George? Or did he know something? Another undercover officer, Nolan Allen, had come to the weekend to back up Susan, giving his name as Sam Crane. As Nolan walked across the motel courtyard, Susan saw Stewart's eyes tracking him. She heard Stewart mutter, "Who *is* he?"

If George was wondering about Susan's identity, he didn't show any signs, at least not to her. Susan pushed ahead, trying to strike up a conversation every time she found George alone. She thought back to another piece of Hagmaier's advice: "Give George a chance to help you, to be your protector. Make yourself a victim of the same type of person George despises. If George disliked Peggy's family because they were crude and loud, complain about a crude and loud person who has ruined your life. Maybe George will say to you, 'I had that kind of problem. Let me help you with yours.' "

Susan devised a plan: She would pretend she was going through a messy divorce. After hearing George's jokes about lawyers the previous night, she decided to make her estranged mate a lawyer. She waited for the right time to tell George her story. Inside the hospitality suite she overheard George telling a friend that he and Diana were thinking about selling their Alturas house. What an opportunity! If she acted as if her divorce had left her homeless, Susan thought, maybe George would invite her over for a look at his house. If she saw potential evidence in plain view—lab equipment, illegal drugs, a book about thallium—it could give her the probable cause needed for a search warrant.

Then Susan had second thoughts. Did she really want to put herself in this position? George could say, "Let's go over and take a look at the house today." What would she do then? She had no gun, no radio, no surveillance team; she would be completely on her own. A smart undercover officer doesn't take that kind of risk. Then again, she thought, I might not get this chance again.

She sat down in the chair next to George and caught his eye. "George, did I hear correctly that you might want to sell your house?"

"Yes," he said, turning to her with a friendly smile.

Susan began telling her story. "I'm splitting up with my husband, and the only thing I'm getting in the divorce settlement is a house," she said. "He's a lawyer and a real jerk." Just as she had hoped, George's eyebrows arched with recognition. Even if she didn't get inside George's house, Susan reflected, this could be a valuable step toward gaining his confidence.

"I'm looking for a job," she said. "If I can find one, I'm going to need a place to live."

George seemed eager to help. "Sometimes Diana needs medical transcribers; they get up to twenty dollars an hour," he said. "Would you be interested in talking to her?"

"That's nice," Susan replied. "But see, I worked an eight-to-five job for a long time and I'm really not interested in that. I'm leaving my old life behind. I want something new."

To this point George had rarely looked Susan in the eye, his gaze flickering nervously around the room. But suddenly he looked right at her. "Well, then, you could deal drugs," he said, his lips spreading into a smile. "You'd make a lot of money, and you could travel, too."

Susan's mind reeled. She couldn't look away; George's eyes were boring into her, studying her, testing. What should she say? If she were on a vice case, it would be simple. She'd say, "Sounds great! Can you help me get set up?" If he took the bait, boom, they'd nail him. But while Susan hoped to make a drug case against George, her first priority was the murder investigation. For an instant she hesitated, a shadow of uncertainty passing over her face. George must have glimpsed it because he laughed nervously and quickly changed the subject. He said he had another idea for making money. "You could approach persons at the airport, say that you have a black belt in karate, and request their wallets," he said. "You could get money that way."

George was obviously joking now, retreating. Susan cursed herself for blowing the chance. But the damage wasn't lasting; in a few moments George had returned to the subject of his house. He told Susan that his wife was feeling overworked in her medical practice, and they were considering relocating someplace where she wouldn't be on call twenty-four hours a day. Susan found that puzzling. According to the police theory, George poisoned Peggy Carr and her family because he and Diana wanted the neighbors gone. Having succeeded, why would they now want to move? Or if they had been planning to move anyway, why kill Peggy? Surely, Susan thought, it wasn't just for the thrill.

George extended an invitation. "Stop by the house anytime," he said, giving her the address and phone number. "Just let me know when you're coming."

That night the amateur slayers and sleuths headed into a shadowy nightclub for the weekend's premier event. Susan read the brochure's description: "Cafe El Sleazo. This hellhole (previously the hotel's bar) is the meanest, nastiest, filthiest dive on the face of the earth. We'll give prizes for the sleaziest costumes."

A big bearded guy wearing a soldier's uniform stood at the door, patting people down, paying particular attention to the women. After enduring his hands wandering down her sides and along her legs, Susan pulled away and went inside. A hard rock band played on the stage in front, its screeching guitars and pounding drums amplified to a painful roar. The drinks were free, and before long people had started moving on the dance floor, tentatively at first, then with increasing abandon, a mad whirl of arms, legs, and gyrating hips.

Susan had worn an outfit from her vice assignments, blue jeans, a black top with a shredded fringe, long feather earrings—and she had teased hair. Another guest, a schoolteacher in real life, had donned a slinky nightgown and a cheap wig. Chuck Allen sported a blue denim jacket with torn sleeves and, on the back, silver studs that spelled out "MENSA." Diana seemed to be angling for the night's sleaziest costume honors, her pale flesh spilling out of a flimsy black negligee and feather boa.

Swaying in time with the music, Susan looked around the room for George. She spied him at a table at the edge of the crowd. As the others danced and laughed, he sat alone, somehow detached. Although he supposedly disliked the music played by Peggy Carr's kids, he didn't look at all unhappy. A smile played on his face, and his feet tapped in time with music. Susan sat down at a table with the missionary and his girlfriend, the two characters whom she had earlier photographed. Next thing she knew, the girlfriend screamed and fell to the floor, dead. Another Mensa murder.

There was another death before the evening ended, but it turned out to be a mistake. A woman in the back of the room cried out, fell to the floor, and was surrounded by confused guests. When they learned that this murder wasn't written in the script, a voodoo practitioner quickly conjured the victim back to life. Sipping her rum and Pepsi, Susan thought, Too bad Peggy Carr couldn't have been so fortunate.

The next morning Susan attended the weekend's farewell brunch. George and Diana were handing out awards to the best sleuths. One of the most successful, it turned out, was Stewart Prince. Maybe that's why he was so curious earlier, Susan thought. He was gathering clues.

Reading from a clipboard, Diana provided solutions to the weekend's murders. In one, she said, a free-lance spy was killed after uncovering a sinister plot by a man named Carlos. "She was going to turn him in," Diana said. "He found out about it and consequently did her in."

Susan laughed with the rest of the crowd, but Diana's words reminded her of the peril of this assignment. For all Susan knew, the glass of iced tea in front of her could have thallium in it, courtesy of the hosts. She left the glass untouched, picking up her camera instead to take a few last snapshots of George.

"I'll be in touch about the house," she called out.

"Okay," he said. "Bye-bye."

FOURTEEN

Driving home from the Holiday Inn, Susan glanced in the rearview mirror and saw the saucers under her eyes. She was exhausted but exhilarated. She had expected to spend the weekend observing George, seeing him move among his friends, listening to him talk. She hadn't dreamed that she would get so much time alone with her suspect—let alone receive an invitation to his home.

Going into the weekend, Susan had seen George's wife as the more likely suspect. But after watching Diana at the Mensa Murder Mystery weekend, Susan felt confident that she had not poisoned her neighbors, at least not on her own. Diana was female, but that was about the only thing about her that matched the FBI profile. After hearing Diana's booming voice and seeing the way she dominated George and their friends, Susan could see that Diana didn't display the other characteristics of a poisoner: a passive person who flees from direct conflict and gets revenge indirectly. If Diana were inclined to kill, Susan thought, she probably would do it with a gun, a knife, or her hands.

But Susan wasn't ready to rule out Diana altogether. There was something dark about her, something cold. Maybe she and George had organized the poisoning just as they had planned this weekend's murders: Diana wrote the scenario, and George carried it out. Maybe Peggy

Carr's death was part of some twisted game, where the line blurred between real murder and weekend fantasy, where one family's mystery script became another's death sentence.

Back home at his computer George Trepal was recounting the weekend's events in a letter to a friend of his.

My Nerf bombs, a weapon commonly employed by terrorists, were well accepted. To make a Nerf bomb get a 4 inch foam ball, spray paint it black, and a put a small firecracker in it. This not only looks like something Wile E. Coyote would have but if the firecracker goes off in someone's hand the foam protects them. Would high IQ people be stupid enough not to throw bombs and let them explode in their hands? You betcha!

During the day people were murdered and came back as zombies under the control of powerful voodoo priestesses. I can't remember ever seeing so many women in strange clothes carrying rubber reptiles. This profoundly impressed some of the hotel guests who didn't know what was going on.

The fourth murder, at the Cafe El Sleazo, went a bit off when the wrong person died. We restored her to life and the murderer (laughing like hell) killed the right person, then explained to the group how he made the mistake. As a result, three people (out of 50) figured out who had committed the murder. My efforts to sell the other 47 swampettes in Everglades National Park failed. They were willing but had spent all their money on the Brooklyn Bridge or the Washington Monument. Some had purchased both.

Other details of the weekend are better left unsaid.

At the office on Monday Susan settled in to write her report. She picked up a booklet George had handed her at the registration table, *Voodoo for Fun and Profit. A Mensa Murder Weekend Report*. George had written the voodoo manual, even drawing the cover illustration: a wretched creature, half monkey and half man, sitting atop a pile of bones, clutching a cross. She opened the booklet and began to read. George had written in the preface:

> This is a project that got out of hand. My plan was to look up a few voodoo spells. Unfortunately, I got too involved in my research and wrote this huge report.
>
> The dictionary says voodoo is a system of primitive rights and practices based on a belief in sorcery and the power of charms, fetishes, etc. The key word is primitive because most of us think primitive people are both ignorant and stupid. These people are ignorant of our ways and not at all stupid. Voodoo priests and priestesses have a profound knowledge of practical psychology and natural medicines, especially natural poisons. . . .
>
> Few voodooists believe they can be killed by psychic means but not one doubts that he can be poisoned. When a death threat appears on the doorstep prudent people throw out all their food and watch what they eat. Hardly anyone dies from magic. Most items on the doorstep are just a neighbor's way of saying, "I don't like you. Move or else!"

Susan put down the booklet, the blood roaring in her ears. She couldn't believe it. Why, so soon after Peggy Carr's funeral, would George write something that so closely paralleled the circumstances of her death? She picked up the phone to call Brad and Ernie.

Susan decided to take George up on his offer of a home tour. When she dialed the number George had given her, Diana answered the phone.

"Yes, is this Diana?"

"Yes, it is."

"Hi, my name is Sherry. I met you over the weekend."

"Okay . . ."

"I had asked George about coming by to look at your house."

"Let me let you talk to George."

George came on the line, sounding much friendlier than his wife. He invited Susan to stop by the next afternoon. "I'll try to get home about three o'clock or so and just be waiting for you."

The next day a Camaro Z28 with gold wheels rolled through the groves and up the blacktop road to George Trepal's house. The clouds hung sodden and gray overhead, dripping April rain. As she drove the last mile to Alturas, Susan briefed another undercover officer, Nona Dyess, on what she had told George about Sherry Guin. Today Nona would be posing as Sherry's cousin Mona.

"We're not going to go into a lot of detail with him about you," Susan said. "Just say you're from Fort Lauderdale. While I'm talking to him, keep your eye out for chemistry equipment, a bag of pot, a plant growing under a lamp—anything we could use to get a search warrant. Maybe we'll get lucky and find a bottle of thallium, although I doubt it."

Susan felt raw, on edge. As excited as she was by the chance to walk inside George's house, she was also wary. George's friendliness at the weekend could easily have been a ploy, a trap set by a killer who knew her true identity but wanted to get her alone. Susan wasn't going to take any dumb chances. She had arranged for a small army of FBI agents and sheriff's deputies to hide in the groves around George's house during this day's visit. A few words spoken into the tiny radio transmitter in her purse, and the backup officers would be inside in seconds.

The scenery was familiar to Susan. For months she and other officers had been riding shotgun on county garbage trucks past the house. They had separated George's trash from his neighbors' and spread it out for inspection. Before she ever set foot in his house, Susan knew that George and Diana had a lot of cats, owed money, and preferred fast food to home-cooked meals. Susan didn't find any incriminating evidence in the garbage, but that wasn't the only goal. She was building a foundation of knowledge, a familiarity she could use to feed a new friendship.

As the Z28 neared George's place, Susan flicked on the transmitter. "This is Special Agent Susan Goreck," she said. "Myself and Special Agent Nona Dyess are going to suspect George Trepal's home on Alturas Road."

She glanced at her watch. It was 3:44 P.M. Speaking to the microphone in her purse, "We'll be turning into his house in just a second." She took a deep breath and looked at Nona, who smiled back.

Here goes.

Leading the way, Susan walked past an anemic flower patch and rapped on the wooden screen door. Flakes of white paint rained down on her shoes, and the hollow sound of her knock echoed across the porch. No answer. Didn't George say he would be home this afternoon? After walking around to the back, Susan knocked again. This time George appeared, wearing shorts, flip-flops, and a T-shirt with a tuxedo drawn on front.

"Hi! How are you?" Susan said. "George, this is my cousin Mona."

"Hello, Cousin Mona," George said pleasantly, gesturing for the two women to follow him inside. "Let me give you a tour, and you can poke around things."

For the first few moments Susan studied him closely, to see if he had learned the truth about Sherry Guin. As soon as George's eyes met hers, though, she knew she was safe. His gaze showed no knowledge, no suspicion, just genuine pleasure that she had come to visit. Susan trailed along, trying to look interested but not too eager. The house was a nightmare of primary colors: yellow curtains, orange cabinets, lime green trim—a decorating scheme right out of George's psychedelic period.

As George led the way, Susan noticed the way he walked. His legs slightly bowed, he moved with an airy, self-conscious shuffle. In the library she saw shelves stacked high with books on botany, biology, and chemistry. On one shelf she noticed a dinosaur statue. Recalling that someone had given George a dinosaur key chain at the Mensa Murder Mystery weekend, Susan saw a chance to stroke his ego.

"These are the dinosaurs you collect," Susan said. "Is that right?"

"Oh, yeah," George replied, his face lighting with pleasure. "They're probably as important as alligators are to ecology. There just weren't as many of them." He moved on to the subject of giraffes, marveling that the animals don't pass out when they drop their heads eighteen feet for a drink. Stretching his neck and running his hand along the length of it, he exclaimed, "They must have glorious internal mechanisms!"

"That's nice," Susan said. In a way she found it charming. George was like a brilliant child, fascinated by the world's wonders and proud of his ability to explain them. She wondered if someone so enchanted with life would also be willing to end it.

"We have the closet here," George said, pulling open a door. Susan felt a jolt of adrenaline; what would she see inside? She poked her head in for a look. After her eyes had adjusted to the light, she saw no chemistry equipment or suspicious bottles. But she saw something else: long black leather collars hanging from hooks, some plain, some adorned with silver studs. Nearby sat a small box of extra studs of various shapes and sizes. George said nothing about the bondage equipment. Instead he pointed at stacks of unopened cans of soda, including Coke. He explained, "Stuff left over from our murder."

George led his visitors into a room full of shelves, tables, and plastic buckets holding hundreds of rocks, gems, and minerals. Looking into the buckets, Susan saw a kaleidoscope of colors and shapes: petrified wood, quartz, crystal that sparkled even in the gray wash of afternoon light.

He explained, "This here is my junk room."

Susan smiled with genuine pleasure. She loved rocks and minerals. When she was a child she and her family often went camping in the mountains of North Carolina and Tennessee, where many towns feature tourist mines. Her father would give Susan and her brother a few dollars to buy a bucket of mud dug from the mine, which they would pour onto a screen and lower into a trough of frigid, rushing water. Shaking the screen with numb fingers, Susan would wash away the mud and dig through the rocks that remained. Mostly they were plain mountain stones, dull and undistinguished. But once in a while she would find a gem. The result never mattered so much to Susan; she loved the hunt, the patient sorting out.

She picked up one of George's geodes, an ugly stone with a core of glittering crystal. "I love these," she said. She had always marveled at how a coarse, ugly rock could hold such inner beauty. "It is so exciting to open one of these and find out what's inside."

"Yes," George said.

Enough small talk, Susan thought. She walked to the window and pointed at the squat mustard-colored structure behind Peggy Carr's house. From reading the files, she knew that George had complained to authorities when Pye turned the garage into an apartment. She feigned ignorance.

"Now, is that a garage?" she asked.

George joined her at the window. "It was a garage until they converted it into an apartment," he said. "I went down to the building board, and I said, 'Look folks, this section is zoned R-one; you can't do that.' The building board agreed with me and sent an inspector out. The neighbors were not happy with me.''

He smiled, warmed by the memory. ''What they've done is moved out,'' he said. ''I'm not sure what they're doing. I suspect they may be selling it. I think they want a hundred and twenty thousand dollars for the house. . . . It's been appraised at fifty.''

''I was going to say,'' Susan replied, ''for this area that seems a little steep.''

George laughed. ''Everybody found that to be outrageously funny.''

George continued the tour, leading them onto the porch, where the screen hung tattered and torn. ''The parakeet ate the screen,'' he said. ''What we've done is leave the outside just to go to hell as much as possible. But we feel it kind of protects us.'' He explained that the torn screen would be a wonderful deterrent to burglars—if Alturas had a crime problem, that is.

''This area of Alturas, the last crime that I know about, which is like break-ins and such, is about nine years ago,'' George said. ''Nobody around here locks their doors.''

Following George back inside, Susan noticed another strange feature of the house. On the first floor two bathrooms sat directly across from each other, so that the occupant of one could look across to see inside the other. His and hers toilets. Stranger still, one of the commodes was equipped with a seat belt.

Susan and Nona exchanged a glance but said nothing as they walked with George up a steep staircase. The master bedroom took up the entire second floor, with a bed at one end and a window that looked over a tin roof to the pool behind Peggy Carr's home. George tugged open a closet door. Inside, Susan could see a woman's arm and head.

''Oh, my,'' she said, ''there's a half a person in there!''

George explained that he and Diana had used the mannequin in some of their Mensa murder parties. "The last time I had her, which was the murder we had here January sixth, somebody sent me, ah, undergarments for the lady. In fact, I'll show them to you."

George reached into a small box and pulled out a black underwire bra and panties. Susan could feel her cheeks flush, but her embarrassment didn't stop her host. He held the underclothes toward her, his hands shaking slightly as he fondled the frilly silk. He said, "I had her nude except for a garter belt and a long wig."

Why is he showing these to me? Susan thought. Is this some kind of test? She gave a little laugh and said, "That's cute."

She saw that one wall held a large bookcase filled with murder mysteries, including a collection of Agatha Christie titles: *Remembered Death, Murder with Mirrors, The Secret of Chimneys*, among others. Somewhere in Diana's collection, Susan knew, there was also an Agatha Christie mystery entitled *The Pale Horse*. Ernie had talked with Diana about it during one of their meetings, but for some reason he had not read it himself. Susan had and found a story that mirrored Peggy Carr's murder.

In the book a British character named Mark Easterbrook sets out to solve the murders of nine people. The search leads him to an inn called The Pale Horse, where witches are said to arrange murders for people willing to pay the price. Easterbrook persuades a woman friend to pose as his intended victim, and then he watches helplessly as she comes down with flulike symptoms and a sore throat. Despite a doctor's assistance, the woman's condition continues to deteriorate. When her hair begins to fall out, Easterbrook remembers the story of some factory workers in America who were accidentally poisoned with a drug called thallium. He discovers that the poison was sneaked inside his friend's house shortly after a "consumer research" group stopped to poll her on favorite foods, makeup, and medicine. He calls in the police, who then find a packet of thallium in a potting shed near the inn. They eventually arrest a pharmacist who has drawn attention to himself by lying to police.

"You've got as many books as the library," Susan told George.

"These are all detective books," he replied. "They belong to Diana. I think she only keeps about twenty percent of what she reads."

"Is she the one that wrote the scenarios?" Susan asked.

"Yes," George said. He and Susan began reminiscing about the weekend's events, laughing about the time the wrong victim was murdered. Susan confessed that she had missed one murder altogether, although it happened under her nose.

"As soon as you revealed who it was, I said, 'Oh, good grief, I saw him do that.' It's amazing how quickly things happen, and I guess it's something you learn to look for, but since I'm not used to people getting murdered sitting next to me, I—"

George interrupted her. "It makes you wonder about eyewitness testimony," he said, "doesn't it?"

Back in the downstairs library George leaned over and pushed against a panel situated under the bookshelf. The panel swung aside to reveal some sort of hidden passage. Susan looked to see what was inside, but she couldn't make out anything in the darkness.

"Look at that," she said. "I've seen things like that on TV, but never—"

"This is our guard against break-ins," George said. "The way many of these burglars operate now, they'll use a metal detector to hunt out precious metals. So you can hide your precious stuff in the clothes dryer, which is great, or else you can have it so far away from anything that the detector won't pick it up, which is what we've done in this case."

"Amazing," Susan said.

"Actually," George said, "you're the only people who know about it—at least the only ones in Florida."

George led them out the back door. Looking across at Peggy's yard, Susan saw that the magnolia tree was in full bloom, its white flowers unfolding luxuriously across the waxy green leaves. On this side of the fence, on George's property, there was another tree, long dead, its branches turned to gray bones. Across from the tree she saw the garage workshop where George had been sawing wood four months earlier, when Mincey and Brekke had paid their first visit.

If George has some kind of drug lab, Susan thought, he would probably keep it away from the main house, to reduce the risk of a chemical spill or fire. Adding a page to her character's story, she created a hobby for herself that George would appreciate.

"Oh, can I look at it?" she said. "I'm interested in doing woodworking."

"Sure," George said. The door creaked open on rusty hinges, and he reached for the light switch. The air inside was thick with sawdust, a yellow fur lining the floors and shelves. Amid the power saw and other tools, Susan saw several jugs holding what seemed to be chemicals. George was still fiddling with the shop light, trying to turn it on. She took the opportunity to look around for signs of heavy-duty electricity, plumbing, ventilation—the utilities needed for a serious drug lab. Susan saw there was electricity, but not much more.

Once again Susan asked about neighbors. She wanted to give the impression that she, like George, had reason to be reclusive. She told him she was looking for a house away from prying eyes. "I want total privacy."

"I can understand that," George replied. "I'm like that, too."

Susan kept pushing, talking about the odds of getting good neighbors. "I guess you stand a fifty-fifty chance."

George laughed a little, but it was a strange laugh, deep and whispery. He began talking about Pye Carr and his family, his voice oozing disdain. George recalled how Pye began trying to sell him things. "He found out what Diana did, so he knew we had money," George said. "Which we didn't. We're in debt like crazy."

"What did he try to sell you?" Susan asked.

"He didn't sell his wife," George said. But Pye did try to sell him just about everything else, George said, his voice dipping into a sarcastic imitation of his former neighbor. "I've got a great pickup truck. Wouldn't you like a pickup truck? You could haul wood in it so easy, you know. Paid three thousand dollars for it. I'll give it to you for four and a half; it's a real deal."

"Anyway," George continued, "this went on for a week, and he came over one evening, and it was obvious that he had one or two beers too many. He wasn't really drunk, but he wasn't as smart as he normally is. He offered to sell me his shop." George said that he agreed, although he had neither the money nor the inclination to buy. George knew that Pye would regret the offer when he was thinking more clearly, and he couldn't wait to see Pye squirm.

"So he went back the next day and said he'd been thinking about it and he doesn't want to sell it," George recalled. "I said, 'Well, I've got a verbal contract. What are you going to do about it?' "

Susan giggled, feigning delight at George's devilishness. "Oh, great!" she said. "And did you get to buy it?"

"Oh, no," he said. "For one thing, I didn't want it, and for another, I didn't have the money. But I pushed it for about a week."

George flashed Susan a conspiratorial smile. Clearly he hoped that she would appreciate his treatment of Pye. Surely she could appreciate the challenges of living in a world populated by lesser creatures, creatures to be enjoyed—and abused.

George and his visitors settled down at the dining-room

table, and the conversation turned to employment. "Cousin Mona" had remained silent during most of the visit, making mental notes about George's house and behavior. But as the visit drew to a close, she began wondering aloud about job opportunities in Polk County. She said, "If you could just stay home and make money . . ."

George jumped right in. "I understand that drugs are fairly easy to refine."

"You'd probably have to be taught to do that," she said. "At least I would."

George pushed on, his voice excited. He explained that the house had plenty of plumbing for an illegal lab. "Yeah," he said, "we've got three bathrooms."

Susan's partner kept the conversation going, pushing George to reveal himself. If they got him talking about his days as an outlaw chemist, the conversation might wind around to the ingredients used in methamphetamines. If George started bragging about how he used thallium as a catalyst, they would have a major piece of evidence. Susan sat silently, marveling at how easily George had shifted from making small talk to plans for making drugs. For most of the visit he had been avoiding his guests' eyes. But now he was studying them, gauging their response to his invitation.

"But what could we make?" Nona said. "What could we make?"

Susan played it dumb. "You're asking me?" she said. "I studied art and literature. I don't know that much about—" She stopped mid-sentence, realizing her blunder: She was playing it *too* dumb. George was most likely waiting for a signal, even a subtle one, that Sherry and Cousin Mona knew something about drugs and would welcome his help setting up an illicit business. Unless the two women revealed themselves, George wasn't about to talk in detail about an illegal lab. He wasn't stupid.

And just like that, George closed up, retreating to safe territory. "Polk County is growing," he said. "An area that

you might want to look at is the north part of Lakeland . . .
the Lakeland Mall. . . . ''

Damn! Susan thought. I blew it.

As the tour ended, Susan stalled on buying George's house.

''Well, what I was really looking for was something not
quite this big,'' she said. Rather than try to persuade her,
George gave her tips on shopping for other houses. Watch
out for termites. Make sure the doors fit. Oh, and have you
considered the house next door?

George walked his visitors to the car, sending them off
with a wave and a smile. ''Nice meeting you,'' Nona called
out to George. Then, to the microphone in Susan's purse,
she said, ''Okay, we are clear.''

The two undercover agents rode in silence down the hill,
looked around to make sure George wasn't following, and
then turned off the transmitter.

''What did you think?'' Susan said. ''Did you think he
was weird?''

''Oh, yes,'' Nona said. ''Definitely.''

They did a play-by-play of the visit, shaking their heads
and laughing at the memory of George's mannequin, bondage collars, the toilet and safety belt.

''Did you see that scale in there?'' Nona asked.

''No,'' Susan said. ''Where was that?''

''In the spare bedroom,'' Nona said. ''It looked like the
kind drug dealers use.''

''That's interesting,'' Susan said. ''And I think he gave
us some good stuff about the neighbors. You could just
see the hatred and how stupid he thought they were. And
isn't it interesting that Diana is addicted to murder mysteries?''

They agreed that the meeting had gone well. Except for
Susan's blunder on the drug lab, George seemed comfortable with them, not at all suspicious. Of course, he hadn't
confessed. Actually, Susan thought, it was what he *didn't*
say that made him look the worst.

Most people, innocent people, would have said something—*felt* something—about the neighbors next door getting poisoned. "Oh, yes," George might have said. "It was the most awful thing: an entire family poisoned. The mother lingered in a coma for months and then died. Her sons are still recovering from the damage to their central nervous systems. You know, it's funny, Diana and I didn't get along too well with Peggy and her family. They let their dogs run loose and played their radios too loud. And Pye Carr, well, I've already told you how annoying he was. We had a few words. But I would never wish this on them. It's really an awful tragedy, and the police seem to have no clue to who did it. To be honest, Diana and I are worried that we might get sick, too."

George had said nothing of the sort. Not a word about Peggy and her family, except to complain. George thought they were so obnoxious, such *rubes*. To Susan, it seemed there were only two possible explanations. One, George was innocent, but he wanted to sell his house so badly that he wouldn't risk scaring her off with the news of a murder next door. But that theory had one big hole: He hadn't seemed at all anxious to sell. He acted more like a friend than a salesman, even offering tips on shopping for other houses.

The other explanation, of course, was that George really did care about Sherry and knew she had no reason to worry. He knew there wouldn't be another poisoning because *he* was the poisoner. The more she thought about it, the clearer it became. Of course George did not mourn Peggy's death, or pity her teenage boys, or grieve with Pye. To do all that, George would have had to think of the family as human, as people with lives that held some value. He had dehumanized them, made them less than himself, an annoyance to be gotten rid of—and quickly.

Two weeks after the murder weekend Susan mailed off another letter.

DEAR GEORGE and DIANA,

I have enclosed some photographs from the Mensa Weekend. . . . I do hope that you enjoy them as much as I have.

Even though I hate to send my valuables through the inept United States Postal Service, I will go ahead and take a chance that you will receive these intact.

The tour of your charming home gave me some excellent ideas on what I would like to do with my future. I have picked out three similar pieces of property in the Polk County area which appeal to me. My problem now being that my ex-husband is demanding to view the properties before okaying any of the purchases. (As I explained, the new home is all I'm getting in the divorce settlement.) Therefore, I must request one more viewing of your home with my malevolent ex-mate, so he can determine if he can justify one last act of retribution.

I am still traveling continuously between Ft. Lauderdale and Lakeland, so the best way to reach me would be through the mail. I remember you saying that Diana and yourself would be doing quite a bit of traveling in the next few weeks, so please let me know when in May would be a good time to set up an appointment.

                                        Thank you,
                                        SHERRY

DEAR SHERRY,

I'm just about back from about two weeks of running all over the country.

Diana and I would be happy to have you come anytime. If you'd like to spend a night or two, feel free. We don't lock the door so wander in anytime. . . .

Since you get one and only one house, our house

would be a poor choice. You need to buy the most expensive one you can find, then resell it and buy a house of lesser value and have cash left over. Perhaps you could work out a deal with the Indian government to have the Taj Mahal shipped to Florida and reassembled in Polk County. You could make a bundle selling it. . . .

GEORGE

Susan picked up the phone and dialed.

"George," she said, "I just got your letter and I was wondering if it would be all right this week. My husband's going to fly in from Texas. I was wondering if I could bring him over to see the house."

"Of course."

"I will try to keep him under control," Susan said.

George said, "I'll sic the cats on him if he gets nasty."

Susan's weekend surveillance was rapidly turning into a full-time job, but she wasn't complaining. George was warming to her, and she didn't want to blow it. She and her bosses called the FBI Academy in Quantico and asked Bill Hagmaier if he would be willing to make a trip to Florida to help map out a long-term plan for breaking down George's defenses. In early May, a month after the Mensa Murder Mystery weekend, Hagmaier arrived.

On the telephone Hagmaier had always been courteous and professional. In person, without a dozen other people demanding his attention, he impressed Susan even more. A tall man with a gentle voice, he seemed knowledgeable but not arrogant, supportive but not condescending. Hagmaier had seen the worst possibilities of human nature and returned to tell about it. Susan hoped he would help her do the same with George.

She showed Hagmaier into a conference room at the sheriff's office and began spreading out the case so far. Hagmaier watched the videos she had shot at the weekend.

He read the brochure describing the various sinister characters created by George and Diana. He marveled at the voodoo manual. He even examined some of the items Susan had retrieved on the trash runs: cake mix in a plastic bag, jokes George had written on his computer, crumpled letters from friends. One of George's drawings showed a man yelling at a computer. The man was shouting, "If you're hiding in there, I'll find you!"

Susan briefed Hagmaier on the fictional relationship she had created between "Sherry" and her estranged husband, "Richard." Richard had enormous power over Sherry, both personal and financial. Sherry had worked for years in her mate's law firm, and she needed him as a reference. He had the money she needed for a house. Plus he was an aggressive, domineering lawyer, just the kind of man George would hate. As he listened, Hagmaier nodded with approval. He said, "That's perfect."

Hagmaier wanted to see the crime scene, so Susan took him through the orange groves and up the hill to Alturas. The FBI man liked the idea of bringing Richard to visit George, particularly if Richard berated Sherry during the visit. "It would show him how aggressive and how abusive your husband is," Hagmaier said. "It would further your kinship. Maybe he'll give you some suggestions about how to get out of the situation.

"See," he said, "it really fits well. Your husband and you are the reverse of George and Diana." If George was the weak partner in the marriage, the one who depended on his mate for money and emotional comfort, he would relate to the beaten-down Sherry. Hagmaier offered some advice: Whoever played the part of Richard should try to be a male version of Diana—aggressive, loud, always in charge.

Hagmaier urged Susan to use the encounter to test George on a key part of the FBI profile. "Poisoners tend to flee from conflicts," he reminded her. "It would be interesting to see how George reacted when a fight broke out in his own home.''

At the end of the day Hagmaier congratulated Susan on her work so far. "I don't know why you thought it was so urgent that I come down," he said with a smile as he shook her hand. "You certainly don't need me to run things."

Two weeks passed. Late one night something awakened Susan, pulling her from an already forgotten dream. She looked over at the clock's blinking red numbers. Two A.M. Dawn was still hours away. Nighttime sounds filled her ears: the air conditioner ticking, a cat scuttling by the window, her husband breathing deeply.

The date was May 23, 1989. It was her husband's birthday. Unfortunately Susan wouldn't have time to celebrate with Gary. Instead, masquerading as Sherry, she would be introducing George to her other husband, "Richard." But first she had to get back into Sherry's skin. Lying in bed, she went back over the murder weekend and her first trip to George's home, trying to remember everything she had told him. Sometimes George seemed more like a computer than a human being, and she was afraid any inconsistency in her story would trigger his memory and scare him off.

She had found the perfect man to play Sherry's husband. Lieutenant Mike Lawton was a big man, mustachioed and gruff. He rarely smiled, brooked no nonsense, and could talk down to anyone. Perfect. She had briefed him about Sherry's life, about how Sherry and Richard met at college in Houston but had lately fallen very much out of love. She arranged for him to arrive at George's house in a brand-new white Lincoln Town Car. A shiny chariot for an imperious jerk.

"Treat me like dirt," Susan told her colleague.

"No problem," he replied.

*   *   *

Before the Town Car's dust had settled in George's drive-way, Lawton was in character. He growled, "This place looks like a dump."

George walked toward them and called out a greeting, but Lawton strode past without a word, beginning his inspection of the property. If the snub shook George, he didn't show it.

"He's checking out the neighborhood, I see," he said.

Susan acted embarrassed, the abused wife. Casting her eyes downward, she said, "Please, anything he says, just ignore him, okay? He's not Mr. Personality."

"I'm not really either," George said. "Do you wish to come inside or—"

"No, I suppose I'd better go find him," Susan said. She walked over to Lawton, who was studying the house with disapproving eyes. Making sure that George could see, she gave Lawton a pleading look, as if to say, "Please don't humiliate me in front of my friend." Lawton sauntered back over to meet George.

"Richard, this is George," Susan said.

Lawton didn't extend his hand, barely looked in George's direction. "How are you doing?" he said, sounding bored.

"Hi," said George. His eyes flickered to Susan, then at Lawton, and finally at the ground. He shifted uneasily on his feet, a creature torn between defending his territory and deferring to a stronger beast. Despite his anxiety, George tried his best to break the ice, pasting on a smile and playing the salesman.

"This could be considered an old country house," he said, opening the screen door and ushering Susan and her mate through the kitchen and into the library. While Lawton scowled, Susan swooned.

"The library," she exclaimed. "I love the library! The little alcove!"

Pointing to a cardboard box on the scuffed pine floor,

George said he had been packing, getting ready to move. While he and Susan talked like old friends, Lawton looked around the room, muttering, *"Great!"* and clearly not meaning it.

One of George's cats appeared and rubbed against Lawton's foot. He groaned. "Cats!"

Oh, Lord, Mike, Susan thought. Don't overdo it. Don't kick the cat! He didn't, and Susan yammered on about how much she loved animals, including cats.

Lawton sniffed. "You're not serious."

Susan replied, "I'm very serious."

George was doing his best to ignore the storm brewing between his guests. A smile pasted on his face, he continued the tour.

Lawton asked, "Do you have any sinkholes around here?"

"Oh, yes," George said. "In fact, the lake is a sinkhole."

Susan could see George's features brighten at the chance to escape the marital strife and, better yet, show off his knowledge. "This lake and the one you can't see used to all be spring-fed," he said. "And then in 1954 mineral mining in another part of the county cut the underground water supply, so the water level dropped desperately."

It was as if some sort of tape had clicked on inside George's head, freeing a stream of pure fact, information uncluttered by human emotion. "In the 1920s this was just a pleasure place," George said, standing in the living room and looking through the orange groves toward the lake. "During World War Two a Nazi spy was caught in the area, and no one can figure out what he was transmitting because there wasn't anything going on here!"

Susan laughed.

George laughed.

"Richard" never laughed.

George was starting to look uneasy, his eyes darting

around the room, as if seeking cover. Susan offered him a way out. On the first trip she hadn't gotten to look in the basement. She wanted to, though, in case George had set up his lab there.

"Now, where is the basement?" Susan asked.

George led them around the side of the house, where a set of storm doors opened to the space beneath. George stepped aside to let Lawton descend.

As Lawton fumbled for the light, George flashed Susan a conspiratorial smile. It was going just as she had hoped; as George saw what a nasty man her husband was, their alliance was building. George and Sherry had seen the enemy, and he was Richard. Wiggling his eyebrows, George lifted a sandaled foot and pretended to kick Lawton down the stairs.

Susan giggled. "Oh, my!"

George's voice dropped. "We'll lock the door on him."

"Does it have a lock on it?"

"We can nail it."

As Susan and George conspired, Lawton was having a look around the basement. There wasn't much to see: pipes, giant cobwebs, small windows crisscrossed with wire. Susan had told Lawton to look for lab equipment, but he saw none. After a few moments he emerged, glared at Susan, and snapped, "You about through?"

"If you are," Susan said.

"I think I've seen enough," he replied. "I'm not impressed at all."

Looking over at George, Susan could see that the tension was wearing him down. His smile had disappeared, and he looked as if he were ready to run into the orange groves and hide behind a tree. Although George talked about attacking "Richard" when Lawton was out of earshot, he did and said nothing when Lawton returned. Susan reflected that George fitted the FBI profile perfectly; no matter how much he cared for his friend Sherry, he was not about to stand up for her.

"Wander around," George stammered. "Feel free, dig through whatever you want, okay?"

Susan saw him turn and scurry upstairs. She and Lawton looked at each other in amazement but kept up their act. Lawton yelled, "What's he asking for this dump?"

"Why don't you wait while I go talk to George, okay?" Susan replied, loud enough for George to hear. "Why don't you just cool it?"

Climbing the stairs, Susan found George in his bedroom, sitting on the bed with his feet folded in the lotus position. Most people caught in another couple's crossfire would hide their embarrassment by pretending to tidy up, dust a windowsill, straighten a bedspread. Not George. His circuits had finally overloaded with the strain of ignoring the tension. His smile gone, he simply sat there, Zen-like.

"I don't know how to apologize," Susan said. "I—"

George interrupted. "There's nothing to apologize for."

"That's why I'm getting out of this," she said. "I'm not going to tolerate it anymore."

George looked at her with sympathy but showed no sign of moving from the bed. Susan walked to the top of the stairs and looked down at Lawton, who shrugged his shoulders and grinned in disbelief. Susan yelled down, "Do you want to say good-bye?"

Lawton walked upstairs, taking his time. He poked his head around the corner and said, "We'll see you later."

"Okay," George said absently. "Bye-bye."

Susan and her partner made a show of jostling each other as they walked down the stairs. Lawton growled, "Are you out of your mind?"

The screen door clattered shut behind them, the racket echoing through a house gone perfectly still.

Two days later, on a hill overlooking another lake, people were getting home from work. They returned to a neighborhood that was comfortable but nothing fancy: one-story houses, driveways poured from smooth concrete, grass struggling to grow between thin sand and hot sun. As the workday ended, the neighborhood symphony tuned up. A dog barked. A car door slammed. A child yelled, *"Mommy's home!"*

Normally the sounds soothed Susan after a day of police work. Not this afternoon. Susan had told George that she didn't have a family or a permanent home. While George thought she was still shuttling between friends' apartments, Susan didn't want him to hear evidence to the contrary. She clicked on the stereo to drown out the television, her children's excited talk about the day at school, the racket of her real life.

After the visit to George's house Susan hadn't wanted to call right away. She wanted to give him time to recover, to think about the ugliness between Richard and her, to come up with ideas on how Sherry could rid herself of her husband.

Let me poison him for you, Sherry.

George wouldn't say that, Susan thought, would he?

When she did call, George answered.

"I wanted to tell you what happened after I left the other day," she said.

"Okay," George replied.

"I won't even ask you what your opinion of Richard is."

"Well, actually, I felt I was seeing him possibly at the worst time."

"I—"

"That's okay."

The conversation stumbled on, George's words sounding clipped, matter-of-fact. He seemed to be putting distance between Susan and him. She wondered what was going on. Had she blown it? In the back of her mind a voice said, "Hang up. It's over."

George hesitated. "Ah," he said, "there is something I've been wondering about."

"Uh-huh," Susan replied, bracing herself for the worst.

The possibilities ran through her mind: George had seen a picture of "Richard" in the paper, a picture showing a cop, not a lawyer. Or, he had recalled a day years ago when a police officer looking very much like Richard had pulled him over and written a ticket. Or perhaps he was simply beginning to wonder why "Sherry"—a woman with no phone number or visible means of support—had dropped into his life shortly after Peggy Carr's demise.

George's voice came over the line. "About you getting a horse," he was saying, "I honestly don't know how much room horses need. Have you checked into it?"

Susan's breathing eased, and she swallowed a laugh. So George hadn't been fretting about her true identity. He had been worrying about something she had mentioned earlier: keeping horses on his land. Susan cheerfully steered the conversation in that direction, and just like that, she had the old George back. He patiently explained that his home was not really a farmhouse, but if she had her heart set on horses, she might be able to board them at a nearby ranch.

George told Susan that his wife had signed a contract to move her practice to Sebring, a small city an hour's drive south of Alturas. Unfortunately George said, they wouldn't be moving out of Alturas anytime soon. Susan told him not to worry, she was in no hurry.

She tried to return to the other day's conflict and how George had fled from it. She wanted to see if he would suggest a less direct solution to her woes.

"The other day," she said. "I've got to tell you how embarrassed I was—"

"Well," George replied, "when you really get down to it, you cannot be responsible for the actions of any other person. So, ah, there's no need to be embarrassed."

"No," she said. "You're my friend. If I didn't care about what you thought, then I wouldn't be worried about it. But it's embarrassing to me to know that I lived with him for ten years."

"Okay," said George. "I'm sure he must have very good traits, too, 'cause obviously you wouldn't have lived together so long."

How strange, Susan thought. George had talked coldly about Pye Carr, a man who had buried his wife and nearly lost a teenage son and stepson. But now he was giving Richard, who had abused her and was an asshole lawyer as well, benefit of the doubt. Who was George Trepal? A man who would kill a family over loud radios or an eccentric fellow willing to understand the peculiarities of other people? Cold-blooded killer or compassionate friend? Maybe, she thought, George is some of both. A killer with a kernel of goodness.

As their phone conversation drew to a close, George invited Susan to his office to look at his computer. This was a good sign. George had lied about the office when he talked to Mincey and Brekke, and he probably wouldn't invite her there if he suspected her true identity. "Come in through the glass doors," George told her. "My office is the one just to the right. It's totally unmarked."

By the end of their talk George seemed to have regained the confidence he lost in the encounter with Richard. While at first he seemed reserved, by the end he was working hard to keep the conversation going. As if Susan's voice were the only friendly one he would hear that day.

George offered to put his new friend in touch with Mensa members in other parts of the state and country. "You actually know a lot of the people because they were at the murder weekend," he said. "Of course, you don't know their real names."

"You know, that was terribly confusing to me," Susan said. "I didn't know what was the real name and what was not the real name. I was beginning to doubt my own at the end of the weekend. I rather liked the name that you gave me."

"Well, if you want to use it," George said. "I mean, if you're starting a new life . . ."

"I might do that," she said. "It sounds mysterious. Oh, well, I won't take up any more of your time, but—"

George interrupted. "I have plenty."

FIFTEEN

An undercover investigation is like a play. There are lines to write, scenes to memorize, sets to erect and tear down. For every word uttered onstage, there are a hundred spoken in planning, rehearsing, getting into character. And always, looming in the background, there is peril. If Susan botched her role, if her audience saw through her words to the underlying truth, there would not be a critical review in the newspaper the next day. There would be an obituary.

Two weeks passed before Susan saw George again. Despite his apparent warmth, she didn't want to push too hard. She had told him she didn't have a phone number yet because she was staying with her cousin in Fort Lauderdale, waiting for the divorce settlement she needed to buy a place in Polk County. She wanted George to think she was calling him on the rare occasion when she was in town.

Although Susan couldn't spend every day with George, there were ways to observe him from afar. She continued to sift through his trash, follow his car to work, watch his home from the groves across the street. Increasingly she was also spending time on what cops call pen registers. With a court order she hooked into a phone company computer that recorded the time and destination of all the calls George and Diana made from their house. Susan identified the most frequently called numbers, then spent hours combing phone listings and city directories for the names and addresses of people and businesses. It was tedious work, but important. She was looking, first, for any calls to chemical supply houses that sold thallium. She found none but continued to monitor the calls, compiling a list of frequently called friends and acquaintances. Susan could not call George's friends yet, for fear of blowing her cover. But the day might come when she would need their insights.

Susan wanted to take George up on the invitation to visit his office, a rented space in a white concrete-block building in downtown Winter Haven. Accompanied by Nona, Susan walked through the unmarked door and found George at his computer, dressed in his standard outfit of T-shirt, khaki camp shorts, and sandals. Surrounded by stacks of paper and computer disks, George made his fingers dance across the keyboard, his hand waving the mouse like a wand. At first he didn't notice his visitors. He stared at the computer screen, utterly focused, a world away.

Susan was getting the impression that for George, the computer was not just a machine but an extension of himself, a window to his soul. As he worked, he showed an ease, a self-assurance, that he didn't have in other settings. When talking to people, George stumbled and stuttered, buffeted by his own insecurities and the inherent chaos of human communication. With a computer George could put his thoughts into a language that, once mastered, offered him complete control. In the computer mind, all information—fact, feeling, even mystery—is reduced to a binary code, a series of zeros and ones ordered by the most rigid logic. While human relations can be irrational, the computer offered George an orderly way of solving problems—and an off switch.

George noticed Susan and Nona standing there and wheeled around on his stool. He smiled with genuine pleasure.

"Do you want to go to lunch?" Susan asked.

"Yes, I'd love to."

George flicked off the computer. Susan said, "How about a hamburger?"

"Sounds good," George said.

At the restaurant Susan and Nona went through the salad bar, while George waited at the counter for a burger. Susan took a seat across from where George would sit, so that she could keep an eye on both her suspect and the door. If anyone walked in who knew her true identity—a good possibility in a county this small—Susan would signal Nona to distract George while she waved off the visitor. As much as anything, Susan was afraid of running into another cop. This undercover operation was a secret not only to George but also to most of her colleagues. Susan didn't want one of them to call out a greeting and spoil the investigation.

This was the first time Susan had sat down to eat with George, and she didn't take her eyes off his hands. His fingers unwrapped the hamburger and lifted it to his mouth. She imagined his fingers carefully prying the caps off Coke bottles, pouring in the poison, and then wiping away the prints. She pictured them opening the unlocked door to Peggy's kitchen and sliding the Cokes under the counter, taking care not to spill any thallium on *his* skin. The images chilled her and reminded her to be wary. Even though she didn't think George was wise to her, why take chances? If he had killed once, he wouldn't hesitate to kill again, especially a cop masquerading as a friend. Susan knew that thallium was tasteless, odorless, and deadly in the smallest doses. Hagmaier had warned her: If George discovered her true identity, he wouldn't confront her directly. He would simply sprinkle something in her drink. To George, it would be the ultimate game: The hunted becomes the hunter.

As the threesome ate, they talked mostly about Sherry's troublesome husband. "He is such a brute," said Nona. "You should never have married him. I told you so, but did you listen?"

George lifted a french fry to his mouth and chewed. He said little, but Susan could see he was listening. This was exactly what she wanted: to draw him in, make him feel some responsibility for her welfare. Hagmaier had told her not to expect George to do anything as obvious as offering to poison "Richard" or confiding in her about the neighbors, at least not yet. But someday, she hoped, George would say, "I might be able to help you with your problem. . . ."

After lunch George offered to take them on a tour. Both Nona and Susan knew Winter Haven; they had worked there for years. But they didn't let on. In George's presence they were seeing it all for the first time. As George directed them out of town, Susan said, "Don't get me lost out here. Is Cypress Gardens out here? Look, look, Mona, there's Cypress Gardens! Now we know where to come."

George directed them to the Audubon Nature Center, a forty-two acre patch of wilderness surrounded by houses, shopping malls, and asphalt streets. They turned off the main road and into the park, through a row of slash pines and laurel oaks where raccoons and rat snakes and cotton-tail rabbits sought refuge from the urban sprawl. Susan wondered why George had brought them here, away from the crowds.

As they began to step out of the car, the weather turned, clouds gathering in angry black clots, warning of a summer thunderstorm. George's plans spoiled, they climbed back in the car and headed toward town. As they pulled out of the park, George cried out.

"Stop!" he said. "Stop here!"

Susan put on the brakes, and George scurried toward a fence. He plucked a handful of tiny red berries from a vine growing there. Climbing into the backseat, George handed the berries to Susan and began talking excitedly.

"These are very poisonous," he said. "Three of them can kill a person."

Alarmed, Susan dropped the berries on the car seat and stared at them. They looked sweet and harmless, like red rosary beads. As they drove off, Nona smiled at George and looked at Susan. Too bad you can't feed some of these to Richard, she said.

George threw his head back and laughed, speechless with pleasure.

George's poison berry tour wasn't evidence, at least not the kind Susan could use in court. "My client's interest was academic," George's lawyer could argue, "an extension of his curiosity about minerals and dinosaurs and other wonders of the natural world." But it gave Susan another piece of the puzzle, took her one step deeper into George's psyche.

Dissecting the criminal mind: It was the thing Susan liked best about police work, especially undercover assignments. In uniform a cop can get only so close. The criminals know who you are, keep their defenses up. In plain clothes, posing as one of them, Susan got a close look at the darkest hearts. Many cops loved the excitement of the chase and capture. So did Susan. But to her the adrenaline rush wasn't enough to compensate for a skinny paycheck and an ever-present risk of death. She needed a mental thrill as well, the challenge of climbing into a criminal's head and unlocking its secrets. With many suspects, the dopers and prostitutes, it took only a few days, or minutes, to get the key. But with George the closer Susan got, the more mystified she became.

She wondered: If George was guilty, if he was as brilliant as he seemed, why would he keep dropping clues? He had taken such care in committing the crime. Having gotten away with it, he should want to continue living anonymously, in freedom. Yet George kept dancing near the flame, dropping hints, some far from subtle: The murder mystery weekend. The voodoo pamphlet warning of poisoned food. The talk about how much he hated Pye Carr and his family. Hints about drug labs. And now, to a woman he had known for only two months, a lesson in poison berries. Why would George talk so freely of things that could link him to a murder? The most obvious reason was, simply, that George was an innocent man caught in an awful coincidence. He just happened to be fascinated with murder and poison. He just happened to live next to a woman who had died from drinking poisoned Coke. He just happened to possess the sophisticated chemistry skills needed to pull off the crime.

No, Susan thought. There are just too many coincidences. By now she had come to believe that George was indeed guilty, and it was her job to prove it. But why was he making her job easier? She remembered what Bill Hagmaier had told her: George loved to relive the murder, to keep it alive in his fantasies. With each day that passed without the police coming to arrest him, perhaps George gained a measure of confidence. Maybe it had become a game, with George dropping clues he knew the bumbling cops would miss.

All that made sense and fitted with the FBI profile of an intelligent, arrogant poisoner. Perhaps George wanted to reveal enough details of the crime that someday someone would know that he had done it. Only then would he get credit for his brilliant crime. But with George, Susan thought, there might be another element: a guilty compulsion. As proud as he was of his deed, perhaps he was also ashamed. Perhaps some part of him wanted to be punished.

Except for the prison term he served during the 1970s, Susan learned, George had rarely felt the consequences of his actions. When he was a child, his mother fought his fights for him and spared him the spankings other children got for misbehavior. When he left home, he flunked out of one college and coasted through another, showing little interest in acquiring the skills needed for a real job. As long as Diana was willing to support him, he seemed happy to play with his computers, write an occasional technical article, and organize Mensa parties. He didn't have to support a family; he didn't even have to support himself. He simply tended to his own needs and didn't worry about the impact they had on others. Even as he moved into his forties, Susan reflected, George lived in a constant state of self-absorption, perpetual adolescence.

When George left Susan, he went home to a house filled with the evidence of that self-study. Over the years he had kept a series of journals in which he chronicled his thoughts on subjects ranging from S&M to ethics. In some of those writings, dating back to the 1970s, he framed the issue of moral responsibility with a peculiar blend of Eastern religion and egotism.

In a September 1976 journal entry George wrote: "There is no reason to stop doing anything unless you want to. If you are going to do something, accept that you are going to do it. Feeling guilt or conflict is the worst thing that can happen, much worse than what you do. A yogi can kill but the deed should be done with love rather than anger."

Less than two weeks later George wrote about Karma, the Buddhist principle that actions in one life shape one's destiny in future incarnations. "Life is a spiritual journey," he reflected. "If that statement is the 'what' then Karma is the 'how.' How the universe operates. Karma is action. As you sow so shall you reap. This isn't connected with morals, it's just simple action and reaction.

"The more you love, the more you are loved. The more you hate, the more you are hated. . . . In karma there is no right or wrong. Do what will create less suffering in others because it will create less suffering in you."

George seemed skeptical of traditional notions that good people find a reward in the afterlife. In 1977 he published a short story in the *Mensa Bulletin* entitled "Heaven." In his story the main character dies in an avalanche and ends up in some other world, standing in a long line.

It was all misty around her and somehow she knew she was dead. She decided to make the most of it—being that kind of person. "Where am I?" she asked the man ahead of her in the line.

"Purgatory," he replied.

"But I'm agnostic!" she exclaimed.

He shrugged his shoulders. "I'm Catholic."

There was a small popping noise as a Buddhist monk materialized in line behind her. He spoke to her, but she didn't understand his question. (His question was, "Where am I?")

At that moment a red, spade-tailed demon walked by with a sign. The sign said, "SADISTS! JOIN THE DEMON CORPS. HELL CAN BE HEAVEN FOR ALL ETERNITY!" And in small letters it said, "Apply at front desk. . . ."

The front desk had a sign. It said, "FRONT DESK." There was a tired looking gray man behind the desk. He talked to whoever was at the front of the line and then they went through one of two doors. One door said "HEAVEN" and the other said "HELL." They were both very impressive.

When she reached the desk, the man asked, "Do you want to go to heaven or hell?"

"I get my choice?" she asked.

"That's right. Anything else you've heard is wrong. Our public relations department on your world is a little behind on getting that idea across, but that's it."

She paused for a moment and then asked, "What are they like?"

"Heaven is eternal bliss, etc. Hell is the opposite. You know."

"If I don't like one can I change my mind later?"

"No."

"I was afraid of that." She paused again. "Does anyone go to hell?"

"Oh, lots of people do. The demon corps is very popular. Other than that, many feel they didn't live a good enough Earthly life and go. And others think it's a trick or the final temptation and go to hell thinking they're outsmarting the system."

"How can I be sure it's not a trick?" she inquired.

"No way that I know of," he replied. A bell sounded. "I'm sorry but your time is up. Either take a door or go to the back of the line." His eyes left her. "Next, please!"

It was with fear that she walked through the HEAVEN door. . . . "Welcome to heaven. This will be ultimate bliss for all eternity. I can't tell you how good you'll feel, so I won't try. We're happy to have you. The ushers will show you what to do. Please cooperate with them. Thank you."

An usher touched her shoulder. "Walk with me, please," he told her. She looked at his wings and halo as they walked in silence. Eventually they came to a place where the clouds were dark and smelly. "Pollution from our plants," he told her. "Don't worry, it can't hurt you."

They walked on past a power plant, and on the other side of it she saw rows and rows of cots. There were more cots than she could count in a lifetime. Massive power cables snaked among the cots and divided many times until they were mere hair-thin wires. The wires went to boxes bolted to the cots. Each cot had a box. Each cot also had a body.

"What's in the boxes?" she asked.

"Transistors," he replied. "Much nicer than the old vacuum tube models."

"I meant to ask what they do."

They had reached an empty cot. "Please lie here," he said. She did and felt his fingertips on her scalp. "It's really technical," he began to explain, "but think of it as a gadget that electrically stimulates the pleasure centers of the brain. You will know nothing but pleasure for all eternity.''

"Wait!" she yelled. "I don't want this! This isn't what . . ." Her scream was suddenly replaced by a smile of pure ecstasy as he flipped a switch.

"Sorry sister, but you can't fight city hall," he said softly as he walked away.

She did not hear him.

Susan called Hagmaier. "Bill, you're not going to believe what just happened," she said, telling him about George's lesson on poison berries. "Do you think this means that he might offer to poison Richard for me?"

"He might," Hagmaier said. "But I doubt it. George didn't walk up to Peggy Carr and shoot her; he snuck some poisoned Cokes into her house and then ran home and waited for her to die. The same principle would apply to him talking about murder; he would probably just hint at it, and hope you pick up on the suggestion."

Susan looked out the window, to where her boys were playing in the yard outside. She was still pumped full of adrenaline, eager to turn today's success into an arrest warrant. "I understand," she told Hagmaier. "But he really seems to be opening up to me. How do I take advantage of that? My bosses aren't going to wait forever for me to make a case against this guy."

"This is going to take time," Hagmaier said. "You need to build a friendship with George, and that doesn't happen overnight. What are you thinking about for your next move?"

"I had an idea," she said. "What if I took George on a picnic? So far I've always had somebody else around, and I'm not sure that he has been able to relax. Maybe if we go to a park, just the two of us, he would open up. Maybe even slip up."

"Now that," said Hagmaier, "is a great idea."

*   *   *

In early June 1989 northerners were just starting to enjoy the summer warmth. By that time in Florida folks had a hard time remembering when it *wasn't* hot. As Susan drove toward George's office, the sun hung inches above the car, pounding through her windshield.

She pulled over and dropped a quarter into a pay phone. She didn't want to give George much notice about the picnic because she didn't want him to offer to pack lunch. So she had rented a Mustang convertible and thrown a lunch into the back seat.

"Hi, George," Susan said. "Would you be interested in going on a picnic today? I know it's short notice, but—"

"Sure," George said.

"Great," she said. "I already packed a lunch. I'll be by to pick you up."

Susan had packed her basket with ham sandwiches, chunks of broccoli and cauliflower, and sixteen-ounce bottles of soda. After picking up George, Susan drove to Lake Martha Park, a sprawl of grass, grandfather oaks, and swing sets not far from George's office. They walked toward where some schoolchildren were splashing in the warm water.

"Do you want to sit down here or up there? It doesn't matter to me." That was what Susan said. But even as she spoke, she was steering George to a particular park bench, one just above the pump house—in clear view of the surveillance team that had been waiting for them to arrive. Two cops sat in a car with dark windows, listening to the conversation piped through a microphone in Susan's purse.

As the children filled the air with shouts and excited laughter, Susan reached into a paper sack and pulled out the sandwiches and bottles of soda. She had brought a variety: Sprite, diet Sprite, Pepsi, diet Coke, Coke—a regular poisoner's taste test.

Susan chose diet Sprite, then pointed to the bottles, saying, "I didn't know what you drank, so I brought one of each."

As George picked out his bottle, Susan saw that his hands were trembling. Is he nervous, she thought, or have I just never noticed this before?

She immediately took control of the conversation; she didn't want George to launch into an hourlong dissertation on the hydrogeology of Lake Martha. Susan had a different agenda: "Sherry" was going to open up, show George that she trusted him enough to share her inner pain and seek some badly needed advice.

Susan told George that she was lonely, that he was the only friend she could count on. "I don't have anybody to talk to," she said. "I appreciate you letting me talk to you. . . . " She let the words trail off into a soft, self-conscious laugh.

"Yes," George said, his voice gentle. "I'm always here."

Susan took off her sunglasses and looked into George's eyes, brown and large behind his thick glasses. George rarely made eye contact, preferring to hold himself apart, disconnected. But today Susan wanted him to look at her, to feel their bond, even if it made him uneasy. She wanted him to feel *responsible*.

She told him she was frustrated that Richard was stalling on their divorce. "I don't know what to do with him," she said. "I can't get on with my life till I end that part of it."

"I can't do anything but listen," George said.

"I appreciate it," Susan said.

George returned her gaze and leaned toward her. His voice was gentle, full of genuine care. He said, "Whenever you have problems, call, okay?"

Encouraged by George's openness, his *tenderness*, Susan decided to push. But she had to be careful. If George offered to poison Richard, she didn't want his lawyer telling a jury that she had planted the idea.

"Have some advice for me?" she asked. "'Cause I don't really know what to do."

"If you're wanting to force a move, figure out what he

would least like and threaten him," he said, his voice deep-
ening, gaining timbre. "I mean, after you tell his secret to
everybody ..."

Susan glanced at his hands; they were no longer trembling. She thought, This is interesting. George is suggesting
blackmail. It's not murder, but it shows that George is not
above doing something unsavory, even criminal. She took
his cue, focusing on Richard's vulnerability to character
assassination.

"He's very worried about his reputation," she said.
"He's built his business on his reputation."

"I assume he knows enough law to just run rings around
you," George said.

"Oh, yeah," she replied.

"You have to attack someplace else," George said, his
smile turning wicked. "Scandal is nice."

An ambulance sped along a nearby street, its siren yip-
ping. George didn't turn to look; he was completely focused on the task at hand, constructing a scheme to
blackmail Richard into submission. His voice was strong
now, his gaze steady. "If you want to play real dirty," he
said, "probably the thing to start with would be the child
molester. The way this works, it would be a letter sent to
him.

" 'Dear neighbor, Mr. Richard Guin, who is a prominent
attorney in town, molested my five-year-old son three
times. He didn't tell me about it immediately, because the
man said that the police would come and take Mommy and
Daddy. Now this man lives' ... and you would describe
where he lives," George said. "Ah, then you end the letter
with 'When I confronted this horrible man, he said, "I'm
a prominent attorney. It's my word against a child's, and
then I will sue you for slander, for everything you're
worth." I believe him. I feel that since you live in the
neighborhood, he probably has molested your children as
well as mine. Hopefully you'll have more courage, and then

I can come forward, and we can send this horrible man to prison.' "

George leaned close to Sherry, his eyes bright with possibility. Sweat beaded on his forehead, pooled on his thick eyeglasses, and trickled down his nose. He went on. "Now if you can imagine this getting to your two hundred closest neighbors, as well as the police and whatever . . ." he said. He explained that she wouldn't actually mail the letter to the neighbors, just send a copy to Richard to shake him. "Of course, it would be free from anything which would mark it as being from you, except it would have a Florida return address."

Inside the unmarked car a tape recorder whirred, picking up every word of the conversation. "It's horribly illegal," George was saying. "But there's nothing to connect you with it."

"I can be one of the most vengeful people," Susan said, "and I never will give up."

"That's nice," George said, chuckling. "I'm gonna like you and always will."

In addition to getting even with Richard, Susan told George, she wanted to get a job, make some money, so she wouldn't have to depend on a man. But there was a problem: The only job she could list on a résumé was working for her husband as a legal secretary. Susan told George she was worried that Richard would give her a bad reference.

George's voice turned quiet and businesslike. He said, "You could lie." Rather than rely on Richard's goodwill, he said, why not simply forge a letter of recommendation from him? George offered to compose the bogus letter on his computer.

"Really!" Susan said, leaning toward her friend. "You are a very talented person."

"No, my computer is very talented," he replied. He laughed, adding; "My specialty is understanding systems, how anything works."

"Well, once you understand it, what do you do?"

"Abuse it," he said.

George was on a roll, peeling away layer after layer of his armor. Maybe Hagmaier was wrong about George, Susan thought. Maybe George *would* open up quickly, tell her about what he had done to get rid of his neighbors, and offer to do the same to Richard.

"Seriously," George was saying, "with Richard you need to use just enough force to get what you want, but not enough force to make it worthwhile for him to get you back."

"Yeah," Susan said. "I will try something subtle, and if it does not work, I'll do *something*."

George laughed. "I can suggest things."

Susan smiled. "Would you?"

Suddenly, inexplicably, George backed away. It was as if he had seen something in Susan—a sideways glance, a whisper of insincerity—that stopped him cold. He began stuttering. "I—I suggested one already," he said. "Believe me, it's very effective."

Susan tried to get him back on track. She said, "All he needs is one real good shock."

But it was too late. George wasn't going any farther, at least not down that path. "Something else which works very effectively is," he was saying, "you just write a threatening letter to the President and sign somebody's name to it. . . . "

"Oh," Susan said, "I see what you're saying."

"All you need is a little letter saying, 'Dear Mr. Bush, I'm very unsatisfied with the way you're running the country and I'm going to kill you,' " George said. "I mean, even if it's an utterly false alarm, he will be checked out very thoroughly."

After dropping George back at his office, Susan ducked into Davis Bros Cafeteria for a glass of iced tea and a dose of air conditioning. She knew she looked like a sweaty mess, but she didn't care. She was elated with progress she had made at the picnic, and she couldn't wait to tell Brad and Ernie.

Standing in the drinks line, Ernie asked, "Where have you been?"

"I went on a picnic," Susan said.

"Who did you go on a picnic with?"

She smiled coyly. "George."

Settling into the vinyl cushions of a corner booth, Susan recounted her outing with George. She felt an adrenaline high, her words spilling out in an excited stream.

"Let me tell you what I did," Susan said. "I let him choose his drink."

"So which did he choose?"

Susan motioned for them to follow her outside. At her car she opened the trunk and pulled out a trophy in a plastic bag: a sixteen-ounce bottle of Coke. It wasn't evidence, at least not the kind she could take to court. But it was another revelation. When George was thinking of a normal soft drink, the sort that could turn up under a kitchen counter without attracting notice, he didn't think of the Pepsi favored by Peggy and her family. He thought of his own favorite drink. Coke was it.

Chapter

SIXTEEN

———

Susan left the Coke bottle at the office, along with Sherry's other things. Sherry wasn't just a name Susan had thought up for her undercover character; she was another person, with her own history, even her own brand of musk perfume. Every time she put on that perfume, she became the killer's friend. Before she went home for the day, she stepped into the bathroom and scrubbed the scent away. There was always the risk of bringing too much home.

Susan needed to remain *Susan*, to keep Sherry what she was: a tool to get George Trepal. It was getting harder to do. Susan had stopped taking the kids to McDonald's or the movies, for fear of running into George or one of his friends. She had even stopped wearing her wedding ring; after all, George thought she was getting a divorce.

Susan's husband tried to be understanding, but the case was draining even his deep well of patience. A man with muscular arms and a wry wit, Gary was also a cop. But he and Susan were worlds apart. He liked classic rock; she liked country. He kept to himself; she was outgoing and bold, the girl who gave high school administrators hell until they made a spot for girls on the school rifle team. He trusted people; despite her outward openness, she trusted no one. They had met in 1972, when he had just graduated from high school and she was completing her senior year. They wed the next year.

In the beginning theirs was a traditional marriage: Gary began his career as a police officer while Susan stayed home to raise their firstborn son. But after a few years Susan got the itch to follow her husband into law enforcement. Although they had chosen the same profession, they followed different paths. Gary joined the police department in Lake Wales, the small city where Susan had grown up. He did no undercover work and liked it that way. On the streets, in uniform, he got to help his neighbors, put away bad guys. By contrast, Susan traded her patrol uniform for a plainclothes job at the earliest opportunity. She liked the independence and the risk. She liked finding her way in the shadows.

Susan and her mate had an understanding. She told him as much as he *needed* to know about her cases. For the first few months of the Trepal investigation that wasn't much. Susan certainly didn't want her husband to know that she was befriending a man who could sprinkle some poison on her food and kill her in an instant. When she had to disappear for an evening or a weekend, she simply told him, "I'm working that suspect again."

As her involvement grew, Gary began to ask—only half-jokingly—if he should set a place for George at the dinner table. When Susan came home at night, she spent hours on the phone, setting up surveillance and mapping strategy for her next meeting with George. Sometimes she would ask Gary to keep the kids quiet in the next room while "Sherry" called George to set up a meet. Even on vacation Susan had to stop and mail a postcard to George.

As the investigation moved into its third month, Susan's distraction was becoming obvious to their family and friends. At the Lake Wales Police Department, Gary's colleagues teased him about Susan's absences. "Hey, Gary, is your wife going to be home tonight?" they'd say. "Or is she going out on a date?" For Gary the joke was wearing

thin. But he kept his mouth shut at home. He knew that
Susan was under a lot of stress, and he didn't want to add
to it. Just a few more weeks, Susan told him, and they could
get back to normal.

Peggy Carr's family was trying to get back to normal as
well, but it wasn't easy. Cissy moved into an apartment and
looked after her younger brothers. Although the thallium
had disappeared from Duane's body, the damage remained.
His muscles ached, and the doctors said it would be months
before he regained his strength and bulk.

Duane was a picture of health compared with Travis,
who had suffered more severely from the poisoning. Although he was out of intensive care, Travis continued to
require painful therapy to regain even simple motor skills.
In medical reports his doctor and therapists noted that
Travis could walk a distance of only six feet, needed help
pulling his pants over his toes, and spoke with a "whispering slow voice." Aided by his father and his own de-
termination, however, Travis made steady advances. As
Susan forged ahead in her undercover investigation, he
worked up to a hundred-and-fifty-foot trip using a walker
and leg braces and was described as making "remarkable
progress" in regaining his mental sharpness and emotional
health.

Susan was following Hagmaier's advice, slowly building
her friendship with George. It appeared to be working. Although George hadn't told her about his role in the neighbors' poisoning, he seemed to be opening up. He was
starting to view her as a friend, and she was encouraged
by his offers to help blackmail Richard. But talking about
blackmail is one thing, Susan knew, and committing murder is another. George had been dancing near the flame long
enough, Susan decided. It was time to shove him in.

She left a message for Hagmaier. He was forever off
somewhere working on a case—Kansas, New York,

Alaska—but when he got Susan's messages, he called right away. He knew she was counting on him.

"Why don't you really push him hard?" Hagmaier suggested. "Put him in a situation where you are threatened, and see what he will do to protect you. See how far his anger takes him." But he cautioned her not to expect anything dramatic. The tension between George and his neighbors had built for years before George acted. It might take Susan months to bring George to a similar point, since her problems with Richard touched George only indirectly. While many killers act in an instant of reckless passion, Hagmaier reminded her, poisoners do just the opposite. Rather than resist an impulse, they have to overcome their passivity. Rather than lash out, they ponder and plan.

George had been wanting Susan to accompany him to Consuelo's, a favorite restaurant of his in Tampa. She decided to take him up on the offer but added a request of her own. Would he accompany her to the Tampa airport to meet Richard? George agreed. Early that morning Susan pulled up to his office in a blue Mustang convertible. She wore green slacks and a nice flowered blouse, explaining that she had dressed up because well, that's what Richard would expect.

"Do you want to take my car?" George asked.

"I appreciate it," Susan said, "but I've got Mona's car. Here's what I'm thinking: Because I know how uncomfortable you feel around Richard why don't we drive separate cars to Tampa, then meet? That way you won't have to ride home with Richard." The truth was, Susan wanted George to see Richard verbally abusing her at the airport, then taking her off in a car to do who knows what. She wanted him to anguish over what had become of his friend Sherry. Perhaps that would fuel his anger and encourage him to help her get revenge.

George headed west on Interstate 4 in his silver Honda, with Susan trailing behind in the Mustang. The two cars joined the stream of rented sedans carrying sunburned tourists, tanker trucks loaded with orange juice, and, unbeknownst to George, a parade of unmarked cars carrying Polk County sheriff's deputies and FBI agents.

Susan was thoroughly wired. Using a needle and black thread, she had sewn a microphone and miniature transmitter into the lining of her black purse. Under the car the techs had installed a tiny, black "bird dog" to transmit a radio signal to the airplane and cars trailing behind.

In Tampa Susan and George rendezvoused in a parking lot. Since there was time to spare, George suggested a visit to one of his favorite bookstores in the nearby city of St. Petersburg. As they drove across the bridge, the wind teased the green waters of Tampa Bay into a froth. Sea gulls wheeled through the air, soaring here, plunging there. George gazed at the scenery and lectured Susan on why she should abandon the American dream, which he described as being happily married, gainfully employed, and raising two children. His voice rose over the wind rushing through the convertible's top.

"Once you dispel this ideology that has been programmed into you," he was saying, "you can concentrate on what's right for you."

Susan felt her anger rise. "Not all of us have the luxury of living life without responsibilities, George. You have a wife who doesn't mind supporting you, who doesn't care if you contribute to the family income or to society. You may call that escaping the American dream, but I would call it being a gray-haired teenager." That's what Susan wanted to say, but she didn't. She just smiled politely, the eager student absorbing George's words of wisdom.

George directed her to Haslam's, a bookstore in a gritty part of the waterfront city. In a neighborhood heavy with streetwalkers and cheap wine, Haslam's was an oasis of culture, a huge building packed to the ceiling with new and used books. George pointed Susan to the guides on building self-esteem, while he headed to the science shelves. Susan looked up to see another detective, a member of her surveillance team, standing across from her, browsing through the titles.

She leaned over and whispered, "Is everything all right?"

"Yes, it's fine," he said. "But we're having trouble picking up your conversation. The reception on the bug stinks."

She shrugged, looking nervously toward where George was scanning the shelves in the next room. "Good luck," she said. "I've gotta go."

She walked to George. "I want to show you a book," he said. She looked at the blue cover and white letters: *Kill All the Lawyers?* George handed it to her, saying, "I want you to have this while Richard's here."

"Great!" she said, taking the book. "Thank you!"

As they walked up to the cash register, George took the book from her hand. "I'll pay for it and I'll loan it to you."

"If I'm going to have it," Susan said, "then I'll pay for it."

"No, no, no," he said. "I like to possess books, but I'll loan it to you. You can have it lying around when Richard comes to visit."

Susan decided not to resist. Clearly it was important to George that he own the book. Perhaps, she thought, it was his small act of war. He knew that the book would upset Richard, a man who had rejected not only Sherry but also her brilliant friend. It wasn't enough that the book was George's idea; it also needed to be his weapon, his little dose of poison.

Susan's stomach churned as they walked to the car. George wanted to eat, but Susan was dreading it. She knew that agents were already at Tampa International Airport, setting the stage for the fight between her and Richard. Susan was edgy, her nerves gone raw and jangly with anticipation.

George, on the other hand, was thrilled. He had been wanting to take Susan to his favorite restaurant for weeks, but she had kept making excuses, saying she was busy or out of town. In truth she had been trying to avoid meals with George. While she felt increasingly secure around him, Hagmaier kept reminding her of the risk. "George is a smart man skilled at keeping his feelings inside," he told her. "He could find out about you, but you wouldn't know until it was too late. Don't give him any more chances than you have to."

Susan and George walked into Consuelo's and settled into a booth. As her eyes adjusted to the dim light, she opened a menu and smelled the taco meat cooking in the kitchen. Her stomach was rumbling like a 747 about to crash. As she contemplated the Mexican food swimming in sauce and spices, Susan thought, Just what I need.

She asked for a glass of water, while George ordered his usual Coke. She chose what she thought would be the least threatening item on the menu: taco salad. George said he would have the same. When the waitress brought the salads, Susan picked at hers, stirring it around so it would look at least half eaten. George dived into his with gusto, devouring the lettuce, beef, tomatoes, sour cream, guacamole, and picante sauce. As she watched him eat, Susan felt ill. Her face was green; she knew it was. She didn't want to vomit right then and there, but she was afraid she might.

George looked at her with concern. "Are you all right?"

"No," she said. "I'm so afraid of what Richard's going to do that it's making me ill."

She expected him to offer words of comfort, to pat her arm, reassure her that everything would be fine. Instead he stared at the tabletop. After a long moment he mumbled, "I've decided not to go with you to the airport. I'm going to make sure you get there, and then I'm going to leave."

"Please, no!" she exclaimed. "I really need you to go with me. I don't want to confront him alone."

George paused for a long moment, then reluctantly nodded. "Well, all right," he said. "I'll go with you."

Susan sighed, her relief genuine. "Thank you!"

She excused herself and pushed open the door to the ladies' room. Inside she pressed her forehead into the wall, its surface cool and steady. "It's going to be all right," she whispered. "It's going to be all right."

Richard's plane still wasn't due, so they had more time to kill. George offered to show her Ybor City, a neighborhood in East Tampa where Cuban immigrants once rolled cigars in red-brick factories. The factory workers are mostly gone now, replaced by galleries, boutiques, and restaurants serving paella and café con leche to suburbanites who liked their ethnic flavor served by people who took American Express. As they drove around looking for a place to park, Susan wondered about her surveillance team. Ybor City wasn't on the itinerary, and she hoped they hadn't lost the trail. She needn't have worried. Rounding a corner in a crowded lot, she nearly ran head-on into one of the undercover cars. The driver's mouth dropped, and he quickly headed in the other direction. But then, a couple of turns later, the two cars were facing each other again. She glanced over to see if George had picked up on the pathetic pas de deux, but he seemed oblivious, staring out the window at the old brick factories.

Finally Susan gave up on finding a space and headed for Tampa International Airport. The flight was scheduled to arrive at 2:45 P.M. George and Susan walked through the airy lobby as travelers churned around them, bags slung over shoulders, tickets popping out of pockets, elevator music following their every step. Susan and George walked to Airside E, where a shuttle train would take them to the gate. Susan looked up and saw the sign. ALL PERSONS SUBJECT TO SECURITY CHECK.

The lights glinted off George's glasses. He began talking about metal detectors, explaining their operation in numbing technical detail. Suddenly it hit Susan: She had forgotten about the microphone and transmitter hidden in her purse! If she walked though the metal detector with it, she

Peggy Carr (left) with her daughter, Cissy (center), and sister, Shirley. (*Courtesy of Cissy Shiver*)

Peggy's new husband, Pye, was out of town on a hunting trip when his family fell ill. At first, police considered him their chief suspect. (*Courtesy of Cissy Shiver*)

Doctors couldn't figure out what had made Peggy and her two sons fall mysteriously ill, but neurologist T. Richard Hostler had a suspicion. Tests confirmed that the family had been poisoned with thallium, a chemical so toxic that the U.S. government had outlawed its widespread use in 1972. (*Robin Donina*)

Police learned that the thallium had been planted in an eight-pack of Cokes. (*Courtesy of Polk County Sheriff's Office*)

Ernie Mincey, a gravel-voiced homicide investigator with the Polk County (Fla.) Sheriff's Office, puzzled over why someone would poison an entire family. Then he learned about an anonymous death threat a few months before. (*Robin Donina*)

A month after Peggy's death, George Trepal and his wife hosted a Mensa Murder Mystery party featuring voodoo, a threatening note, and "death" by poison. (*Courtesy of Polk County Sheriff's Office*)

One of the guests at the murder party was a woman who introduced herself to George as Sherry Guin. Unbeknownst to George, his new friend was actually Susan Goreck, a young undercover officer assigned to bring him to justice. This photo of Susan ("Sherry") and George was taken at a later date. (*Courtesy of Polk County Sheriff's Office*)

George Trepal—a reclusive thirty-nine-year-old computer whiz—lived next door to Peggy. He would emerge on occasion to stage bizarre fantasy scenarios with his wife and high I.Q. friends in Mensa. (*Courtesy of Polk County Sheriff's Office*)

"Sherry" accepted George's offer to visit him at his home in the middle of an orange grove. To George, "Sherry" came across as pleasant and unassuming, even naive. It would be a year before he learned the truth. (*Robin Donina*)

During the yearlong undercover investigation, Peggy's family tried to carry on. Cissy told her daughter, Kacy, who was two years old when the family was poisoned, that her "Me-Me" had gone to heaven and couldn't come back. (*Robin Donina*)

The poison didn't kill Peggy's teen-age son and stepson, but it withered their bodies and spirits. Her ailing son, Duane, is shown here next to his healthy brother, Allen. (*Courtesy of Allen Dubberly*)

Susan's boss, Sheriff Lawrence W. Crow, Jr., had begun collecting Coke memorabilia long before the poisoning. He was outraged that someone would use the familiar soft drink as a murder weapon. (*Robin Donina*)

Susan received invaluable support from Bill Hagmaier, one of the rising stars at the FBI's Behavioral Science Unit. Before he began to help Susan understand George's sinister mind, Hagmaier (*left*) helped extract a final confession from serial killer Ted Bundy. (*Courtesy of FBI*)

Susan got so close to George that she moved into his house. There, she found a tiny bottle containing damning evidence. (*Courtesy of Polk County Sheriff's Office*)

George had been careful not to leave any fingerprints on the poisoned bottles, so it fell to prosecutor John Aguero to prove that the circumstantial case was more than just "coincidences." (*Robin Donina*)

When police searched George's home, they found the hardware needed to turn their suspect's S&M fantasies into reality, including handcuffs, a leather riding crop, and a black hood bearing a distinctive set of teeth marks. (*Courtesy of Polk County's Sheriff's Office*)

George sat silently throughout his murder trial. Only when the jury had delivered its verdict did George speak to his friend and nemesis, Susan Goreck, aka Sherry Guin. (*Courtesy of the* Tampa Tribune)

On the anniversary of Peggy's death, her family gathered at the cemetery to pay their respects. They brought Cissy's newborn baby, Ethan, the grandson Peggy never met. (*Robin Donina*)

realized, the alarm would sound. Guards would scurry over, demanding to see the inside of her purse. They might even rip out the lining in search of a bomb.

The shuttle train squeaked to a stop, and the passengers began rushing inside. As George moved to join them, Susan held back. If I step on this train, it's all over, she thought. I won't be able to turn back. She needed an excuse, quickly.

She clasped her hand to her chest. "Wait a minute," she gasped. "Before we go over there, I've got to go to the rest room. I'm getting ill again."

Before George could respond, she raced across the carpeted lobby. Around a corner and safely out of George's sight, she punched the elevator button and looked nervously at her watch. As the elevator climbed toward the level where she had parked the car, Susan wondered, Why is this thing taking so long? Finally she reached the fourth floor and ran to the Mustang. "I've got to take this out," she whispered into her purse, hoping the surveillance team could hear. "I've got to go through the X-ray machine." She ripped the lining out of the purse, tore out the microphone, and threw the whole mess into the trunk.

The sound of her trunk slamming echoed behind Susan as she sprinted through the garage and back to the lobby. Running a hand through her hair and across her slacks, she took a few deep breaths and walked around the corner to where George stood in the same spot, pacing in a small circle.

"My gosh, I got lost," Susan said, still breathless. "I couldn't find you anywhere."

If George sensed something wrong, he didn't let on. "Oh, yes," he said mildly. "This is a large place. It can be confusing."

The X-ray machine was silent as Susan walked through. "We've still got a half hour before Richard arrives," she said to George. "Want to stop by the snack bar?"

Susan had a diet Sprite, George a Coke. They sat at a

tiny table amid a swirl of travelers: businesspeople with tense faces and briefcases, moms giving in to children's pleas for ice cream, college kids hunched over paperback classics. George began talking about how he was constantly looking for ways to experiment with life.

"Once," he said, "I lived on the streets, just to see what it was like. I lived inside a cardboard box, ate in soup kitchens, and went for days without a bath. I found out that I fit in as well with homeless people as I do with Diana's doctor friends and Mensa people."

George was boasting: nothing new. But Susan heard something different in his voice, a note of sadness. He held his glass of Coke with both hands, clutched it as if it were an anchor. "I feel like I'm almost a mutant," he was saying. "I'm intelligent, but people think I'm funny-looking."

Susan looked at George. He was wearing his usual ratty T-shirt, shorts, and old leather sandals. He had a five-dollar haircut, an unruly beard, and glasses coated with dust and sweat. On one level she despised him. But on another she couldn't help feeling a flash of pity. As he spoke, Susan sensed his vulnerability. What have people done to him to make him feel this way? she wondered. If he were a friend instead of a murder suspect, she would have reached over, grabbed those scrawny shoulders, and said, "If that bothers you, why don't you do something to help yourself? Why don't you put on a suit and some decent clothes? Just because your glasses are thick doesn't mean you can't fit into normal society."

But Susan didn't say that; it wasn't her job to be George's counselor or his mother. Instead she stored away another lesson about George: Despite his claims of indifference, it anguished him to be an outsider, a stranger in his own land. If he feels shunned by society, Susan wondered, does he also feel exempt from its moral and legal codes?

*   *   *

"Continental Airlines Flight Four Ninety now arriving."

George and Susan pitched their soda cups and walked across the carpet to where an escalator carried passengers from the airplane. Below, Mike Lawton, aka Richard, had been waiting on the ramp with a suitcase, waiting to blend in with the flight's genuine passengers.

"Are you sure you want to go through with this?" George said.

"Yes," Susan said, her tone unconvinced. "It's all going to work out."

Lugging bags and craning their necks to look for friends and family, the travelers begin rising toward the gate area on the escalator. Susan peered down, trying to see her partner. When she spotted him, she said, "Here he comes, George."

Hearing nothing, she turned around. *"George?"*

George had vanished. Susan swiveled around, scanning the lobby for her friend, her protector. He was nowhere in sight. Susan felt anger, real anger, boiling inside. Just moments ago she had let her heart go out to this guy. Yet at this moment, when "Sherry" needed him most, George had vanished. She said under her breath, "How could he do this to me?"

Lawton came up the escalator. Seeing that Susan was alone, he gave her a questioning look. But he stayed in character, not knowing what had become of George. "There you are!" he boomed, grabbing her arm. "I need to talk to you."

"I've lost George," she whispered. "I don't know where he went." But she couldn't just stop the confrontation; what if George was hovering nearby, watching? She glared at Lawton and shook her arm free. Sensing that she needed time, Lawton snapped, "Wait here! I've got to go to the bathroom."

Other passengers were slowing to watch the spat, but Susan saw no sign of George. She walked toward the bathroom, peered into the snack bar and over at the newsstand.

Nothing. Just as she was about to give up the hunt, George reappeared from behind a pillar, looking furtively around, a cockroach caught in the kitchen.

She walked over and touched his arm. "George," she said, her voice edging toward sarcasm, "I just wanted to thank you. I found Richard, and I wanted to thank you for supporting me."

He pulled away from her like a scared animal. "That's fine," he muttered. "That's fine. I knew you would want to be alone, so I was just going to go ahead and leave."

They walked a few steps together, and then George looked up to see Richard bearing down on them. "What the hell's he doing here?" Lawton yelled. "What's he doing with you?"

Busy travelers paused to take in the fight. Without another word, George ran to the shuttle and disappeared inside. The doors closed, and he was gone.

Jana Monroe, one of the FBI agents who had been monitoring the scene, sidled up next to Lawton and Susan. She was chuckling. She told them that she had been hiding behind a pillar to observe the confrontation. Next thing she knew, a nervous man with a beard and thick glasses had taken up surveillance beside her. It took her only a moment to recognize his face.

Lawton and Susan rode the elevator to the parking garage, stifling their laughter as they walked toward Susan's car. Susan couldn't tell if George's car was still there, so she said to Lawton, "You'd better make it look good." He obliged, dragging her across the floor to her car, then filling the air with the sound of squealing tires.

In a car parked nearby a man crouched in the shadow of the seat. George Trepal, Mensa genius, master chemist, and murder suspect, waited patiently for his chance to make a getaway.

The next day Susan felt genuinely ill. It had taken her days to set up the airport trip, and she was beat. But it wasn't just nerves and fatigue wearing her down; it was also the mounting toll of slipping in and out of Sherry's skin. She wasn't getting much sleep, and she worried that in her exhaustion she might slip and tip off George. She called Hagmaier for advice.

"It's relentless," she said. "It's draining me. I'm starting to have a hard time separating Sherry from Susan. It takes so long to get into my role as Sherry that I'm afraid of stepping out of it."

Hagmaier had worked with a lot of undercover officers, and he knew that Susan's problem was a common one. When you spend that much time playing another person, the lie becomes the truth. It has to, in order for the undercover operation to work. But with Susan, Hagmaier had a special worry. Many of the undercover cops he worked with were tough types, nearly as dangerous as their suspects. But Susan was an extraordinarily sensitive person, and Hagmaier worried that the empathy she felt toward George might blind her to his threat.

Hagmaier looked at the picture of Ted Bundy on his wall. He remembered how charming Bundy could be, with his easy smile and quick mind. But Hagmaier didn't have to worry; every time he met with the killer, prison guards stood nearby. Susan's situation was considerably more perilous, and he urged her to keep reminding herself of that. "Read over those case reports again," he said. "Remember what this man has done."

After the airport scene Susan wanted to keep the pressure on. She decided to continue the drama, convincing George that Richard had beaten her up after leaving the airport. One of her bosses, Colonel Paul Alley, had suggested having a makeup artist give Susan a black eye. As it turned out, though, Susan didn't need makeup. After getting home from the airport, she stumbled into a door. It was just the bruise she needed.

The next day Susan donned a beat-up pair of blue jeans

and a blouse, then drove to a gas station. She ducked into a bathroom, scrubbed her eyes until they were red and swollen, and dropped a quarter into the pay phone.

George answered. "Sherry, I was concerned about you," he said. "Are you all right?"

"Yes," Susan said, making her voice shake. "But I need to talk to you. Can you meet me at the park?"

"Sure," he said. "I'll be right there."

They sat on the same bench as before, with the same surveillance team recording their conversation. Susan's voice came out flat and numb, drained of feeling. "It took me a long time to work up the nerve to call you," she said. "I feel so bad about what happened yesterday."

"Ah, what happened?" George said nervously.

"At the airport."

"Oh," he said, nodding but avoiding Susan's eyes. "Oh."

"I guess I don't need to tell you that he's not gonna go along with what I want."

"Oh, well, that was kind of obvious," George said, looking down at his hands. He swallowed and went on. "Ah, let me tell you how my thoughts were going yesterday, which may clarify things a little bit, okay? It was kind of a normal George personality, and there is this bit of my brain which I call the Watcher because it just sort of sits in the background and really understands what's going on. And if anything of interest occurs, it alerts the rest of me.

"So," he continued, "we're talking about Richard, I think it was at lunch, and you're saying, 'Well, I'm not exactly sure why he's coming. I think maybe he's gonna pay me.' And this is when the Watcher wakes up, and it's going, 'Wait a minute! Something's wrong here,' and ah, then the Watcher really starts screaming.

"The way I'm seeing this," George said, his words gaining momentum, propelled by their own curious logic, "you are his worst enemy. You, and you alone, have ruined his marriage, threatened his career, and have a good chance of taking money away from him. I'm going, 'Wow, I mean if I have a bad enemy, I'd love to have her in a situation like this.' "

Choked with heat and humidity, the air around the bench barely moved. Some children splashed and giggled in the water nearby, but neither Susan nor George looked at them. George pushed on, apologizing for hiding when Susan's angry spouse was confronting her.

"This is where the cowardice comes in," he said, "because I think I've done all I could."

"I know that," Susan said. "I'm shocked, to say the least, at what he did. I don't know why I'm surprised, okay? Because that's just his . . . I don't know," she said. "Needless to say, it went downhill from there."

"Yes, I kind of thought it would," George said, leaning toward her. "I was worried about physical harm."

"Well . . ."

"Are you okay physically?"

"Yeah," Susan said. "I've got a nice goose egg on my forehead, but I'll live. I, all right, let me tell you what his ultimatum is: He's giving me until Tuesday to come back."

George looked at her bruise, nodding. "Uh-huh."

"He said he has found a way to tie up everything and I don't get one penny. I mean nothing."

"Uh-huh."

"And I have to believe him because he's got these judges and lawyers as friends. What else am I gonna believe? You know what I'm saying?"

"Uh-huh," George said. "What I really recommend that you do is find the meanest divorce lawyer that you can."

Get a lawyer?

That was the last thing Susan expected to hear. Just the other day George was suggesting blackmail and other nefarious plots to get rid of Richard. Today he was offering logical solutions, solutions that work within the system—instead of abusing it.

What has happened? Susan wondered. *Is he on to me?*

Or when it comes down to it, is he really nothing but talk? Maybe he doesn't have the courage to harm somebody, even by an indirect method. Maybe we're just wrong about him.

No. She couldn't just walk away. Maybe she wasn't pushing the right buttons. After all, George had been in prison, and he was running from a crime that could put him there for the rest of his life, could even lead to the electric chair. He wasn't just going to incriminate himself casually. Susan tried a different tack. Maybe George would open up if he thought that she too, had a hidden criminal past. She told George that she worried about attacking Richard, then having it boomerang.

"I did something a few years ago that he knows about," she said. "And he said that it would all come out if I went through with it."

"So what?" he replied.

"Well, it would probably ruin me from working anywhere."

George didn't push for details. His chin rose, and he looked her in the eye. He said, "I can make you disappear within twenty-four hours."

"How is that?"

"Oh, I can give you a new identity, anything you want."

"Really?"

"Yeah," he said. "I understand the system."

George began to squirm on the bench, and his words spilled out in a breathless torrent. "What you do, you go to Orlando, to the public library building, and down in the basement they have the county records. Now you toss through those until you find somebody your age who is dead; that's your new name. You get a copy of the birth certificate . . . go and apply for Social Security . . . get yourself a new driver's license."

Susan nodded appreciatively. This all was very interesting, but she wanted George to propose a more direct solution.

"I've put up with him so long," she said. "I'm so filled with hate."

"Okay," he said.

"You're so nice and you're so understanding," she said. "I don't know. I don't know if anybody can realize how much rage . . . I feel like a whipped child."

George offered more understanding words but no concrete solutions. As they spoke, a grasshopper jumped between them on the bench. George smiled and shooed it away with gentle, almost fatherly care.

"Go on now," he said to the grasshopper. Smiling at Susan, he said, "I don't want to hurt the creature."

Susan tried one more approach. Maybe if she talked directly about drugs, George would tell her about his experience with the North Carolina crank lab. She told George she was thinking about another trip to Fort Lauderdale.

"I want to lie on the beach," she said. "And in all truthfulness, I've got some old friends down there that would . . ." She paused, as if trying to decide whether to go on. "I'm looking at old habits," she said, "and right now I feel like I need something from an old habit."

"Okay," said George, curiosity flickering in his eyes.

"And I think they can get it for me."

"Okay," he said, beginning to laugh. "Interesting crystalline patty, something like that?"

"Something like that," she replied.

He tipped his head back and smiled, as if he had just taken a hit of something strong and delicious. Normally it was George who dropped the hints; he seemed pleased that this time his new friend was suggesting something illicit.

He said, "If you run across a good source of acid, let me know."

"Okay."

"I'm serious."

"Okay."

"I just love playing with that stuff," he said. "I mean,

not enough to synthesize it, but ah, if it were offered, I certainly wouldn't pass any up.''

More laughter. George was warming to the subject.

"Okay," he said. "What's your specific interest?"

"In regards to?"

"Altering your mental molecules, which melts in your mind rather than your mouth."

Susan spread her hands a foot apart. "Right now," she said, "I would settle on a joint about that long."

George bounced excitedly up and down on the bench. For his part, he said, he preferred LSD, little drops of acid that could transport him from a banal world. "Most people use it recreationally," he said. "I mean, it's the most beautiful psychic . . ." His voice trailed off, then picked up again. "This way I can see what the trash is, and I can grab on to it and get rid of it.

"So, in other words, I'm using this very much the way the Indians used it," George continued. "With drugs, if you use them for short term, like with acid, you're ripping open the door for perception." Acid also has the advantage of being inexpensive, he said. "If I got desperate enough, I'd simply synthesize."

"Really?" Susan said. Hadn't he said just a few minutes ago that he *wouldn't* want drugs badly enough to make them?

"Remember," George was saying, "I have training in chemistry and psychology." He launched into a technical discourse on making illegal drugs, his voice swelling with wonder, the way a teenager talks about his first time in the back seat. "The thing that is hard for me is, part of the molecules—a seven-membered ring with an interesting carbon—hooks like three across. . . . ''

Susan could see that she had touched George, broken through a layer of his self-defense. This was the first time he had done more than hint at his drug days. He hadn't told her yet about his arrest and imprisonment, but Susan hoped he was getting close. If he told her about that, it would show that she had truly won his trust.

"So it's like analysis work on amphetamines," George was saying. "Turned out about two hundred and fifty-six analogs for hallucinogens based on one molecular base. . . . " He began to laugh, then apologized. "If I get started, I guess I'll go on forever—because I know a hell of a lot about it."

"It's fascinating," Susan said. She told him she appreciated his not condemning her past drug use. "I wasn't real sure how you were gonna take that. I thought you would say, 'Ooh, bad person, go away.' "

"I don't think highly in terms of child molesters," George said, grinning. "Anything else I do not care about, or else I probably do it myself.

"When you get down to it," he said, "I have a relatively secluded life. I play with computers, and I'm happy about it. My religion prevents me from doing real harm to anybody."

"What is your religion, if you don't mind me asking?" Susan said.

"Oh, it's more Buddhist than anything," George said. "I'll give you a five-minute lecture on Buddhism if you want. It's a great way to get through life."

"I tend to be more agnostic," Susan replied. (In reality she considered herself a Christian.)

"Ah, Seven-Day Avoider. No, it's a Jehovah Bystander," George quipped. He explained his interpretation of the Buddhist worldview. "The first noble truth of Buddhism," he said, "is the world sucks.

"The second noble truth, it talks about attachment." He continued. "Let's say that we are looking at somebody in a mental institution, and he has this hang-up about fecal odors. I mean he had to wipe very thoroughly. So he got the ten rolls of toilet paper, but that's not enough. So he gets a hundred rolls, and then finally a thousand, and then he thinks there could be a nuclear war. *The toilet paper plants will be shut down, dammit! This is not enough! I need ten thousand rolls, a hundred thousand.*"

She could only nod. "Uh-huh."

The lesson in this tale, George explained, was that the man could never be happy because he was *attached* to his toilet paper. The price of attachment—to toilet paper, to emotions, to people—is pain. That brought George to another noble truth: "If you ain't attached, it don't hurt."

And another: Live only in the moment. "You can have your mind running all over the past and future, but that does no good," he said. "You sit right in the present. When something comes up, you react."

Susan said, "That's a good philosophy."

"It's a wonderful philosophy," he replied. "I mean, hell, it's a major religion."

"That's right."

"It also has a nice way of dampening down emotions," George said. "When my mother was dying and I was sitting with her, ah, I'd start getting very uptight about this and I'd just have to sort of grab on to myself . . ."

Susan stared at the man sitting beside her on the park bench. Even a killer's eyes might well up at the memory of his mother's death, but George's remained dry. His voice cool and rational, he repeated the dialogue—apparently between himself and "the Watcher"—that played out in his head as he sat by his mother's side.

" 'George, what are you doing?'

" 'I'm sitting here, watching my mother die.'

" 'Then sit and watch your mother die. Don't worry about anything.' "

"That is amazing!" Susan exclaimed, the flesh rising on her arms.

"And so," George said, "I just pulled myself back."

"I wish I could do that," Susan said.

He smiled. "It takes practice."

Chapter
SEVENTEEN
———

It is more shameful to distrust one's friends than to be deceived by them.
— La Rochefoucauld,
  Quoted in one of George Trepal's journals

Five days after their trip to the park Susan telephoned George. She said she was still in Fort Lauderdale but would return the next day. "What have you been up to?" she asked.

"Oh, playing with computers," he said. "As always."

"It's just nice to hear a friendly voice. I want to hear nice things."

"All right. You're a nice lady."

"Thank you. Tell me something good. Tell me something wonderful."

"Oh, I wish you hadn't put it that way."

"Don't you know something good?"

"Well, I have a new kitten who's quite good. She's turned into a real foot eater, but otherwise . . ."

"And what have you named her?"

"Tigerlily."

George's voice came across the line like a breeze, light and free of care. Susan, on the other hand, sounded listless and glum. It wasn't entirely an act. After a long weekend out of character she was struggling to become Sherry again.

"As you know," she heard George say, "I'm a good listener."

"I just can't tell you how much I appreciate it," Susan replied. "I'm just lonely, and I just wanted to hear a voice, so . . ."

"Yes," he said. "I'm somewhat lonely, too, except for a kitten chewing on me."

"I've got my television set," she said, "which is not a real good friend. That's the only voice I've heard, too."

"What would be a good place to go?" George said. "I don't know much about Fort Lauderdale, so you're on your own, unfortunately."

"The beach. There's lots of people, but you're still alone."

"Yeah, um. I've had problems like that at times, too, sort of being in a crowd but alone," George said. "It's like being in a glass box, not really able to touch anybody."

"That's right," she said. "But—"

George interrupted. "So, uh, a really good way to introduce yourself is to throw up on somebody. It's because, really, nobody suspects that you do it on purpose and then you can start a conversation of 'Gee, I'm so sorry. Let me help you out of your clothes. Golly, I—I'm so embarrassed about this.' And it just goes on from there, and they never suspect it's really a pickup."

Just when Susan was sure that George had a killer's heart, pure ice, he would show that strange vulnerability. *Like being in a glass box.* That was so true for George, Susan thought. He sees the world, but he can't touch it, or let himself be touched. The people outside the box won't accept him, or at least he thinks they won't. He's too smart, too strange.

Once in a while George ventured outside the box, as he just had. But then he got nervous and scurried back inside. Susan was beginning to see a pattern: George would lay himself open, then retreat with a clumsy joke. It was a pathetic routine, but she found herself feeling sorry for him. She felt something more: a trace of empathy, a connection.

As she got to know him, she felt tiny shocks of recognition. George's father had been a television repairman; Susan's had worked on small appliances. George collected rocks; so did Susan. George studied Buddhism; so had Susan. The similarities ran deeper; Susan realized that she and George were, in some ways, kindred spirits. Like George, Susan was an intelligent person who had never fitted in with the crowd, never wanted to.

When she was growing up, before central Florida was paved with theme parks and hotels, she had roamed a magic kingdom of rolling fields, wild flowers, and meandering streams. Dressed in cutoffs, she splashed in the tea-colored water of Tiger Creek, dropped a hook into Lake Parker, and learned to shoot her own .410-gauge shotgun before her tenth birthday. Like George, she read voraciously and chose activities that carried her away from the crowd. In high school Susan took flying lessons, organized a girls' rifle team, and went to a different church almost every week. She wrote letters to newspapers in countries from India to Iran, looking for pen pals. While her classmates wore dresses to a school dance, she donned a sari.

A thread ran through Susan's interests: They indulged her intellectual curiosity, and they gave her distance. While other kids were satisfied to drive cars on Polk County's winding roads, she soared above them in a plane. While others unthinkingly followed their parents to church, she explored different faiths. While Susan enjoyed hanging around with her high school friends, she devoted much of her time to correspondents she would never see.

It was only logical that Susan chose to become an undercover cop. With a badge and an ever-changing list of identities, she could plunge into the middle of a crowd but never be part of it. But there was a risk. The longer she acted like George's friend, the more she felt herself becom-

ing one. When the investigation began, her colleagues at
the sheriff's department had warned her about the Stock-
holm syndrome. But Susan had dismissed their concerns.
She would play the part, make the arrest, then walk away.
At least that was what she thought.

On a certain level she wasn't surprised to feel some empathy for George, to see some goodness in him. While most
police officers see the world in terms of good guys and bad
guys, Susan had never felt that way. She liked to say,
"There's nobody on this earth that doesn't have some good
in them."

Her feelings didn't just stem from her faith in human
goodness. There were also practical advantages to acknowl-
edging George's sympathetic side. For one, it helped her to
make her character believable. While many undercover
cops have no trouble acting friendly toward someone they
hate, Susan could not. By focusing on the good in George,
on his vulnerability, she could make "Sherry" seem a genuine friend.

Something gnawed at Susan, though. George wouldn't
be revealing himself unless he trusted her, and Susan knew
his trust was rooted in her deceit. If her plan worked, Susan
would arrest him and move on to another case, while he
awaited the electric chair, betrayed by a woman he thought
a friend. She knew that shouldn't bother her—catching a
killer surely justified a lie—but it did. After she had finished talking to George that day, she called Hagmaier.

"You know, Bill," she said, "it would be so much easier
if George was nothing but a jerk. Then I could just look at
him as a bad guy who needs to go to jail. But it's not that
simple. I find myself feeling sorry for him. Is there something wrong with me?"

Hagmaier poured himself a ginger ale. He had been expecting this. Many undercover officers never feel a trace of
emotional involvement, no matter how long they pursue a
suspect. They simply focus on getting the criminal off the
street, driven by a desire to protect the public or win a

promotion. But Hagmaier knew that was not Susan's way.

"There's nothing wrong with you, Susan," he said gently. He reminded her that George was a typical poisoner, helpless in the face of direct conflict, always looking for someone to recognize his vulnerability and protect him. In addition to being a cop, Hagmaier knew, Susan was a mother. "George seems to need a mother," he told her, "and it shouldn't surprise you that you respond to him as a mother."

Hagmaier urged her to accept her feelings but not to let them cloud her judgment—and put her life at risk.

"I know what you're going to say," Susan said.

"What?" he replied.

"You'd say I just ought to take a step back and look at this, maybe read the case file again and see what the man was responsible for."

Both of them started to laugh.

"Good-bye, Susan," Hagmaier said. "Keep your antenna up."

The next day Susan stopped by George's office. As usual he was hunched over the computer, his fingers working the keys. He looked up and smiled.

"Come in," he said.

"Am I disturbing you?"

"No, no." George explained that he was working on a computer program. "I'd be dangerous if I were out there loose."

Susan laughed and invited him to a ride in her new car, a Monte Carlo with plenty of miles on the odometer. As they drove through Winter Haven, George talked about the pleasure of flying in his wife's small plane.

"One of the more glorious things with small planes is to see the space shuttle go off," he said. When the big white spaceship launches, it sends giant waves of smoke and fire rolling across the ground, George said. "It's like an atomic bomb going off upside down."

Susan liked this side of George, his wonder at the incredible potential of the human mind. She thought, Why hasn't he done more with his intelligence, something that would set the world on fire?

Then again, she said to herself, maybe he thinks that he has.

Back at his office, Susan sat in a chair, clutching her purse on her knee. She didn't want to spill its contents: money, perfume, a microphone. Looking around, she noticed a painting of Hawaiian mountains hanging on the wall.

"I've never been to Hawaii," she said. "It's so green and beautiful."

George looked at the picture and recalled a time when he had been there. He described a particularly enchanting road. "It's so winding the tour buses can't even get on it. It goes by the ocean," he said. "Everything blooms. You have waves underneath. I mean, I just want to pack a tent and portable generator with me, plug in the computer, and go live there."

"It sounds beautiful," she said. "You have pictures from there?"

"I have one postcard."

"You're not a picture freak?"

"No, it's silly. And that goes against my religion."

"Really?"

"Yeah. The idea of Buddhism is that you're operating in the moment."

George's interpretation of Buddhism intrigued Susan. Operating *in the moment*. Did that mean that if George did something horrible one day, it wouldn't matter the next? Susan had studied Buddhism when she was younger, found it fascinating. But she didn't see it, or any other system of belief, as a way to scrub away responsibility. Susan believed that most actions have a moral component, with consequences that stretch beyond the moment. George apparently did not.

In many ways, Susan reflected, George was an intellectual Peter Pan, forever young, forever enchanted with his
own perspective on life. Diana allowed him that luxury, by
paying the bills, taking care of the real-world worries. Susan wondered if that support carried a price.

When Diana exploded in anger at Peggy Carr and her
kids over the loud radios, maybe she had said to George:
"God, I could kill those people!" Of course, she couldn't
act on that rage; she was a doctor, respected in the community, and she would not throw that away in a flash of
anger. Her husband, on the other hand, already lived at the
edge of society, playing by his own rules. Maybe, with or
without Diana's help, he had decided to take care of his
wife's problem.

George also had his own reasons for wanting the Carr
family gone. Pye and his kids had been tormenting George
for years, letting the dogs run loose, cranking up their radios, scoffing at his complaints. For all George knew, they
were laughing at him behind his back. Here he was, a
Mensa-certified genius, and these truck-driving rubes were
laughing at him!

Maybe George had decided to come out of his glass box
for a while. Show them how smart he really was. Make
sure they never laughed again.

A week later Susan drove to George's office and found him
inside, playing a computer game. He invited her to sit beside him and try her hand at moving marbles through an
on-screen maze. As Susan moved the computer's mouse,
George began talking about Diana. For the first time since
they had met, Susan heard a trace of bitterness in his voice.

"She's a lot like a five-hundred-pound gorilla, the way
she pushes people around and gets what she wants," he
said. "She's not intimidated by anyone."

George changed subjects, launching into a story about a
trip he had taken to California in the early 1970s. Back
then, he told Susan, he used to chum around with a guy

named David Warren. David had a girlfriend in California whom he wanted to pick up and bring back to South Carolina, and he asked George to come along. They planned to drive straight through, so George brought along a thermos full of coffee and a bag of Oreo cookies.

David picked up George at 3:00 A.M. in a brand-new Ford Maverick. George threw the cookies and thermos on the seat, then settled in for a nap while David drove the first leg. It was a rainy night, very dark, and the first part of the trip carried them through the mountains of western Carolina. David reached for the cookies and chewed them, sipping coffee, as George slept.

When George awoke and noticed that David had eaten the cookies, George told his friend that each Oreo had twenty milligrams of amphetamine in it. "No wonder I'm so wired," David had said.

As George recalled that night for Susan, he grew progressively more animated. His voice rose and his hands fluttered as he recalled how the men then stopped to pick up a hitchhiker, a woman who said her name was Ruby. Ruby stood five-feet seven inches tall, with curly auburn hair, and she wore a flowing skirt and T-shirt. She seemed a little nervous, so George gave her some of the cookies— without telling her their secret ingredient.

It wasn't long before Ruby began to hallucinate, her mind spinning upward through layers of drugs and sleeplessness. When she began seeing colors, George played psychedelic tour guide. "She told me what colors she was seeing, and I would analyze what was happening," he boasted. "She thought I was a god."

Susan sat quietly, nodding from time to time and smiling to show her interest. George recalled that his friend had an idea: David wanted to tell his girlfriend in California that Ruby was George's lover. "I said, 'I can't do that,' " George told Susan. "I was going through a period in my life then when I had sworn I was not going to lie. So to make it true, I had sex with Ruby.''

Susan smiled and nodded. She thought, Is he making it up as he goes along, or is this the truth?

Chapter

EIGHTEEN

Susan stepped out of the sheriff's headquarters and walked toward the Polk County Courthouse. It was late June, and she needed some guidance. The Richard scenario seemed to be going well, but only to a point. George was sympathetic to Sherry's problems with her malevolent ex-mate, but he hadn't offered to help poison Richard, let alone revealed his role in poisoning the neighbors.

Although Hagmaier had counseled Susan to be patient, it was getting harder. Inside the sheriff's office, she began to hear skeptical rumblings. Nobody had said anything directly, but the signs were unmistakable: Her base of support was eroding. When the investigation began, she had had no trouble getting a carload of deputies to run surveillance; now she had to scrape to find one officer to back her. Then a lieutenant shuffled personnel, giving every undercover officer a new partner—except for Susan, who was left to work on her own. Even Ernie Mincey seemed to be losing enthusiasm; he had begun talking about bringing George in for an interrogation.

Susan resisted that idea. While a confrontation might make another killer crack, it would most likely terrify George into silence—and almost certainly blow Susan's cover. She knew that she needed to draw George with subtler traps. She wanted to stage one more scene with Richard, to turn up the heat and see if George offered to help her get rid of him. But she wanted to make sure that she didn't push so hard that George could later argue entrapment.

Susan walked across the street to the Polk County Courthouse. After clearing security, she took the elevator to the second-floor office of Assistant State Attorney John Aguero. A mustachioed man with the courtroom demeanor of a bulldog, Aguero was the prosecutor who would ultimately decide whether police had enough evidence to charge George with first-degree murder.

Settling into a chair in his office, Susan looked at Aguero's bookshelves. They held photographs of the things nearest to the prosecutor's heart: his wife, his three daughters, and Florida's wooden three-legged electric chair, known as Old Sparky.

Susan told him her worries. "If George poisoned the Carr family, I don't want him to go free on some technicality," she said. "What if I just came out and asked him, 'What should I do to get rid of my husband?' Would that be entrapment?"

Aguero posed a question of his own: "If a friend came up and said, 'I can't stand my husband. I've got to get out of the marriage,' what would you do?" he asked.

"I'd suggest a divorce lawyer, or some counseling," she said. "Maybe I'd offer to let her stay with me."

"What if she came back and said, 'I have five billion dollars. Will you kill my husband?' " Aguero said. "Would you do that?"

"Of course not," Susan said.

"That's the difference," Aguero said. "Entrapment is when you entice somebody to do something he wouldn't otherwise do. When you ask George for advice on your troubled marriage, you aren't enticing him to suggest murder. If he comes up with that idea, he does it on his own. Do you think you're enticing George?"

"No, all I'm offering is a friendship," she said. "And all I'm asking for is friendly advice."

"Then don't worry," Aguero said. "Just do your job."

A few days later Susan and George were driving toward Tampa. Susan had planned one more trip to the airport, telling George that she needed to pick up "Sam," the friend (really Lieutenant Nolan Allen) who had accompanied her to the Mensa Murder Mystery weekend. As Susan drove away from George's office, a construction worker in jeans and a safety vest suddenly appeared in the road. Susan had plenty of time to see him, but she overreacted, veering sharply away. She muttered an apology.

"I don't want to run anybody over," she said, laughing nervously. "I tend to be a little overly cautious."

In truth, Susan's jitters had little to do with traffic. The pressure was on. Unless George talked today about poisoning Richard—or, better yet, the neighbors—she feared her bosses would make her abandon the undercover operation. She thought back to the heady days after the Mensa Murder Mystery weekend, when she and her colleagues were amazed at her success in getting close to George. Everyone, including Susan, thought that by now George would be wearing jailhouse blues.

They were wrong.

Since the murder weekend Susan had learned that George was no easy prey. He held himself open but just long enough to tantalize, give a glimpse. But then he got edgy, pulled back into his shell. Was it because he suspected her? Or did he suspect everybody, even his friends? Susan was going to push the issue today. She wanted George to think she had spent the weekend trying to do Richard in. Of course, she couldn't come right out and say that. Even if it didn't constitute entrapment, that line might make George suspicious. He wasn't the type to say things directly—or to trust someone who did.

"I have a very positive attitude," she told George as they drove along. "Yep. A very nice weekend."

"Fort Lauderdale?" he said.

"No. Let me put it like this. I was only gonna be gone a day or so, but because of a storm, I could not go anywhere, so I kinda got locked up for a couple of days. But that's why I was late getting home. I think it was fruitful."

Susan hoped he would get the message. Over the weekend Tropical Storm Allison had charged through Texas, Richard's alleged home state, ripping off roofs, flooding roads, turning trees into deadly missiles. She wanted George to think she had been there, close enough to take revenge on her malevolent mate.

George seemed to get the hint. His voice quiet and his hands folded in his lap, he said, "Can I offer help or information on anything?"

But Susan didn't want to go any further, not just then. She was planting a seed for later in the day, when they would pick up Sam at the airport. She simply wanted George to remember that she had been near Richard over the weekend.

"Maybe," she said, concentrating on the road ahead.

"Just keep going straight for another five or so miles," George was saying. "This little community is called K-ville."

They were driving on Polk County Road 542, a blacktop road that meanders through the oak trees and meadows, past tiny houses with jalopies rusting out front. "This has less crowds," George said. "It's more scenic."

The route may have been scenic, but Susan was having trouble enjoying it. George had taken her off the planned route, and she worried about her surveillance team. On a busy road the unmarked cars could blend in with traffic. But on a quiet one George might see the same car following them and begin to wonder.

Susan looked in the rearview mirror, but it was empty. Another worry crept into her mind: What if George had chosen this remote road for reasons other than scenery? If the surveillance cars couldn't stay behind her, could they reach her soon enough if there was trouble? Worse yet, what if they had lost her? She remembered the microphone sewn into the armrest and began sprinkling her conversation with tidbits on their location. "Now I remember . . . Old Dixie Highway . . . I've seen that intersection on Ninety-two . . ."

Finally she caught a glimpse of a familiar red sedan. Relaxing for the first time, she turned back into the conversation. By then George had launched into a lengthy discourse on a trip he had taken with a friend named Carlos. Carlos, it seemed, was able to talk on George's level about science and technology. Smacking his lips, George talked about what a treat it was to hang out with someone who spoke his language.

Susan felt irritation flash inside her. This guy is such a snob, she thought. She had been acting naive, playing to his ego. But it was getting old. She wanted to say, "Don't get arrogant with me, you dweeb! If only you knew . . ."

But she held back. "That's great!" Susan said. "I may not be able to communicate on your level of physics, but I enjoy your company anyway."

"Thank you," he said, smiling graciously.

Susan couldn't resist. She dropped a clue of her own.

"I love to study people. I have an uncanny way of picking up on feelings," she said. "I tend to be very quiet and reserved, and I think that's a lot of repressed feelings over the last few years. I guess I study myself more than others."

George didn't care to hear about her self-analysis. "Yeah," he said, "I've done quite a lot of self-studies."

In the beginning Susan and her colleagues had been intimidated by reports of George's intellect. But Susan had learned that no matter how high George's IQ was, his ego would always tower above it. And while that arrogance got on Susan's nerves, she recognized it as her greatest defense.

As long as George was dazzled by himself, he wouldn't pay attention to her.

"Has it gotten you anywhere?" she said.

"Oh, yeah," he answered. "I found myself when I was about twenty-five. I truly loved myself. And I do think that's when I found the ability to love truly." Susan studied his face, waiting for the smile, a flicker of irony. There was none; he was absolutely serious.

He went on, recalling the time when he had reached too deeply inside. He was meditating, and his nervous system went haywire. His words rolling out in a joyful lilt, George recalled, "So, I'm just rolling around on the floor, barking and shitting . . ."

Susan cringed. "I don't even know how to visualize what you did," she said. "Maybe I don't wanna know."

George didn't hesitate. "If you can imagine being dumped with burning gasoline, with electricity going through it, you got an idea," he said, grinning and beginning to bounce in his seat. "Looking up and inward, release the serpent, and then all hell broke loose. Now I'm profoundly impressed that you can do this with your own nervous system."

He told Susan about how a college had once hired him to teach ceramic chemistry. She guessed he was referring to his days at Central Piedmont Community College, when he had worked with a teacher on developing new glazing techniques while also launching a secret narcotics lab. Thallium, she had learned, can be an ingredient in ceramic glazes.

"They had a wonderful ceramics lab," he said. "But budgets got cut, and they're saying, 'George, we can't pay you.' I say, 'That's okay because I make enough money doing other things.' "

He continued. "So a typical glass lab in, say, a university will have a particular arrangement of chemicals. They had well over a hundred, some very exotic. It's just a wonderful place to experiment."

As they neared the airport, the car tires bumped across the seams in the road. Duh-dump. Duh-dump. Duh-dump. George had moved away from chemistry and into a droning dissertation on the art of silk screening. As his voice blended in with the sound of the road and the wind rushing by, Susan's mind drifted. She had learned a great deal about George in the last three months, but little about his wife. He never brought Diana along, and when he mentioned her these days, it was generally to criticize her. Diana had recently been in a serious car accident, but George made it into a joke. "She's bruised in places," he told Susan. "It looks like I've been doing a better job than normal, beating her."

Susan laughed. But she heard not only mirth in George's voice but also a coldness. George wouldn't be the type to come right out and say, "I hate my wife," but why did he seem to resent her? Diana gave him money, made love to him, and apparently shared his affection for black leather. With her physician's income and forceful personality, Diana had the power to free George from financial and social responsibility. But maybe her power didn't bring George just pleasure. Perhaps it also brought him pain.

The car had pulled onto the road leading to Tampa International Airport. Shit! Susan thought, seeing her turnoff whiz by the car window. Glancing apologetically at George, she looped back around the airport terminal and eased up to the mechanical arm outside the parking garage. She reached out to take a ticket.

George said, "Have you heard from Mona lately?"

As Susan began to answer, something caught her eye. It was "Mona," sitting no more than five feet away in the passenger seat of the surveillance car beside them. Her eyes bulged as she saw Susan and George, and she quickly pulled up a magazine to hide her face.

"Right," Susan stuttered. She had forgotten George's question, and she fretted that he would see the shock in her eyes and turn to look at the car beside them. She prayed for the mechanical arm to rise, and finally it did. She raced up the ramp into the garage. Once again George seemed oblivious.

"I think we need to go through one of these little green arrows," he said.

"Green," Susan stammered. "What is, is this green?"

"Oh, yes," said George. "So how's Mona? You—"

"She's gonna get married," Susan said quickly. "I'm trying to talk her out of it."

"Well, if he's a pretty good man, you ought to join her in it," he said. "He'd welcome two for the price of one."

Susan managed a smile, then glanced in her rearview mirror. The surveillance car was nowhere in sight.

Susan and George walked toward the airport restaurant, where they were supposed to meet "Sam." She steered the conversation back to her troubled marriage, telling George, "It took me a long time, many days of thinking, to see exactly what Richard was more afraid of than anything else."

"So what is it Richard is afraid of?" he asked.

"He is superstitious."

George brightened. He said, "I happen to know lots about voodoo charms you can send him."

Before he could elaborate, they came across Nolan Allen—Sam—sitting at a table in the restaurant, smoking a cigarette and sipping a CC and Coke. "Wait a minute," she said to George. "I think I see him."

"Hey, girl!" Nolan cried out.

"Hey!" Susan replied, hugging her friend.

"How you been?" he said. "You're a sight for sore eyes."

Sam looked tired. "It's been a rough week," he said. Holding up his empty glass, he looked at George. "Drink?" he said. "Please, I hate to drink alone."

"Uh," George said, looking up at the waitress, "Coca-Cola for me."

Nolan launched into the script he and Susan had rehearsed the night before. Turning to her, he said, "At the risk of seeming impertinent, where have you been?"

"Today?" Susan replied, looking mystified.

"No," Nolan replied. "The weekend."

"In Fort Lauderdale," Susan said weakly. George knew she was lying, but he said nothing. They were partners in silence. He just toyed with his Coke, listening.

"I tried down there," Nolan was saying. "I tried Mona's. And I tried a couple of other places."

"I forgot to tell—"

Nolan interrupted her to say he had even tried to track her down in Texas. "I even called Richard's office looking for you," he said, pausing for emphasis. "He was in the hospital."

"Why would I go out there?" Susan said.

"I don't know, but I thought it was a possibility," Nolan said. "And he's in the hospital."

"Gee," Susan said, real breezy. "That's too bad."

"They don't know what's wrong with him. There's some sort of strange intestinal virus," Nolan said. He paused, then pointed his finger at her. "You know I can tell when you're lying."

"No!" she exclaimed. She looked over at George. She imagined his brain at work, trying to solve the puzzle between Sherry and Sam. What *had* she been doing over the weekend? But if George reached a conclusion, he kept it hidden behind a neutral stare, saying nothing.

The threesome paid up and walked to Susan's car. "Sam" stretched out in the back seat, while George rode in front with Susan. As they drove toward Polk County, the talk about "Richard" continued. Finally George had something to contribute to the discussion.

He said, "I've heard that FTD sends poison flowers."

Chapter
NINETEEN

There's no science in being a cop. You follow your gut, hope for that blend of hard work and good luck that brings an arrest. Susan had been following her hunches for better than four months, and where had they gotten her? Close to George, closer than she would have ever dreamed—but not close enough.

George's mention of poison flowers was one more tantalizing clue, one glimpse of his evil dimension. But it wasn't enough to make an arrest, or even get a search warrant for his house. It was making Susan crazy. George would reveal the elements of his guilt: hatred of the neighbors, a sophisticated knowledge of chemistry, and a willingness to break the law to hurt those he disliked. But these revelations came in tiny pieces, so thinly connected that they would never hang together in court. It was as if George really did know who Susan was but was playing dumb, taunting her. Or maybe he didn't know, and his revelations revealed an inner conflict—between the George who wanted to get away with his fiendish crime and the one who wanted nothing more than to be caught.

June, July, August. The summer burned on, the air harsh as dog's breath. It had been weeks since Susan had seen George; she had told him she needed to go on a trip north, to help ''Sam'' with some business and pick up a little extra cash. Meanwhile, she was doing more background research, hoping to find some hard evidence in George's phone calls or chemical purchases. Because she was at the office more, she could hear the talk. Down the long, shiny corridors, behind the closed doors, she heard her name echoing.

"This case is going nowhere."

"Goreck's milking it."

"I could have brought this guy in by now."

"That's what you get for sending a woman on a man's job."

"Maybe she should come on to him, loosen him up."

"Why don't we just bring this guy in, before he gets wise?"

"Aw, forget it. It's already too late."

Were the voices real or Susan's imagination? Just as she was having trouble separating Susan and Sherry, so she was having trouble finding the place when reality ended and her anxiety began. It had been four months since she went to the Mensa Murder Mystery weekend, and her bosses had been letting her set the agenda. But Susan knew that they, too, were starting to wonder.

One day in August Susan was poring over the log of phone calls made at George's house, looking for a lead. She heard footsteps, saw a pair of sharkskin boots. She looked up to see one of her bosses, Lieutenant Francis Hart.

"Susan," Hart said, "I've been meaning to talk to you about something."

Hart looked the part of undercover cop: long hair and aviator glasses, T-shirt and sinewy arms, blue jeans and boots. He and Susan went way back; both had grown up in Lake Wales, gone to junior high and high school together, and ended up at the police academy. While they weren't close friends, they knew and respected each other as professionals. If Susan was going to hear straight talk from anyone in her office, she expected to hear it from Hart.

Until now Hart had been running interference for Susan, taking the internal heat so she could focus on George. It

seemed as if they had been teetering on the edge of something big for months, and people were beginning to ask
why Susan hadn't been able to push George over the edge.
It wasn't anything against her necessarily. Nobody expected
miracles from her. After all, George was the slipperiest
killer they had ever come across, shrewd and dangerous.
They expected Susan to protect herself; after all, George
could easily poison her. But they wondered if she was beginning to fear too much—so much that it paralyzed her.
Like his colleagues, Hart was starting to wonder if Susan
was still up to the job.

The lieutenant settled into a chair across from her.
"There's a concern," he said, "that there's a reason that
this case hasn't progressed any further."

Susan's back stiffened. What was this? She struggled to
contain her anger, but it spilled out. She sputtered, "I beg
your pardon?"

Hart winced a little, as if he had swallowed something
bitter and now had to make Susan do the same. "There's
a concern," he said, "that maybe you're too afraid of
George to successfully complete this case."

Susan put down the phone log she had been studying
and glared across the desk. "Where were you during the
months when I was having to eat with him? When I was
spending all day with him? When I was sitting in his
trash?" she demanded. "He could have killed me at any
time. If you thought I was afraid of him, why wait until
now to say something?

"Sure I'm afraid of him," she continued. "If I wasn't
afraid, then I'd be a fool." She reminded Hart that George
could kill her in a moment. All it would take was a speck
of thallium in a drink or sandwich. But she said she used
that fear the way a cop should: to stay alert, on guard. She
never let it get in the way of pursuing George.

Hart didn't argue with her. He simply held up his hand
and said, "I just wanted to bring it to your attention." He
got up and walked out.

Susan drove home, tears boiling from her eyes. I have tried so hard, she said to herself. I killed myself working extra cases so nobody would say I'm milking this one. What does he mean, I'm not putting my heart in it? He could have told me that I wasn't turning up the heat enough, he could have told me that I was too close to entrapment, but don't tell me that I'm afraid of the man, not when I've spent that much time close to him. You can call me a lot of things, but not a coward, not *ever* a coward.

At home Susan sank into a chair in the living room and began weeping. By now Gary had a better idea of what the case involved. When he heard what her boss had said, he exploded. "I just can't believe it!" Gary said. "Let me go talk to him."

"No," Susan said. "Let me cool down and think it out."

As Susan reflected on the trouble at work, it seemed clear that some of the questions had nothing to do with her performance and everything to do with her sex. There wouldn't be so many doubts if she were a man, she was certain. Despite its risk, the poisoning case was a choice assignment; the press was paying attention, and Sheriff Crow had made it a high priority. If a man had landed the assignment, he would have encountered some jealousy, some ribbing in the locker room, but the old boys ultimately would have supported one of their own. As one of the few women detectives Susan didn't feel she had the same support network, probably never would. No matter how well she did, she would never quite measure up.

But Susan had to be honest with herself. Most of the pressure she felt had nothing to do with macho colleagues or wagging tongues. She had to prove her worth to others, sure, but she really needed to prove it to herself. Until she arrested George, she wouldn't be happy. Couldn't be.

The office wasn't the only place where things seemed to be falling apart. At home Gary and the kids were also losing patience. A lot had been happening in the family while she was off masquerading as Sherry. Gary had won a promotion to sergeant. Steven, her younger son, was about to turn three. He was changing from day to day, talking up a storm, getting into everything, his big blue eyes soaking up a world made just for him. Greg, her firstborn, was twelve, getting ready for his teenage years, combing every hair just so, making sure his clothes had the right brand name. ("No, Mom, not *Open* Pacific. *Ocean* Pacific!")

Susan was missing most of it, and a space had opened inside her. Even when she was home cooking hamburgers for the boys, she was thinking about George. What had she told him yesterday? What would he say today? She needed to think about him; her life might depend on it. But my life isn't worth a nickel without my family, Susan told herself. I'm shortchanging them.

The guilt was cresting, pushing against the levee she had built to contain her feelings. When the kids were home from school for the summer, it just got worse. Again and again they asked to go to the movies, to go skating at the indoor rink, to get ice-cream cones. Again and again she had to say no.

One day Greg asked if she could drive him to the mall. Steven's birthday was coming, and Greg had seen a green toy tractor he wanted to buy for his little brother. Any other time it would have been a routine request; Susan would have grabbed her car keys and driven her son to the mall, maybe stopped by McDonald's for a cheeseburger.

"I can't do it," she told her son. "I'm investigating a man who works near the mall, and I don't want him to see me." But Greg didn't understand, couldn't understand. Susan wasn't about to tell him that she had assumed a different identity to get close to a murderer. At twelve Greg couldn't be expected to see beyond his own frustration. For months his mom hadn't been there for him. And it looked as if that weren't changing anytime soon. He stormed off.

"You just don't want to take me," he shouted over his shoulder. "When is this going to stop?"

Susan was speechless. She wished she could answer that question. Wished it in the worst way.

She knew that Gary, too, was losing patience. He had tried to be a help to Susan at home, not complaining about the late hours, keeping the boys quiet in the living room while their mother made another call to set up a meeting with George. As the case went along, Susan had told her husband more and more about it. He knew she was under a lot of stress, and she could tell he was trying not to add to it. She kept telling him she was getting close, just a few more weeks.

But the weeks turned to months. Instead of closing in, Susan seemed to be stalled. To make up for the lack of progress on the undercover investigation, she had taken on other cases and spent even less time at home. As her hours got longer, so did her face. Although Susan didn't talk much about her troubles, Gary could see it in the shadows ringing her eyes, hear it in the flatness of her voice. It used to be that he was the homebody, the one Susan would have to drag out to a night on the town. Now Susan didn't want to go anyplace, didn't seem to have any time for fun. She was so busy and preoccupied that she didn't even have time to go to the post office. She had passed most of the work of running the household to Gary.

A lot had changed in the decade and a half since they married. When Gary first started in police work and Susan was staying home, she planned her days around his work schedule. If Gary worked the midnight shift, Susan stayed up all night, had breakfast with him, then went to bed. When Greg came along, Susan stayed at home while Gary went off to work. Gary hadn't complained when Susan wanted to start her own career, and he came to have great respect for her abilities as an undercover cop. The way she could read people, Gary just knew she was the one to nail George Trepal. But some days Susan could tell he felt more than a little nostalgic for those simpler times.

After dinner one evening Susan was standing at the kitchen sink, finishing up the dishes. Just a few months ago she had loved moments like this, listening to Greg talk about school or Gary recount the crazy sights he had seen on patrol. She had savored those small moments. But now she didn't have time for them or for much of anything else beside George.

"Would you mind mailing a letter for me?" Susan asked, her eyes fixed on the plates below her, her thoughts elsewhere. Gary said something but Susan missed it. She looked into the dining room, where Gary sat in a chair, staring at her with a blend of confusion and anger.

"What is wrong with you?" he snapped. "You don't even act like yourself."

"There's *nothing* wrong," she said.

"Well, just tell me this," he said, his normally soft voice swelling with anger. "Who are you today? Are you Susan or are you Sherry? I don't even know you anymore."

It all came to a head the weekend Susan and Gary had planned a small party at their house. Nolan Allen and a lady friend were going to come over, and they planned to throw some steaks on the grill, uncap some cold beers, maybe go for a swim. Susan was on the phone with Nolan, firming up the plans, when Steven toddled over. She had made a lot of business calls at home while Steven played nearby, coloring in his books or stacking plastic blocks on top of each other. He was so little, just starting to talk, that she didn't think he would understand what she was talking about. George this, George that. By making some calls at home, Susan thought she could get some work done and still spend at least some time with Steven.

So there she was, sitting on the couch, talking to Nolan. When she got off the phone, Steven crawled up on the couch beside her, his eyes bright with pleasure.

"Mommy," he said, "who's coming to the party?"

"Nolan Allen, a friend of mine from work," she replied. "And he's going to bring a friend of his, too."

"Mommy," Steven said, "is George coming?"

She just stared at the boy. Oh, my God, she thought, George has even violated my home. And I let him do it.

One afternoon Susan drove by George's house to have a look. They hadn't spoken for weeks; she had told George she was up north, had even written a postcard, signed Sherry's name, and arranged for some friends to mail it from Montreal. Seeing George's car in the driveway, she decided to give him a call.

"I'm glad you caught me," George said. "I'll be leaving soon to take a trip with an old friend of mine."

George told her that he and Diana had decided to put their house on the market. Diana was getting ready to move her practice to Sebring, he said, and they needed to start thinking about buying a place down there. Susan wondered if he would be upset by her failure to buy his house, but George sounded as friendly as ever. In fact, he said they had put a clause in their contract with the real estate agent providing that Sherry could buy the house without paying commission.

"That's great," said Susan. "I'll certainly think about that."

"How is Richard?" George asked. "Has he gotten out of the hospital yet?"

"Yes," Susan replied. Her voice bitter, she added, "He's fine."

"Well," George said, "I guess I'll see you in a couple of weeks. Jay and I are driving to a computer show in Chicago, and we may stop in a few other cities along the way. I'll write you with all the details."

"That sounds great," Susan said. "Have fun."

A few weeks later a letter from George arrived in the post office box Susan had rented for Sherry. Sitting in her car, she tore open the envelope and began to read.

Hello,
    I'm back from about 4,200 miles of driving. My

route was Columbia to meet Jay then to Chicago by way of North Carolina, Tennessee, Kentucky, Ohio, Indiana, and finally Illinois. From Chicago we went to Boston by way of Indiana, Michigan, Indiana (again), Pennsylvania, New York, Connecticut and then Boston, Massachusetts. From Boston it was Rhode Island, Connecticut, New York, New Jersey, Delaware, Maryland, DC, Virginia, North Carolina and then South Carolina. The whole trip took almost two weeks.

We stayed on the interstate highways for most of the trip and went through just about every big city on the east coast. Mostly we traveled at night which makes city driving easier. There's almost no traffic at three AM. Sometimes we slept in motels and other times we'd take cat naps in the car and just keep going.

Such a trip can only be spoken of in superlatives.

The pothole award goes to Boston.

The best chocolate milk award goes to Sumter Dairies of South Carolina. We tried chocolate milk every place we stopped.

The oddest name for a convenience store chain award goes to Sheetz of Pennsylvania.

Pennsylvania also takes top honors in the bathroom graffiti category. Someone had written, "Docile male slave, 37, wishes to find dominant male master . . ." and so on. Someone else had written underneath, "So join the army."

The foul air award goes to the purple haze of New York City. We went through at a rather odd hour so we couldn't stop to buy smog sculptures from the natives.

The best driver award goes to Chicago. The folks there are uniformly polite and will always let you into the flow of traffic. They never failed us.

The worst driver and worst traffic awards go to

Washington DC. It took us over an hour to move a mile. Rush hour would probably have been worse.

The ugliest city award goes to Chicago.

The oddest sign award goes to the La Quinta Inn outside of Chicago. It said, "In case of fire use stairs." How could stairs put out a fire. How would you get the stairs loose?

Best Pizza award goes to a Pakistani pizzeria named Hi-Fi Pizza & Subs just off the M.I.T. campus in Boston.

Susan gave a little start. She had told George that she and Sam were going to M.I.T. on their trip. Had George been checking up on her? Or did he want her to think he had been? She read on.

The corn award goes to Indiana hands down. That sucker is covered in corn and is absolutely flat. I think it's a facet on the planet rather than following the normal curvature.

The Amiexpo show in Chicago was a disappointment since nothing really new was there. I made a few contacts there so I now have more places to sell my software.

The SigGraph (Special Interest Group for Graphics of the Association for Computing Machinery) was really fine. There was a supercomputer every twenty feet. I hate the term state of the art but no other description fits. The machines were running everything from cartoons to fourth dimensional models of mathematical sets.

The rest of this letter should interest you.

George had attached a letter from a friend of his who was serving time in prison on a forgery conviction. Susan turned the page and read on:

Time in,

I was looking through the letters I received from you, and I just realized that I got so involved in the atomic stuff that I did not answer a question you asked—namely about the ID stuff for the friend of yours.

First of all, an ID change is simple, especially for a woman, so if she is, in fact, even remotely concerned about her husband tracing her—then having a second identity is not a bad idea at all.

I don't know anything about her husband, i.e., experience and IQ level—so I don't know just how deep he would be able to trace, so I will start with the casual, surface change—and work up to the full blown identity change. That way you can take the degree of action you deem proper.

Yes, one of the oldest methods of ID change revolves around getting the birth certificate of another person—someone dead is ideal, and someone who died as a minor, and therefore had no real record (i.e. SS card, school, etc.) is best of all.

But there is a number of problems with that approach. First of all, with modern computerized record keeping many states have now automated their systems—so birth records are also cross-referenced to death records. And, to make things worse, many states have worked backwards in their files—so not only are the newer deaths cross-referenced to birth records, but a lot of the old records have been keyed in now also.

Therefore you take a chance of picking a birth record that is already keyed to a death record—and the moment you apply for a birth certificate you trigger a chain of events that you may not care to.

That brings us to the second problem—in most states it is NOT illegal to change one's identity (except if they can prove an attempt at fraud) but it is illegal to take the identity of a specific person with the intent to pass yourself off as that person. That is the actual test used in law—you can legally call yourself JOAN SMITH if you are not contending to be a specific and actual person who is alive or was at one time.

So the use of a birth certificate that actually exists is in many cases a crime—especially as most clerks require you to file a certificate of identity, or at least intent, when you apply for a birth certificate. Therefore, as there are many other ways of proceeding, I do not recommend that avenue.

But, as I said, that route is not needed—there are many other ways of proceeding, ones which are not a crime. So let's look at them.

One simple way, which many people overlook, is to simply do it the formal way—to wit, file an application with the court for a change of name. At first that might seem useless in this case for, of course, the change of name is a public record. But that is not really a problem—for while it IS a public record, it is only discoverable if you know EXACTLY where to look. . . .

But putting that aside, the next best route to go is the sky chief routine, so called because it takes advantage of the religious institutions. As you know, everyone will accept a baptismal certificate in lieu of a birth certificate. Therefore if you send the required few bucks (usually $10.00–$20.00) to one of the mail order minister credential places (like universal life church) you can become a ordained minister of your own church, and that includes the legal right to baptize persons into your religion. In fact, most of the places you obtain your minister credentials from also sell birth certificates and marriage certificates. . . .

P.S. you can also usually get a recognized church to issue you a baptismal certificate without a problem—walk in and say you were brought up with no religion, have "found" their god, and want to be baptized. $2.00–$5.00 and a few drops of water later, you have a baptismal certificate. I have NEVER had any church ask me for any form of ID, and I've done it a lot, they just put down whatever you say.

Warning!!!! Make sure she picks a COMMON name. While weird names look good—they lead to problems. Sooner or later she will end up on someone's mailing list, and while that seems harmless one of the BIG ways immigration finds illegal aliens is buying mailing lists and running cross checks against social security records. A common name Sue Jones will pass as there are hundreds of them in the computer, but something like Soliel Gurgle might not make a hit, and immigration starts a search to see if she is an illegal.

I could go into some of the other, more complex routines, but I doubt they will be needed as the one above works in every case I have known of when used by a person NOT wanted by the police, and in most cases if they are. Persons who have to fool the system also (i.e., cops) need to go a bit further. . . .

Another two months passed, and Susan was no closer to making an arrest. Her bosses called a meeting to decide whether to continue the undercover investigation or end it.

"So where do we stand on this, Susan?" said Colonel Paul Alley. "What are your plans?"

Susan looked around the big conference table at the men seated there. There was Ernie Mincey, his bosses, and a whole array of other supervisors, right up to Sheriff Crow. There were coffee cups all around, men leaning back in chairs, good-natured bantering. The atmosphere seemed friendly and collegial, but Susan could focus only on the underlying tension. How many of these men are on my side, she wondered, and how many of them want to abandon the undercover approach?

She told the group that she had been busy with some other cases but was spending a few hours each day gathering more background information about George: monitoring his phone calls, driving by his house and office, waiting for him and Diana to settle into their new home. "I'm just waiting a little bit for him to get his life back in order after being in this traveling mode," she said. Before someone else could jump in, she said, "But I've had a lot of time to think about it, and I don't think we should just give up the undercover role."

Susan knew that her attitude in this meeting was crucial. If she pronounced the case hopeless, her bosses would probably be happy to walk away from it. She was tempted; it would be nice to focus on some other case, something she could *solve*. It would also be great to get her family life back to something approaching normality. But she didn't want to give up, couldn't give up—not after she had invested so much. Not after she had gotten so close.

She told her colleagues they had plenty of circumstantial evidence against George: his hatred of the neighbors, his chemistry background, the Mensa murders, the voodoo manual, the drug-filled cookies, the offers to help Sherry establish a new identity and get rid of her troublesome husband, even religious beliefs that enabled him to forgive himself past sins.

But it wasn't enough. All the signs pointed toward George, but they still lacked that crucial piece of evidence. Without a witness they needed George to say something only the killer would know. Without fingerprints they needed to find some record that George had purchased thallium or, better yet, find a trace of the poison inside his home.

"Let's go over some of the possible angles of attack," Alley said.

What if she took George up on his offer and let him help

change her identity? Alley asked. Susan said she didn't think that would be enough. "At best," she said, "it might yield a misdemeanor charge."

"What about a drug charge?" said another of the men. Hadn't George asked her to buy him some LSD? Susan didn't think that would do much except alert George to the police on his trail. "The key is the house," she said. "We need to find a way inside it, and soon. Diana has already moved her office, and they've put their home up for sale. If we want to get inside and search it, we need to do it soon."

"What about buying the house?" one of the men said. "If we owned it, we could search it."

"Wait a minute," said another. "They want a hundred thousand dollars for it. Where are we going to get that money, and what if the search turns up nothing?"

The television show *Unsolved Mysteries* had offered to feature the case, Sheriff Crow noted. "What about bringing them in, put the murder story on national television, use that to shake George up a little?"

Susan shook her head. "No," she said, "he probably wouldn't even see the show. He doesn't even read the paper that much."

Crow listened to Susan; he had from the beginning. He was in a tough spot; the press was starting to work on the "one year after" stories, spotlighting the pitiful state of the victims and the lack of progress by police. It seemed as if a reporter called every day to ask, "When is this case going to be solved?" Many people in Crow's position would have let the shit roll directly downhill, hounding subordinates to produce some results, and fast. After all, it wouldn't be so long before another election would come around and Crow would have to defend his decisions on the biggest murder case in years.

Crow didn't roll over. He had been a cop long before he was a politician, and he knew how tough Susan's job was. He told her he would support her all the way and then backed that pledge by overruling the objections of some of his staff and pronouncing that the investigation would continue. He wanted to get George Trepal, and he was convinced that the undercover approach was the only one that would work. He asked Susan if she had any other ideas.

"I do have one," she said. "I'd like to go to the FBI Academy and see what suggestions they have." Hagmaier had offered to assemble a panel of specialists from the Behavioral Science Unit. "I'm kind of stalemated here," she said, holding up her hands and looking around the table. "If we can go to Quantico, get some more ideas, maybe we can nail this guy. If not, you all can do what you think is best."

Before anyone could object, Colonel Alley stood up. Smiling at Susan, he said, "Okay, the ball's in your court."

On a breezy afternoon in October 1989 Susan, Brad, and Ernie boarded a jet bound for Washington, D.C. It had been one year since Peggy Carr pressed her hand to her chest and fretted that she was having a heart attack.

The airplane banked and began the steep descent to Washington's National Airport. Susan clutched the armrests with sweaty palms; although she had taken flying lessons as a teenager, she was getting more nervous about airplanes as she got older. The longer she lived, it seemed, the more she saw life as a precarious business. She smiled grimly as Brad tried to small-talk her through the ordeal. With a scrape of rubber and a loud reversal of engines, she could breathe easily again. They were down and rolling toward the gate.

The threesome took their rental car across the Potomac and into Virginia, where the FBI Academy gleamed against the autumn leaves. Bill Hagmaier greeted his visitors and ushered them into a conference room with a big table, where a panel of experts gathered. Brad led off, explaining that the FBI had got involved in the early days when police suspected product tampering. He and Ernie described how they had chased after a half dozen potential suspects, including Peggy Carr's husband, before stumbling across George Trepal. Then it was Susan's turn. She told them about the Mensa Murder Mystery weekend, the voodoo manual, the meetings at which George skated near self-revelation, then retreated.

The experts began to brainstorm. They decided to focus on prompting George to be more specific about his knowledge of thallium and other poisonous chemicals.

"Tell George you have a friend who's a chemist, and look what he gave you," one suggested. "Show him some lab equipment, the kind he knows would let you make drugs. Let George volunteer to be the chemist."

Susan frowned. "I'm not sure he would commit to something like that," she said. "He hasn't even told me about getting arrested on a drug charge in the 1970s." To Susan, this was an important point. If she had really succeeded in winning George's confidence, she thought, he should open up about his criminal record.

Hagmaier gave her a puzzled look. He said, "From what you've told us, he wouldn't tell you about his drug arrest."

"Why not?" she said.

"Telling you about his arrest would be admitting failure. And with his ego, he's not going to admit failure, particularly to you. Remember, he's trying to impress you."

Susan allowed herself a small smile. Maybe she wasn't such a failure after all. She looked over at Ernie, who sat scowling and silent beside her. She wondered what his problem was. As the discussion turned back to the chemistry scenario, she got her answer.

"That's not going to work," she heard Ernie say, "You can't do that."

"Why not?" she asked.

"Because my supervisors are already talking about pulling the plug," Ernie said. "They're not going to let you do anything long term."

Susan couldn't believe it. She had suspected that Ernie

was one of the people back home who was questioning her work, but he had never said it so bluntly. Why was he doing it now, in front of these FBI experts? Here Hagmaier and the others have gone out of their way to help us out, Susan thought, and Ernie picks a fight. Maybe she was wrong about Ernie; maybe he didn't support her after all.

(Years later, Ernie said he was not trying to undermine Susan's undercover work. He simply wanted the FBI experts to weigh in on his plan for directly confronting George.)

An uneasy silence settled around the table, until it was broken by the gravelly voice of one of the FBI men. Winston Norman had worked more than two decades as a homicide detective before joining Behavioral Science. He knew the streets as well as, probably better than, Ernie.

"George is not going to talk," Norman growled. "Why would he talk? If you just went ahead and interviewed him, what do you think the odds are that he's going to confess?"

Mincey said he thought there was a good chance, but Norman and his colleagues disagreed. George had been to prison once, they reasoned; he wouldn't want to put himself there again. To help settle the dispute, they turned to another man sitting at the big table: Richard Broughton, the federal drug agent who had broken up George's drug ring two decades earlier.

Broughton sided with Susan. "George thinks he's smarter than you guys," said the Drug Enforcement Agency agent. "You couldn't get a confession out of him."

Broughton recalled how difficult it had been to catch George back in North Carolina. As early as 1969 federal drug agents had heard that George was involved in manufacturing illegal drugs. First it was mescaline, then methamphetamines, "crank." Every time they'd bust a dealer, agents would ask, "What do you know about George Trepal?" Many of the dealers knew about him, saying he was the chemist in a big-time crank lab. But George had carefully hidden himself behind layers of distributors and street dealers, and it wasn't until Broughton came across George's pal David Warren that he was able to build a case.

Confronted by federal agents, Warren confessed to being a partner in the operation. He told them it was George who made the drugs, in a lab set up at his parents' house. George had boasted that it was the perfect site; the police would never think to check inside the home of a former New York City cop. (Decades later George's father said he had had no idea of what George was doing.) After Warren had told his story to a grand jury, George was indicted on charges of conspiracy to manufacture and distribute illegal drugs. On September 16, 1975, Broughton knocked on George's door and told him he was under arrest. Broughton handcuffed George and led him to the police car, where George settled into the seat, turned to Broughton, and said, "I'm so scared. Would you hold my hand?"

The story brought a wave of laughter from the group. With a wry smile, Brad quipped, "I don't care what you say, I'm not getting in the back seat of a car and holding George's hand."

Ernie joined in the laughter. He said, "Well, don't look at me."

As the laughter died, Broughton finished his story. Despite George's show of vulnerability, despite the overwhelming evidence against him, he had never confessed. Even in the car that day, clutching Broughton's hand, George told nothing but lies.

Walking with Susan to the rental car, Hagmaier told her that she should be pleased with her progress. The investigation might not be moving as quickly as your typical murder case, he said, but George was not your typical murderer.

"Susan," Hagmaier said, walking through oak trees, "you've got to remember, you're not just trying to get George to talk in the abstract about drugs and poisoning. He's talking about his *life*, and he knows what that means.

If he tells anyone about his crime, he could be putting himself in the electric chair.''

They reached the car and waited for Ernie and Brad to catch up. "Let's move an inch or a foot ahead rather than trying to go two miles," Hagmaier said. "He's still George Trepal. He still wants to live. He knows what loose lips can do.''

Susan nodded and smiled. As always, Hagmaier made her feel better. "It is a very long and tedious process, and if you want to do it right, it's going to take a long time,'' Hagmaier said. "It's a miracle that he gave you as much as he did, as quickly as he did.''

Susan drove away, smiling at her luck. In addition to sharing his expertise, Hagmaier had become a friend. When she felt the most bewildered and alone, Hagmaier was there to offer a comforting word. Without his support, she thought, she might not have come this far. With it, she felt ready to "whip the world.''

But as Hagmaier watched her go, he worried. George would like nothing more than to do in a cop. By urging Susan to keep at it, Hagmaier hoped he wasn't pushing her toward a deadly trap.

Chapter
TWENTY

Susan stepped out of the swimming pool and grabbed a towel. For the first time in months she felt a measure of calm. The trip to Quantico had lifted her spirits; even if Mincey doubted her, it helped to know the FBI experts and her bosses did not. She was doing this the right way. She knew it. She just needed to be patient and wait for her break.

Susan figured that George would be back from his trip by now, and she wanted to get in touch with him. But since she had told him that she was staying in Fort Lauderdale for a few weeks, she had to log a couple of days by the pool, building her tan. "Tough assignment," said Gary. But he wasn't complaining; it was nice having the old Susan back.

Later at the office Susan dialed the number for George's office.

"Good afternoon. Gordon Rowan, Realtor."

"Yes, is George there?"

"George Trepal?"

"Yes."

"No, George doesn't have his office here anymore."

"He doesn't?"

"No, he gave up on me."

"Well, that little rat."

"Yeah, isn't that awful?"

"This is Sherry, and I was just moving back up here, and I was trying to track him down."

"Oh, golly, well, you better hold. I'm sure he would want you to have the information."

Susan jotted down the new phone number. She called George and found out that he hadn't entirely moved out of Alturas. He told her he was still making trips back and forth to the house, moving things.

George asked her to visit him at his new home in Sebring. He even offered to have her spend the night.

"We have extra beds," George said eagerly.

"Oh, great!" Susan responded.

In truth Susan wasn't happy to hear that George and Diana had moved. Because George had moved to another county, he now lived in the jurisdiction of another sheriff's department. Not only would Susan have to drive farther to see him, but it would be harder to arrange for surveillance.

There was a more pressing concern: Susan still wanted to poke around inside George's home in Alturas, to look for evidence that George had poisoned the Cokes and then planted them next door. Susan knew the chances of finding such evidence were slim, especially now that George had moved out. But she wanted to try anyway. The FBI lab had told her that thallium doesn't dissipate easily, that traces might remain. George could have spilled some on a counter while filling the Coke bottles. He could have poured some down the sink before moving out, leaving a trace inside a drainpipe. A few grains might have lodged in an air conditioner filter, inside a vacuum cleaner bag, or maybe in that secret room under the stairs.

The legality of searching for such clues was tricky. While George was still living in the house, Susan had the right to visit and look around as long as he had invited her inside. Now that he was gone, she and her colleagues would need a search warrant. But she didn't think they had enough evidence to persuade a judge to give them one. Her mind still running through the options, she stepped out into the night, feeling the drizzle against her face. An early-winter storm was moving in, and as she drove across the flats near Alturas, the raindrops crossed her headlights like tiny, translucent meteors. She watched them, transfixed.

"What can I do?" she said to the empty car. Then it struck her. Spying a pay phone, she pulled over and fished a quarter from her purse. She called her boss at home. "Francis," she said, "what do you think about this? Can I ask him if I can rent his house?"

Susan feared Hart's reaction. She had just persuaded him to let her rent an apartment in Winter Haven to use as a home base. The idea was to have a place where she could invite George over to dinner, so that he wouldn't wonder why she still didn't have a permanent home. Just yesterday they had put a phone in the apartment. What would Hart think now when she told them she needed more money?

His reaction surprised her. "I think that will work," Hart said.

Hanging up the phone, Susan looked down at her blouse, plastered to her skin by the downpour. She grinned and pumped her fist into the air. "Yes!"

The next afternoon Susan went to the Winter Haven condo and called George. She remembered that George had told her how much he hated condominiums; he called them "pandemoniums."

"I moved into my new condo," Susan told him. "I didn't realize how much I hated them until I moved back into one. I don't like being in a place where I can hear everything that's going on next door or above me. By January it's going to be over between Richard and me. I really want to be someplace where I could think freely and make up my mind about what to do. Would you consider renting your house to me for a couple of months? Of course, if you sell it in the meantime, I could just leave immediately.''

George didn't hesitate. "Diana and I have already discussed it,'' he said. "You can move in anytime, and all you have to pay is part of the utilities.''

Well, that was easy, Susan thought. But she couldn't accept George's offer in its entirety. The sheriff's lawyers had told her that she wouldn't be able to conduct a legally defensible search unless she could demonstrate that she had taken possession of the house by giving George a rent check.

"Oh, no,'' she told him. "That's very kind of you, but if I live there, I'm going to rent it. I will pay rent and the utilities.''

George didn't put up a fight. "Oh, fine,'' he said. "And we've got a watchdog who moved in next door, so you don't even have to worry about locking your doors.''

"What do you mean, a watchdog?''

"Oh, a deputy moved in next door.''

A few weeks later, after the sheriff's lawyers had signed off on the idea of renting George's house, Susan called him to close the deal. She told him she would like to rent his house, but only for a few weeks. Just enough time, she told George, to get things settled between Richard and her so she could get a permanent place. "Hopefully it's just going to be till Christmas,'' she told George, "if that would be all right.''

"Oh, sure,'' he said. "Just move on in.''

George said he'd left the house unlocked, but Susan asked about getting a key. Another legality. She could use the key to prove that George had turned over the property. There was a practical benefit, too: She could lock the doors so George didn't walk in while she had technicians scraping the bathroom sink for thallium. George told her the key was hidden under a rock by the front door.

"We've never bothered to lock the house,'' he said. "So

it's kind of superfluous. In terms of moving in, what can I
do to help you?''

"Oh, not much," said Susan. "I'm quite self-sufficient."

George offered a tip on getting along with the "watchdog" next door. "What you need to do is go knock on the
door next door, which is Deputy Hicks, and say that you're
just moving in and watching the house, and that way you
won't have a passel of cops on you."

"Okay," she said. "He's not real nosy, is he?"

"I haven't the slightest idea," George said. "But to be
honest, I don't really trust police types too much. So if you
let him know what's up, they tend to be much less nosy—
'cause it takes all the fun out of it."

Susan laughed. "I'll take your advice on that!"

"My father's a cop," George said. "I know about these
folks."

"Oh, really?"

"Well, he's retired, but he is an old New York policeman."

George told her that he might stop by the Alturas home
while she was getting settled. "There's a little bit of stuff
in the house I need to clean up," he said. "I'm still cleaning out the garage slowly. So I may or may not show up."

Susan tried to swallow her dismay. George showing up
unannounced was the last thing she needed.

George said, "I will at least knock."

On December 12, 1989—a year after lab technicians discovered the thallium in the Coke bottles—Susan told
George she was moving in. Because she was having trouble
getting furniture, she said, she would probably just start out
with a sleeping bag. If George popped in unannounced, she
didn't want him surprised to find the place empty.

In truth Susan was happy not to be moving anything in.
She didn't want any of her belongings, a change of clothes
or even a toothbrush, where George had lived and schemed.
She had been trying to reclaim her life, to build a wall

between Sherry and Susan. It wasn't easy. George still had power over her, a strange, primitive hold. She was drawn to his evil side, his dark half. No matter how close she got, she wanted to get closer. She wanted to understand, but she feared what that understanding might do to her.

How many times can someone, even a person as fundamentally decent as Susan, cross over? How deep an understanding could she acquire before she, too, grew accustomed to the darkness? Having passed over the line again and again, could she return completely? These questions may not have risen to the surface of her mind, but they tugged at her. Made her look for ways, even small ways, to hold back. To stay in control.

As the light drained from the evening sky, Susan met Brad and a group of crime scene technicians at the Circle K convenience store near George's house. One officer was staking out the Sebring home, so he could sound a warning if George decided to visit his new tenant. The group drove up the hill, and Susan invited her guests inside.

The air inside the empty house was stale and harsh, but Susan decided not to open the windows, for fear of attracting attention. Although the "watchdog" next door worked for the Polk County Sheriff's Office, Susan had not alerted him to their visit. The fewer people who knew about the investigation, she reasoned, the smaller the chance that word would inadvertently leak to George.

The evidence technicians drew the shades and began unloading gear from brown paper bags. They dipped cotton balls in nitric acid and began rubbing them across surfaces that might hold a trace of thallium: the floor of George's secret room, the inner walls of cabinets, the dark hollows of sink drains. Before long the floor was covered with cotton swabs, all carefully sealed into plastic evidence bags that would be shipped to the FBI lab.

An hour after they began, Susan was in the library, taking photographs of George's secret room. She heard a knock.

"Oh, no," she said. She turned to the technicians and held a finger to her lips. "Stay here," she whispered. "Be quiet."

Checking to be sure her pistol was tucked inside her jacket, Susan walked to the back of the house. Once in the kitchen she could see a figure waiting outside the screen door. It was Sheriff's Deputy Charles Hicks, holding a flashlight and peering inside. The watchdog had arrived.

Susan hadn't seen Hicks for years. Then she had been wearing the green uniform of a road deputy. Tonight she wore jeans, a T-shirt, and a windbreaker. She held her breath, hoping that Hicks wouldn't recognize her. It would be simpler that way.

"Hello," Hicks said, his tone even but wary. "I'm wondering what you're doing here."

"Oh," Susan said, smiling, "I just moved in. I thought maybe George would have told you. I rented his house."

"Oh, all right," Hicks said, his voice warming some. "I told George I would keep an eye on this place. I heard you over here, and I thought I'd come over here and check it out."

Susan flashed another smile, this one genuine. Hicks had not recognized her. She said, "I appreciate it."

With a neighborly wave Deputy Hicks walked off.

"We need to get out of here as quickly as possible," Susan told the technicians. "Let's not give Hicks, or anyone else, reason to sniff around."

As the technicians moved upstairs, Brad and another officer headed for the garage woodshop. Susan showed the way, opened the door, and shone a flashlight inside. As she looked around, she realized that George hadn't done much cleaning inside his workshop. Everywhere there was junk: pieces of scrap wood, empty spray paint cans, rusted and bent nails, broken chairs, garden supplies, glass bottles, a bureau that seemed as old as the house, all coated with sawdust.

The sawdust was a problem, Susan realized. It would stick to the cotton swabs and make it hard to pick up traces of thallium. "I don't see any need to swab out here," she told Brad and the detective helping him. "Just look around." She went back inside the house.

Brad pulled on a pair of rubber gloves, then a pair of cloth ones; who knew what he would be touching in here? Shining a flashlight through the dusty garage, he spotted the cord to an overhead bulb and gave it a tug. Looking around in the yellow light, Brad saw the old jugs of chemicals Susan had seen on an earlier visit. As he started to pick one up, the liquid inside began to foam and thicken, like something from an old Frankenstein movie. When he tried to pick up another, the contents spilled out, filling the garage with a bitter, acrid smell. "Oh, that's good," Brad said to his partner. "We're going to die."

He put the jug down and walked over to a big rolling door, thinking he could open it and air out the place. Brad pulled at the handle, but the door was stuck. Trying not to breathe too deeply, he went back to work on the other side of the garage, moving quickly. He grabbed a vacuum cleaner bag; it might have swept up some grains of thallium. He scuffed across the pitted concrete floor but saw nothing except the nails, woodchips, and shards of glass. He moved on to George's workbench, which looked homemade and was covered with a coat of faded green paint.

Atop one shelf Brad found a small bottle containing a green fluid, thick as ink, really creepy-looking. He carefully placed the bottle in a plastic dishpan he had found on the floor. He began opening the workbench drawers. Most held nothing but rags, nails, and assorted clutter. Inside one drawer Brad saw a circular wad of rags and newspapers. It looked as if a family of mice had made themselves a cozy little home. Pushing the nest aside, he found another bottle, this one made of brown glass, topped by a red cap. The bottle was the size of a small finger, and it looked empty. Brad picked it up, unscrewed the cap, and shone his flashlight inside. The bottle did have something in it, a white, crystalline residue. It didn't look nearly as sinister as the foaming jugs or the thick green liquid. Brad put it in the dishpan anyway.

Susan tied off another evidence bag and saw that the techs were almost done. "All right," she said. "Let me run back out and see if they're through in the garage."

It was getting close to 9:00 P.M. The man watching George's home in Sebring was about to knock off. They needed to clear out or risk George's catching them. Brad came out of the shed, carrying the dishpan filled with bottles.

"Susan, we're not going to be able to stay in there," Brad said, his eyes watering. "Wait till you smell it in there."

She inspected the bottles Brad had picked up. Some of them looked pretty strange, but she knew nothing about chemicals. She would have to ship them off to the FBI lab. And they would have to come back later for the bottle that leaked the acidic stuff; she wasn't about to take any chances with transporting that.

As the crew drove off, Susan couldn't help feeling deflated. She had hoped for a big break tonight: a chemistry set, a bottle-capping machine with traces of thallium on it, something solid. But there was nothing so obvious. She hoped the lab would find something on the swabs or in the bottles. But once again she would have to wait and wonder. It would be awhile before she knew; Brad had told her that the FBI chemists were working full-time on another case. They weren't sure when they would have time for the Florida poisoning.

After mailing the bottles and cotton swabs off to the FBI lab, Susan and the others settled in to wait. With Christmas approaching, they decided to take a few days off. Ernie was relaxing at home when the sheriff's office operator called to say she had an urgent call to patch through. It was the owner of the Alturas groves where Pye Carr said he had buried his dead dog. He told Ernie that his men had made a find while installing sprinklers in the grove.

"They found some bones," the farmer said. "I told them to leave them alone."

"Good idea," Ernie said. "We'll be out in a little while."

It was late afternoon on one of the shortest days of the year, and Ernie could see darkness coming. He called in a crime scene crew, and they descended on the grove with shovels, trowels, and a powerful light. Ernie called Susan on his cellular phone.

"How many people have you got?" she asked.

"Not many," he said. "If you want to come help, wear your jeans and tennis shoes. It's nasty out here." Rain had begun to fall, quickly turning the soil to mud and drawing a cloud of mosquitoes. Already Ernie had so many bites he looked as if he had the measles.

Susan was intrigued by the prospect of finding the dog's

bones. Hagmaier had told her that many murderers work their way up a chain of violence, carrying out "attacks" on inanimate objects such as clothing or photographs before moving on to a succession of living creatures: bugs, small animals, and finally, human victims. Susan remembered the break-in reported by Margaret Carr; that might have been the first step in George's assault. The poisoned dog could easily have been the second. She told Ernie, "I'll be right out."

She found Ernie and the others on their knees in the mud, using the trowels to sift through piles of grove sand. They worked slowly, methodically, carefully picking out the bones and collecting the dirt around them for evidence of thallium. Susan joined in, and before long they had gathered a pile of small, round bones.

Ernie's cellular phone rang. It was Colonel Alley. "Have you got the bones yet?" he asked.

"Well," said Ernie, "we're not sure yet." He told Alley that Susan had found a veterinarian who had agreed to look at the bones.

Susan and Ernie carefully loaded the bones, many still crusted with mud, and headed for the vet's office. They left the crew behind in the grove; if these were the dead dog's bones, they stood ready to begin a major excavation. Driving through the downpour, Susan and Ernie didn't say much, but both felt a quiet exhilaration. After all this time and trouble, this could be it, their break. If these bones had come from Pye's dog, if they contained thallium, they would have a major piece of evidence against George. Who else would have hated the dog enough, and had the chemistry skills, to poison it? And what would have stopped George from using thallium again years later?

It was after 9:00 P.M. when they arrived at the vet's office. "Be careful," Ernie told the doctor. "These might have thallium in them."

The doctor flicked on the light over a metal examining table, pulled on some rubber gloves, and began sorting through the bones. Scraping a little dirt off each, he laid them neatly in a row atop a sheet of plastic. He took one of the larger bones, scraped off a thick coat of mud, and walked toward the sink, saying, "I need to wash this off."

As the doctor scrubbed the bone clean, Susan and Ernie stood dripping muddy water onto the shiny floor, exchanging anxious glances. Finally the vet looked up and smiled. He had a positive ID, he said. "You've got a turtle."

After a long moment of silence Ernie and Susan exploded in laughter. They thanked the veterinarian, apologizing for calling him out so late on a false alarm. The doctor piled the bones back into a bag and held it out for the detectives.

"Susan," said Ernie, "you want this bag?"

"No," she replied. "They're your bones."

Walking out of the office, they passed a picture of a collie hanging on a door. Pointing to it, Susan said, "Ernie, *that's* a dog."

Chapter
TWENTY-TWO
———

As 1990 began, Susan learned it would be months before the FBI lab could analyze the bottles and swabbings from George's house; federal judges had been getting mysterious bomb threats, and the feds were devoting all their resources to that case. Meanwhile, there was little Susan could do. She and George had drifted out of touch over the holidays, and Susan had run out of ideas for opening him up. The chemistry equipment scenario had sounded good in Quantico, but she couldn't drum up any enthusiasm for it back at her office.

Even Susan's friends in the department were urging her to give up the case gracefully, telling her she had done all she could. Susan was discouraged, but she wasn't willing to give up, not yet. She had one more idea. She called Ernie and Brad and asked them to meet for lunch. An hour later the three were sipping iced tea at the Davis Bros Cafeteria.

Susan laid out her plan. "I want to meet with George and tell him that you guys came by his house in Alturas, asking about the poisoning, asking about him. I have never let on that I knew about the poisoning. Why not do it now, to see if he flinches? What have we got to lose?"

Ernie frowned. "Okay," he said. "But if this doesn't work, I really think we can do something by interviewing him."

Susan felt her cheeks flush with anger, but she kept her voice calm. "Ernie, bear with me," she said. "It's worth a try. And maybe by the time I do this, we will have heard from the lab. I want to have the chance to ask George about the neighbors. We've come too far to just give this up."

Brad had been sitting quietly, listening. A smile spread across his face. He said, "Why don't you give him our business cards?"

Ernie's frown melted, and before long all three were laughing. The detectives had given George their business cards when they first interviewed him more than a year before, but Susan later found them when she was digging through the trash. George, apparently, had decided that he didn't need to worry about these dumb cops.

"Why don't you give him the ones you found in the trash?" Ernie said. "I'd love to see the look on his face."

On January 25 Susan drove to Sebring, George's new hometown. She pulled up to a pay phone in her battered Monte Carlo and dropped a quarter into the slot. She didn't bother with small talk this time; she tinged her voice with urgency.

"Hello, George?" she said. "This is Sherry. I need to talk to you about some things."

"Sure," George said. "What's going on? Do you want to come by the house?"

"No, I'd rather not do that. Can you meet me at McDonald's?"

"Sure."

Susan drove to the fast-food restaurant, where a surveillance team was waiting with a video camera trained on a table outside the restaurant. It was a perfect day for lunch outside; the sky was a pale blue, and the palm fronds tossed in an easy breeze. Susan pulled up in the Monte Carlo, grabbed a bag from the seat, and walked to the picnic table. She was wearing blue jeans, a red tank top, and a white pullover shirt. Although she was in the shade, she kept her sunglasses on. The microphone in Susan's purse picked up her voice and piped it into the surveillance vehicle.

"He just walked in front," Susan said. "He's parked on the side of the Village Inn parking lot. He's got on shorts and T-shirt. He should be coming back out in a minute. There he is."

She walked toward George, waving a greeting. "Hey!" she called out.

George walked toward her, wearing khaki shorts and a turquoise T-shirt. They sat down at the table across from each other, and George smiled at his friend.

"How's your world going?" he asked.

Susan folded her hands in front of her, forcing a smile. "Well, not real good," she said. "That's why I need to talk to you." She took a deep breath. "Well, let me start from the beginning, okay? When I first moved into the Alturas house, Mona and Sam helped me move in."

"Okay," said George, resting his chin on his hand and looking at her.

"The first night the lovely neighbor came over and wanted to know what I was doing there," she told him. "The watchdog."

"Yeah."

"He wanted to know if I was partying or breaking in or what. And I explained that we were moving in. Well, from there I think you neglected to tell me something."

"Oh, what's that?" George said.

"That something had happened in the neighborhood," Susan said, her voice beginning to quaver. "I had a lot of well-meaning people scare me out of my wits."

"Oh, yeah," George said, his voice matter-of-fact. "Somebody got poisoned next door. So, uh . . ."

"That might not be a lot to you," she said. "But it's a lot to me."

"Oh, well," he said, giving a little laugh. "Sorry."

Until today Susan still wasn't entirely sure that George was the killer. Until this moment she had seen a sympathetic side, a fumbling nerd who had a strange sense of morals but at least seemed to care about his friend Sherry. Her mind had said George was guilty, but her heart hadn't been quite there. But as she listened to him talking, she knew the truth. His voice held no grief for the senseless poisoning of his neighbors. No fear of what the poisoner could have done to him and his wife. No concern for the friend who had moved into his house.

Something else didn't fit. George loved murder mysteries, and a real-life one had unfolded right next door to him in Alturas. If he were innocent, he would have told her about it long before, impressed his new friend with his sleuthing ability. "I have a good idea who it was," he might have said, "but the cops are too stupid to figure it out. Let me tell you my theory. . . . "

Instead he had told her nothing.

"They said they never caught the person that did it," Susan continued. "It really frightened me."

George's face remained blank. "Oh," he said again. "I'm sorry."

"You don't seem overly concerned," Susan said. "That's not why you moved out, is it?"

"Oh, no."

"You weren't afraid, were you?"

"No," George said, his voice taking on a soothing tone. "Apparently it was some sort of personal vendetta. I mean, it's not like they're running around poisoning everybody."

"Okay."

"Plus, this is right around two years ago."

"Okay," Susan said. She held her hand to her heart. "It just caught me off guard. Second thing, after that I had a visitor."

"Uh-huh."

"And when they talked to me, I lied to them."

"Uh-huh."

"And that's why I don't really want to go to your house.

I know I'm overly paranoid and all, but they questioned me about some stuff and about you.''

Until then George had been nonchalant. Suddenly, though, he seemed startled. All he could manage was "Oh."

"They gave me business cards." Susan rummaged through her purse. "I told 'em I was living in Naples with Sam. I thought, well, that'll be the end of it. I'll never hear from them again."

"Uh-huh."

"And Monday, they called Sam wanting to know where I was," Susan said. "Well, I started to throw away their cards and . . ." She pulled two business cards out of her bag and handed them to George. He took the cards, cradling them in his left hand, staring at the words. "Ernest Mincey, Detective, Polk County Sheriff's Office." "Bradley Brekke, Special Agent, Federal Bureau of Investigation."

"Thank you," he said. "Hmm. That's interesting."

Susan went on as George continued to study the cards. "They wanted to know what I was doing there. What contact I had with you. I told 'em that y'all moved out of county and I didn't tell 'em where."

"Yes," George said, not looking up. "Huh."

"And I don't wanna go to your house," Susan said. "I know I'm being paranoid, and I know they don't have the money to follow me around or anything. But I don't want . . ."

Any other day George would have taken over the conversation, rambling on about the police, how stupid they were, while his friend Sherry listened and nodded politely. This time he seemed at a loss for words.

"Uh-huh," he said.

Susan kept the conversation going. She said, "I mean, I know enough from working in law offices that cops aren't that smart."

"Uh-huh."

"I just don't want to take any chances, and I don't want

to get involved in this 'cause if my name keeps coming
up—''

''Uh-huh.''

''—Richard's bound to find me.''

''Right,'' George said, still staring at the cards.
''Uh . . .''

''Now it's up to you,'' Susan said. ''I don't care what
you do. If you want to call them and find out what they
want, that's fine. Or if you want me to do something, I'll
be glad to do it for you.''

''Uh, it shouldn't be terribly hard to find me if they really
want me.''

''They really haven't called you or anything?'' Susan
asked.

He shook his head.

Susan said she hadn't told the investigators about
George's moving to Sebring. Instead, she said, she told
them she had located his home through a real estate agent.
''And I know if they check that, they're gonna find out I
lied about that,'' she said. ''But I never thought they'd call
Naples looking for me.''

''Gee, that's really weird,'' he said. His eyes bored into
her. ''What are they asking about me?''

He just can't let it go, Susan thought. He wants to know
more, but he's afraid of seeming too interested. And after
all this time he doesn't trust me enough to tell me what
this is really all about. Hagmaier was right: George would
probably never come right out and tell his secrets, not even
to a friend.

She told George that the detectives had asked lots of
questions: ''Where you were. What was my relationship
with you. Where your wife was. All sorts of things. And I
just played it off, that I'd met you and y'all were nice
people.''

''Hmmm,'' George said, still studying the business cards.
He paused, then drew out the words ''I would guess there's
not that much to worry about.''

"Maybe not for you!" Susan replied. "But for me, you know, just to have my name brought up—especially this one guy scared me to death. He said he was federal."

"Yeah, the FBI got involved in the case," George said. "The next-door neighbor was poisoned by something put into the Coke bottles. That makes it a federal sort of case."

"Okay," said Susan.

"And you say this was Monday?" George asked.

"No, no," she said. "This was, oh, the week between Christmas and New Year's."

"Oh, I see."

"And then they called Monday in Naples for me."

"I see."

"Like I said, I don't want to get involved in it, and I wanted to know what you want me to tell 'em if they do get hold of me."

"Just tell 'em the truth, I guess. That's probably the best thing," he said, nestling his chin in his right hand. "This is all very strange. Let me think. Hmm."

Susan piped up. "I didn't even ask you. You want something to eat?"

He waved away her offer. "Oh, no, I'm fine," he said. While Susan munched on a french fry, George stared off across the parking lot and chewed over her news, unaware of the video camera whirring nearby. He said, "I mean, it shouldn't take 'em a month to track me down, should it?"

He paused. "Wait a minute," he said. "Something's not right here."

Susan could see the computer whirring inside his head, processing the information and looking for the missing piece. She hoped he wouldn't find it.

George said, "What it comes down to—"

Susan jumped in. "Well, do you think it would hurt if I tell 'em I found your phone number or, you know, what do you want me to tell 'em?"

"Well, your best bet probably is just to stick to your original story."

"Okay."

"I mean, this would seem reasonable," he said. Nudging his glasses back up his nose, he continued. "And you know also you don't have to talk to these people."

"You mean just tell 'em to get lost?"

George shifted in his seat. His voice normally swelled when he was dispensing advice to the helpless Sherry. But today the words dribbled out, sounding limp and dispirited.

"Uh, you can do that," he said. "The first thing to ask is whether you're under criminal investigation."

"Okay."

"If they say yes, well, that is a problem in itself, and then you say 'Well . . . I'd like to talk to my lawyer first, and I don't wanna say anything more.' "

"Okay."

"And if you're not under criminal investigation, why are they bothering you? Just go away."

"Okay, okay."

"You know, basically all I can think of is, uh . . ." George said. "Something just isn't falling in place here."

A horn honked in the background, but George paid no attention. Susan peered at him, saying, "Explain it to me."

"Okay," he said. "If they're interested in me, they should've found me by now."

"I agree," said Susan. "And that's why I'm wondering why they're bothering me."

"Really."

"I don't wanna be involved."

"Right," said George. "The only reason they could be interested in me, of course, would—"

"They didn't tell me what it was in reference to."

His voice sharpened in irritation. "Of course, they wouldn't," he snapped. "What I'm doing is just working through various possibilities."

"Okay."

"So leave me alone for a moment."

"Okay, I'm sorry."

"If they're interested in me, it would be because of the, uh, probably the poisoning next door a few years ago. Which, just because I lived in the area, I might be a suspect."

"Have they questioned people or anything?"

"I talked to them twice," he said. "And Diana's talked to 'em. I think everybody in Alturas has talked to 'em."

"Okay."

"I hope I'm not a prime suspect," he said. "That could be messy."

Excusing herself, Susan walked to her car. She had another idea for testing George, to see how shaken he was by her news. While Susan was on a family vacation in Tennessee, she had purchased him a geode and a tiny dinosaur carved out of rock. Most days either gift would delight him and, more than likely, send him off on a long conversational tangent. She wondered how he would react today.

As Susan fetched the bag, George stared off across the parking lot, lost in thought.

She handed him the geode. "Thank you," George said.

"Yeah, I had it cut in half."

"This is quite pretty," he said, without enthusiasm.

"Oh, wait, wait," Susan said, pulling out the dinosaur. "There's one more that I found."

"Okay."

"A dinosaur."

George glanced at it. "That's nice," he said. "So, if they are interested in me, of course, they would not come to me and ask about it, right? Okay, let's assume I am a prime suspect for whatever reason, in that case they . . . all right now, if they're interested in you, what would they be interested in you that the FBI would be called in?"

"I don't know."

"Well, I would tend to think that I'm probably a prime suspect for whatever reason and that you have nothing to worry about."

Bicyclists pedaled by with orange flags flying, and a

Dumpster lid slammed in the background. George took no notice.

"What can I do to help you?" Susan said.

"Oh, nothing," George replied. "It's kind of a shock, but I think they've suspected everybody else. I mean, it's probably just my turn."

"I understand," she said.

"If they get back to you," he said, "you just say, 'I don't like cops.' "

"Okay," Susan said, laughing. "That should make their day."

As the meeting wound down, after he had plumbed as much information as he could, George tried a polite gesture. "So do you want a grand tour of the house?"

Susan declined. "I guess I'm just a little paranoid right now," she said. "Can I take a rain check?"

"Oh, sure," George said, "I understand."

"Okay."

George drifted back to the visit by the homicide detective and the FBI agent. " . . . still asking and trying, trying to gather evidence. But evidence to what? I don't know. I suspect that's why . . . Uh, several years ago there was a bombing someplace in Texas, I think Houston. Some bigwig got killed. It's never been traced. I know the FBI had followed about two thousand dead leads."

"Yeah," Susan said, wondering what had prompted him to tell that story. Hagmaier had told her that poisoners and bombers share a psychological profile, passive people who find ways to kill without being on the scene. She wondered why the Texas bombing had come to George's mind. Was it just coincidence, or did he have some personal knowledge?

"Since they have infinite money and manpower," George was saying, "they can afford to bark up trees and all forever."

"I guess so," Susan said.

The meeting over, George walked Susan to her car and then strode off, a queer smile plastered to his face.

"Okay," she said to her purse. "The time is eleven-thirty, and he's leaving. And he's very worried."

TWENTY-THREE

Susan walked into Lieutenant Hart's office and sank into a chair. "Francis," she said, "I am really frustrated. I've used every idea I can think of and I don't know what else to do. I can't believe I spent a year of my life, I can't believe this man did these hideous things—and there's nothing we can do."

At the McDonald's meeting two months earlier, Susan had given George a shock and awaited a reaction that would help her make the case against him. Maybe he and Diana would pack their things and flee the state. Maybe he would turn to his friend Sherry for advice, taking her into his confidence, telling her everything. True to form, though, George revealed nothing.

Once in a while Susan drove by George's new home. It was a sprawling lakeside house with wooden floors, huge rooms, a pool out back, a guesthouse that George was fixing up for his father, even an elevator. Susan wondered what was going on inside that house, behind the wall George had built around himself. She could only wonder; he had not called.

Barring a confession, the police could only wait for the FBI lab to finish analyzing the materials gathered from George's house. As the weeks passed, Susan's optimism faded. She busied herself with other cases and tried to get used to the idea that this one had failed. Despite the kind words from Gary and her friends, she couldn't help wondering what she had done wrong. It used to be that when she invested enough time and effort, something good would come of it. But in this case there had been nothing but dashed hopes. No matter how close she got to George, she wasn't close enough.

As he listened to her pour out her despair, Hart shook his head, his face a blend of affection and dismay. Although he and Susan had followed similar paths, they were as different as two people could be. Hart rarely let things get to him. He tried to help Susan look at this for what it was: an investigation in which she had done her best and there was nothing more she could do.

"Susan, don't beat yourself up about it," he said. "There're only two things that you've got to remember in this life. Number one, you worry only about the big things. Number two, there are no big things."

Hart's pep talk angered Susan. How could he think she would just walk away? She wasn't a quitter, never had been. She went home and told her husband about the exchange. She said, "How can he say something like that?"

"The man is right," Gary said. "You did your best. Nobody is going to look down on you because you didn't get anything else. You know in your heart that you did what you could, and your supervisor knows. You've got to move on now."

Susan still wasn't sure. She walked outside the house, where the kids were playing in the yard. It was early March, a year after the doctor had unplugged Peggy Carr from life support. Susan could feel the spring wind stirring, carrying the first hints of summer warmth. She looked around. It was so beautiful. The flowers were just starting to push out of the ground. Oak and pine branches fidgeted in the breeze. There were more important things than George Trepal.

Susan tried to persuade herself to let it go. I've done what I could, she thought. This is what life is; you can't be consumed by something like work. I knew all along that it might come to this, so what's the big deal? I guess Francis was right.

The next day Susan walked into the office, her step lighter than it had been in months. She found Ernie upstairs in his office.

"It's your case again," she told him. "If I can do anything to help you, let me know."

Settling in at her desk, Susan wrote a note to Hagmaier at the FBI. "I finally decided that no matter how hard you try, you can't solve everything," she wrote. "Regardless, I want to thank you for all your help. You have really been great. I owe you a steak dinner." She read over the letter, signed it, and sealed it in an envelope. After dropping it in the mail, she called Brad to tell him about her decision.

"But you know what?" she said. "I feel lighter. I think this is the right thing."

"Wait a minute, Susan," Brad said. "There's another phone call. Can you hold on a minute?"

Elevator music. A few moments later Brad came back on the line to say he had another call. "Let me talk to them, and I'll call you back."

She went back to her paperwork. The phone rang.

"Sorry about that, Susan. That call was from the laboratory."

"What was it about?"

Brad let out a bored sigh. "Some of the tests."

"What tests?" Susan said.

"On the stuff we found in George's house," Brad said. "Some of the bottles. That green liquid; they can't identify it. There might have been one other bottle or something; I can't remember what it was." Brad's tone confirmed Susan's suspicion. Once again the lab had not found any evidence to link George to the poisoning. The case really was over.

As if struck by an afterthought, Brad said: "That one brown bottle out of the garage—it had thallium nitrate in it."

"What?" Susan demanded.

Brad, still in a flat tone, replied, "Thallium nitrate."

Walking by Susan's desk, Lieutenant Hart heard her excited voice. He paused to look at her curiously. Susan felt the flesh rising on her arms, but she wanted to be sure. "Brad, you are lying to me," she said. "Come on, Brad, tell me the truth."

Susan looked at her boss, mouthing the words "Don't leave! Don't leave!"

"Brad, are you sure? I'm about to make a fool out of myself."

"Susan, you can call for yourself."

All Brad could hear on the other end was a happy scream. He began to laugh. "We did it, Susan," he said. "We did it. It's there."

Susan thanked Brad, then said she had to go. She hung up the phone, her mouth agape. "Francis, you won't believe it," she said. "They found thallium in the samples we sent."

"Calm down, Susan, calm down," he said, a grin appearing on his face. "Let's go see if the colonel's in."

As she followed him up the stairs, Susan could barely contain herself. She clenched her fists in triumph. "I can't believe it! I can't believe it!" she said. "You give up on something and what happens?"

They walked in on a meeting between Colonel Alley and Sheriff Crow. Lieutenant Hart smiled and said, "Susan has something to tell you."

Susan stepped forward, beaming. "We found thallium!"

Sheriff Crow leaped to his feet and wrapped Susan in a bear hug. He exclaimed, "I can't believe it!"

She called her husband at the Lake Wales Police Department. "Gary, don't leave the station. I've got to tell you something,'' she said. She jumped in the car and raced over.

Gary wheeled around to see her standing there, flushed and breathing fast. ''What is it?''

''You just won't believe what good news it is.''

''The last time I've seen you this excited is when you found out you were pregnant. Is that it?''

''Gary, no!'' she said. ''We found thallium.'' He looked a little disappointed, as if to say, ''Well what did you expect?''

The lab results led to a monthlong grind of preparation: meetings with prosecutors, gathering boxes full of evidence, preparing to present the case to a grand jury of citizens who would decide whether there was enough evidence to charge George with murder.

Susan couldn't resist. She ran down to the Hallmark store to shop for some cheerful stationery. Something Sherry would send. It showed a smiling little man holding an armful of lines and the words ''Dropping a Few Lines.''

GEORGE,

Hello! I certainly have good news this time. I've been in Houston for several weeks now, and it appears that within a few days, I should be a ''partially'' free divorcee. It won't be final yet, but I don't believe anything can stop it now.

After talking to you, the depression and loneliness really started getting to me, so I made up my mind that I could no longer continue to live like that. I never knew when or where he'd show up, or when the whole mess would just explode in my face. So, I sold everything I could find, hired one hell of a good attorney, and went for Richard's throat. As expected, I will not end up rich, but my attorney did get me enough to allow me the lifestyle I wanted, and better yet, the freedom I wanted. I'm only sorry that you had to see Richard as he is now, because he wasn't always that way. But then, this is the last time that I will ever apologize for him. In a few days, the final papers will be signed and except for the legal hearing, it's over.

Do I need to celebrate!!!! When I get back to Winter Haven, maybe you and Diana can go out with me one evening. Maybe I can even talk Sam into coming along if he'll leave his work long enough to drive up there. Well, enough of that.

I trust you and Diana are doing fine and continuing to make a showpiece of your new abode. I've obtained a lease for that condo I told you about until June, which is when the owner moves back in. So, I'll have time to make some decisions; rationally this time. I wish I wasn't so afraid of moving back in your home, but I have come to the realization that I'm not as strong a person as I thought I was, and I do admit I was scared after the neighbor told me what had happened there. Oh—that brings to mind—I called those "people" I talked to you about (the ones who left me their cards) and they never even called me back. I guess it wasn't important.

Well, see you soon!! Please drop me a line or give me a call. You're still one of the only "friends" I have. Which is different from the "acquaintances" that I have learned to tolerate around the condo. What a trip!

SHERRY

On April 5, 1990, Susan called George.

"I've been meaning to ring you," George said, "but I misplaced your letter with your address and such." He explained that he and Diana were preparing to go to Arizona the next week. "I've been there before. It rained all the time; it was great. No, really, 'cause when it rains, the desert blooms and that's really beautiful.''

"Oh, well, you'll have a good time," Susan said. "So, nothing new?"

Nope, George said. Nothing at all.

BOOK III

Poison Mind

Chapter
TWENTY-FOUR

It was 4:30 A.M., ungodly early, but the air inside Fat Boy's Bar-B-Q was already thick with cigarette smoke and bacon grease. Susan, Ernie, and Brad settled down at a table with cups of coffee. Since getting the lab results a month earlier, they had worked sixteen-hour days assembling evidence, filling out search warrants, and planning the arrest. At last the paperwork was done.

It was April 7, 1990. Soon the threesome would drive to a parking lot near George's new house and rendezvous with a small army of other cops. Masquerading one last time as Sherry Guin, Susan would call George on the phone. She would make sure George was home and get a sense of whether he and Diana had any visitors or other threats to the officers about to descend.

At 8:00 A.M. Susan dialed the number. Diana answered.

"Hi, this is Sherry. I'm sorry to disturb you. Is George around?"

"He's in his bedroom. I'll go get him."

"Hello?"

"Hi, George, this is Sherry." Susan's voice shook with genuine anxiety, but she didn't mind George's hearing it. She wanted to sound needy, desperate even, so he wouldn't blow her off. She said, "Those two investigators came to my house again this morning. They were asking about you again, something about some chemicals. I don't know what they're talking about. Do you?''

"Calm down, Sherry," George said. "Calm—"

She cut him off, her voice urgent. Tears had actually begun to well in her eyes. She said, "But I don't know what to do."

"Calm down," he said. "Now . . ."

As they talked, Brad and Ernie drove toward George's home in a Crown Victoria sedan borrowed from one of her superiors. George would be riding to jail in style. They pulled up in front of the sprawling blue wood-frame house. Beyond the house the lawn spilled down a gentle slope and toward the glassy water of Lake Jackson.

"This is it," Brad said, smiling nervously at Ernie as he stepped out of the car. The men walked to the wooden front door and knocked. They heard a voice inside, followed by footsteps. Diana peered through the window and opened the door. Dressed in a flowered dress and knit sweater, she looked confused.

Ernie and Brad spoke at the same time.

"Polk County Sheriff. FBI. We'd like to come in and talk to George and you."

"What's this about?" Diana said, her face reddening. Without waiting for an answer, she tried to shut the door.

Brad pushed back, pulling out the arrest warrant and waving it in the rapidly narrowing space between his hand and the door. "We have to come in," he said. Brad knew they could break the door down; they had a warrant after all. But they had decided in advance to keep the whole process as low-key and professional as possible. Diana clearly did not share their goal.

"George isn't here," she insisted, again trying to shove the door closed. Seeing that her unwanted visitors weren't leaving, though, she turned and called up the stairs, "George!"

George and Susan were still on the phone, continuing their discussion about the police. Susan heard a commotion, and George interrupted. "Sherry, by coincidence, the police are here," he said, his voice strangely cool. "You'll have to call back Monday."

As he hung up, Diana had stopped trying to shut the door and was instead trying to block the way with her body. Within moments police cars converged on the house, tires screeching and lights blinking. Brad had to stop himself from laughing out loud. What else could go wrong? he thought. Here I am playing all-star wrestling in the doorway, and George is nowhere in sight.

Ernie's boss, Lieutenant Juanita Crawford, came running up the lawn to help. The two men had hesitated to engage Diana in combat, lest she later accuse them of brutality. But Crawford didn't hesitate; the woman lieutenant yanked Diana out the door and pinned her face first against the outside wall, ordering her to calm down. Diana continued to struggle, polluting the air with curses.

Free at last, Brad and Ernie went inside the house, calling out for George. At last their suspect appeared at the top of the stairs, wearing only a pair of bikini briefs. In contrast with his protesting wife, George gazed down at them with placid curiosity.

"George, we want to talk to you," Brad said.

"Okay, just a moment," he said agreeably, before disappearing inside his bedroom. Brad and Ernie bounded up the stairs. They couldn't let him out of their sight; what if he went for a gun? As they rounded the corner, they saw that George was simply grabbing a T-shirt and a pair of cutoff shorts. They allowed him to get dressed, then led him downstairs.

George seemed befuddled but pleasant, as if some old friends had surprised him by stopping by at an inconvenient hour. But he knew this was no social call. Outside he could hear his wife still shouting at Crawford. Other officers walked through the yard and into the house, their heels drumming the old wooden floors, radios crackling on their hips, badges flashing in the day's new light. Brad and Ernie took George into the kitchen and asked him to sit down at a table.

"Nice kitchen," Brad said.

"Thank you," George replied.

Ernie told him he was under arrest for the murder of Peggy Carr and attempted murder of her family. He pulled out a tiny card and read George his rights.

"Would you like to talk to us?" Ernie asked.

"No," George said quietly. "I'll talk to an attorney."

That was it; Brad and Ernie couldn't ask George another question about the crime until he had a lawyer present. Still, it would be a long ride to the Polk County Jail, and they hoped George might volunteer some information, about himself and possibly about his wife. Although they hadn't found enough evidence to charge Diana in the crime, Brad and Ernie had their suspicions. Once under arrest, perhaps George would decide he didn't have anything to lose by talking.

After searching George, Ernie and Brad cuffed his hands behind his back and led him to the car. Suddenly the air swirled and filled with the roar of an approaching helicopter. They looked up to see Sheriff Crow, who had come to survey the scene and shake the hands of the arresting officers. It was a bit of spectacle, the big chief descending from the heavens, but nobody minded. The sheriff wasn't just coming in at the end to take credit for his subordinates' hard work; he had quietly kept the investigation alive through its hopeless hours, and everyone agreed that Crow deserved any credit he might claim.

Ironically, Susan was the one person who couldn't take part in this final drama. Instead she sat in a car parked in the church lot across the street, watching from behind tinted windows. To Susan, to any cop who had invested as much as she had in the investigation, the arrest was an important moment, an affirmation. But she couldn't savor it, at least not now. She had to stay under. If George implicated his wife or others in talking to Brad and Ernie, "Sherry" might be able to go in and cement the case.

Brad and Ernie pulled away from the house with their prisoner. Ernie drove, while Brad stayed with George in the back seat. They had a plan: Susan had told them George didn't like cigarette smoke, so Ernie planned to smoke during the entire hour long drive to the Polk County Jail. They wanted to unsettle George, in hopes he would blurt something out. The investigators later acknowledged that the smoke was also a payback, one of the little cruelties cops allow themselves when dealing with cruel people.

George sat in the back seat, hands cuffed behind him, legs arranged in the lotus position, his face impassive. Brad tried to strike up a conversation. The investigators had agreed in advance to play up their roles as city cop/country cop, hoping that George would relate to the FBI man with the expensive clothes and sophisticated ways. As they drove by a trailer park, Brad sniffed. "There seem to be more trailers every day."

George took the bait and began to gripe about all the people moving to Florida with no brains or useful skills, saying it was too easy for them to park a trailer and spoil the landscape. As he spoke, Brad could see him loosening up, his shoulders relaxing and his face hinting at a smile. George didn't seem the least bit angry; he didn't even seem to mind the handcuffs. It was almost as if he were used to wearing them.

As they drove past a billboard where a business advertised its European flair, Brad sniffed. "I bet they do it *just* like in France." George snickered along with his new pal. Meanwhile, though, Brad noticed that Ernie wasn't acting out his part of the plan. For the first time in two years Ernie was saying nothing—and not puffing on a cigarette.

"Ernie," Brad said, "did we forget anything?"

"Oh, yeah," Ernie said, smiling sheepishly and lighting up. As the car's interior filled with smoke, George cringed, his nose wrinkling and shoulders tensing in a futile attempt to lean out of the cloud. Suddenly what seemed like a good joke before the arrest now seemed to Ernie like a cheap trick, and he cracked his window. As the fresh air flowed in, George relaxed again. He asked Brad questions about the life of an FBI agent: How much education do you need? Do you travel a lot? Then, as if he had only just recalled why he was there, he began to ask about what was happening to him: What is the next step in the process? Where is the jail? By the time they reached Polk County, George had talked about a lot of things—except the murder.

Before booking their suspect, Brad and Ernie made one more attempt to open him up. Bill Hagmaier had suggested that they try to rattle George by showing him that this arrest hadn't just happened, that it was the product of long months of stealth and surveillance. They couldn't reveal Susan's undercover role yet, but they had another idea. Recalling *The Pale Horse*, the Agatha Christie mystery whose poisonings mirrored the crime in Alturas, they had converted a room upstairs at the sheriff's office into a phony command post. The sign on the door read OPERATION PALE HORSE.

As George was led inside, his eyes widened in recognition. In addition to the *Pale Horse* reference, he could see other familiar sights: manila folders bearing the names of his Mensa friends; pictures of himself taken through a long lens; images of Peggy Carr, now dead. It wasn't so much that the investigators expected the room alone to prompt a confession, but they hoped it would whittle away at his confidence, crumble any belief that he could beat this murder charge. Another payback: They wanted to show George that maybe cops weren't as stupid as he thought.

After his initial shock, though, George pulled the mask of insouciance across his face and said nothing. When a beefy jailer led him off to be fingerprinted and booked, George smiled at Ernie and Brad and pleasantly said, "Thank you."

* * *

Down the hall at the sheriff's office, television crews and newspaper reporters milled around in a conference room, grousing about being called out on a weekend, speculating on the reason for the hastily scheduled press conference. This was big; that much was clear. Many of them had begun to think that the cops would never solve the Alturas poisonings, but apparently they were wrong. Top officials with the sheriff's office and the FBI took center stage, announcing that one of Peggy Carr's neighbors had been charged with murdering her and poisoning her family. One after another the officials stood up to have their pictures taken and to answer questions.

In the back of the room Susan stood outside the lights. Most of the reporters didn't recognize her, and they paid her no mind. Susan knew she shouldn't resent the attention being showered on her colleagues, but she couldn't help feeling cheated. For most of their careers police officers work with little to show for their efforts but low pay, curses from the people they arrest, and a feeling that society takes them for granted. On the rare occasion when the press and public pay attention to a job well done, cops relish their measure of fame. Ernie certainly was enjoying it, standing up there and grinning.

Susan's beeper went off, and she welcomed the excuse to leave. Alone in her office she returned the phone call, then leaned back in the chair and felt the fatigue crash down. For weeks she had been running on caffeine and adrenaline. Now that George was locked away, she needed some rest. She closed her eyes, just for a minute . . . and heard Brad and Ernie walk in.

"They want to have a conference upstairs," one of them said.

"Am *I* allowed to sit in?" she asked sarcastically.

"What's wrong?" said Brad.

Susan smiled apologetically. "I'm really tired," she said. "We've been going nonstop."

His voice kind, Brad suggested that she go home and get some rest. "No," she insisted. "I'm fine."

At the meeting they mapped out strategy for the weeks ahead. Although George was now under arrest, they still had a lot of work to do to build a strong case for court. It was one thing to charge George with the crime and quite another to assemble the evidence needed to convince a jury.

Posing as Sherry, Susan would contact Diana to see what she had to say. The others would start interviewing George's friends and acquaintances, something they hadn't been able to do during the undercover investigation. Before doing any of that, though, Susan and the others wanted to return to George's house to see if the search team was turning up anything interesting.

Susan and Ernie rode south through the orange groves, speculating about what they might find inside George's house in Sebring. They had the thallium bottle, but no fingerprints to prove who had used it. Susan hoped that they would find something inside George's house that would clearly tie him to the murder: chemistry equipment with traces of thallium, a typewriter whose keys matched the typewritten death threat sent to Pye and his family, a record of George's purchasing thallium from a chemical supply house. She had a hunch they would find some sort of secret hideaway, similar to the one George had shown her behind the bookcase in Alturas. Maybe it would be inside the basement George had spoken of renovating in Sebring; he had laughingly referred to it as "the dungeon."

When Ernie pulled his car up to the house, it was packed with crime scene technicians. By now, early afternoon, Diana had given up the fight and gone off someplace. Most of the neighbors who had gathered to watch the morning spectacle had returned home. Inside the house the searchers worked quietly, the silence broken by the rustle of plastic evidence bags. Susan and Ernie first went upstairs where George and Diana had apparently taken separate bedrooms. In Diana's room Susan saw an exercise bicycle sitting next to an unmade bed. George's room was filled with clutter: a pair of running shoes on the floor, a desk stacked high with books, a catalog from Frederick's of Hollywood. His windows were covered not by blinds but by a crinkly layer of aluminum foil that kept the room dark even at midday.

Ernie walked into a closet, then came out holding a whip with dozens of leather flails. "What is *this*?" he asked.

As it turned out, the closet was full of bondage equipment, a much more extensive collection than Susan had seen on her first trip to the Alturas house. There was a library of magazines and books devoted to the forbidden arts: *The Satanic Bible*, *Whipped Women*, *Studies in Sadomasochism*. One of the magazines, *Advanced Bondage*, depicted a woman on its cover, clad only in a leather chastity belt and stockings, her arms locked by wrist cuffs, her face and neck bound in black leather, her mouth gagged. Next to the picture a drawing showed an elaborate torture rack, with a winch ready to hang a prisoner by the arms.

The searchers found that George had the hardware to turn S&M fantasies into reality: a pair of stainless-steel Speed King leg irons, a well-used pair of Smith & Wesson handcuffs, three leather riding crops, a black leather whip, even a black wizard's hat adorned with golden stars. Those were the more conventional items. The searchers also found a black leather hood with a flap that snapped shut over the eyes and a mouthpiece bearing a distinctive set of teeth marks. There was also an electronic collar that promised a jolt of electricity to its wearer and a heavy steel winch with a label warning, "Not for the movement of human beings." In the upstairs laundry cabinet there were two photographs of George, his beard graying and his chin upturned, a gold cape on his shoulders, holding what looked like a black and silver ray gun. The picture made George look half regal, half ridiculous: King Lear meets Captain Kirk.

A crime scene technician walked up to Susan. She said, "Did you see the bathroom?"

"No," Susan said.

The technician led her down the hallway. "Look at this door," she said. Susan could see that the wood was cracked in a circle around the doorknob, as if someone had tried to break out from the inside. The technician opened up one of the cabinet doors inside the bathroom. On the wall of the cabinet Susan could see that someone had scribbled in pencil, "Help, We Are Being Killed."

Another officer came up. "You've got to come see this book," he said. "It talks about thallium."

He led Susan and Ernie into the kitchen and through a door. Lit by a single bulb, the stairs descended into the darkness. "My God," Susan said, "this *is* a dungeon."

Downstairs Susan found herself in a maze of rooms. Against one wall she saw bookshelves lined with science texts. Computer disks filled several racks, lined up like tiny, silent soldiers. In an alcove she saw cartons full of beakers, tubes, and other chemistry supplies wrapped in 1970s newspapers. There was an old issue of *High Times* and amber bottles with handwritten labels, all apparently containing chemicals. (Tests later showed that the bottles found in George's Sebring and Alturas houses contained the chemicals sodium cyanide, barium chloride, cobalt nitrate, potassium ferricyanide, chromium trioxide, lead chloride, and radioactive uranium oxide. Not exactly an amateur chemistry set.)

Standing not far away was George's mannequin, now dressed in black lingerie. Some of the searchers were posing with the mannequin, yukking it up. Susan walked past them to where a book from one of the shelves lay open. She saw that it was a loose-leaf binder filled with pages from scientific texts. The pages were discolored and worn, apparently from use. On the cover George had scribbled a title: "General Poisoning Guides."

Taking care not to put her own fingerprints on the notebook, Susan began leafing through it. She saw that it contained lengthy excerpts from books used by homicide investigators.

Susan read one excerpt, from a police manual with a chapter entitled "Death by Poison."

Determining whether a person died as a result of natural illness or as a result of poisoning is one of the most difficult types of investigation both for the officer and for the medical expert. Symptoms of different kinds of poisonings include vomiting, convulsions, coma, dilatation or contraction of pupil, paralysis, changes of respiration, delirium, cyanosis and the like; however, unfortunately for the investigator and for the medical expert, these symptoms are also present in various types of normal deaths. The first prerequisite in this complicated field is suspicion. . . . It must be observed that poisoning is one of the easiest ways for a person to commit murder and get away with it.

Another excerpt, from a book titled *Poison Detection in Human Organs*, gave more details:

The criminal poisoner is cunning—to quote Mr. Justice Diplock in the "insulin" case—"poisoning is a cool, calculated, premeditated crime." Only systematic analysis can reveal such murders. A forensic toxicologist cannot hope to perform analyses for all known poisons in all cases that come to his attention, but he can perform a large number of very simple screening tests. . . . It is the aim of this book to present the analyses in such a form that a sequence of tests is performed so that not only is there the greatest probability of detecting any poison, but also that the complications arising from different routes of administration (oral, injection, inhaled, through the skin, into orifices) as well as differing times between the onset of the illness and the taking of the samples, are taken into account.

The book went on to give a detailed lesson in the work of solving a poisoning homicide: how to analyze blood, stomach linings, the tissue of the liver and kidneys; how to preserve samples and seal containers; how to exhume a body without attracting a crowd.

It is often thought that exhumations should be performed at midnight by the light of a policeman's torch so that secrecy can be maintained. This, however, is a fallacy—nothing is more likely to excite the population than a crowd of uniformed police officers watching digging in a graveyard in the dead of night. Daylight exhumation behind screens causes no abnormal suspicion.

Susan didn't have to guess why George would have such a book; she remembered what Hagmaier said about the way sophisticated killers map out their crimes months in advance, carefully studying police procedures to minimize the chance of capture. As she read on, the book became harder to understand, detailing technical procedures that would be understood only by someone with a background in chemistry. After giving general instructions, the book began detailing techniques for identifying particular poisons. On page 138 Susan found the one she had been looking for:

Thallium is a highly toxic rodenticide and is favoured by criminal poisoners. The outstanding point of interest for the toxicologist is that symptoms are delayed for several days after ingestion and death for much longer. The outstanding symptoms are burning sensations over the lower extremities, so that even bedclothes become an intolerable burden, and the loss of hair about 14 days after ingestion. . . . The minimum lethal dose for an adult is said to be about 0.8 g.

Susan remembered the amount of thallium found in the three full bottles of Coke found in Peggy Carr's home. One contained 0.4 grams of thallium, the second 0.8 grams, and the third 0.9 grams. The vial found in George's garage contained 0.64 grams—about enough for the one bottle of Coke that was found broken in the carton.

As she read, Susan felt the hair rise on her neck. The books George had copied from were not standard reading for most people, even cops; poisoning murders were just not that common. But George had left no page unturned. He was declaring war, and he wanted to know everything about his weapons—and his enemies.

Jim Madden, the sheriff's lieutenant supervising the search, came up to Susan. "We looked all around for secret compartments," he said. "We didn't find any."

"There has to be one," Susan insisted. She couldn't believe that George wouldn't have a secret place, not after he had boasted about the one in Alturas. She suggested looking behind the bookcases George had built. The searchers fanned out, pounding on the walls with their fists, listening for the echo of a hollow panel.

Madden was examining a wall where some tools hung from a pegboard when he stopped, a frown scrawling across his forehead. "Wait a minute," he said. He summoned a searcher with a tape measure. "Measure this wall here," he said. Sure enough, the wall was shorter on one side than on the other. Madden examined the pegboard. He tugged at a corner where some saws were hanging, their teeth still coated with woodchips. Instead of coming off the wall, the board swung open on hinges attached to a pair of heavy springs. By now Susan and the other searchers had gathered around, and when they saw Madden open the panel, even the most seasoned drew sharp breaths. Behind the panel was a heavy wooden door, painted black. Madden pushed it open and shone a flashlight inside.

He turned to Susan. "You've got to come look at this."

Following the flashlight beacons, Susan stepped inside

the hidden room. Her nostrils filled with the smell of fresh paint. Someone pulled a cord in the center of the room, and a single bulb threw a harsh, grainy light across the room. Susan could see no windows, only walls covered with black wooden panels. She saw an electric screw gun on the floor. Strange. She and Gary had put up some paneling at their place, but small nails were all they needed to hold the thin sheets of wood. George would need screws only if he were putting up thick panels. Why would he do that?

The answer stood in the corner of the room. There George had apparently been putting the finishing touches on a wooden platform the size of a bed. For a moment it didn't register.

"What in the name of God did he put that there for?" Susan asked.

Brad had also come along for a look at the house. He walked over to the foot of the platform and rotated an L-shaped contraption shaped from two-by-fours. "Look," he said, "this is where you put the feet."

Susan's head swam with the realization: George had been building a platform for tying people down, part of what seemed to be a torture chamber. The knowledge surprised her, knocked her off center. She had come to see that George had the makings of a poisoner, a killer who doesn't stick around to see the effects of his crime. She could even accept the S&M gear, figuring that George played the submissive role, the love slave. But what of this? Did George enjoy torturing people as well? Did he like to see suffering up close as well as from afar? Susan wouldn't have thought so. But this room was clearly George's creation: He was the one who worked with wood, and he had made it clear that the basement was *his* project. Maybe there was a side of him she didn't know, a side that would enjoy the sight of leather digging into flesh, would relish the sound of a human scream.

For some reason Susan resisted the idea. She asked the searchers to pull one of the panels off the wall. When they did, she could see that the wood was thick; hence the need for heavy-duty screws. Behind the panels George had packed more than a foot of dense insulation between the panel and the outside wall. Susan climbed the stairs and walked outside. Because the house had been built into a hillside, one of the basement walls was visible there. She could see a ring of fresh cement over what used to be a window. Clearly George had been trying to seal his room. Constructed as it was, nobody could break in, and no person—or sound—could escape.

Susan's heart pounded. Had George been planning to bring her to this place? The more she thought about it, the more likely it seemed. As far as he knew, "Sherry" had no family, nobody to keep track of her from day to day. She could have wasted away for weeks before anyone noticed. For more than a year Susan had worried about George's slipping some poison into her food, then walking away. But maybe George wasn't as cowardly as she thought.

"Ernie," Susan said, turning to her colleague, "you don't think he meant that for me, do you?"

Ernie said nothing; what could he say? As they surveyed George's handiwork, the investigators began to wonder: Was the attack on Peggy Carr and her family George's first murder, or was he an old hand? Were there other bodies somewhere?

Susan remembered seeing a place where the basement floor consisted of nothing but dirt. She went over to ask Madden to assign a crew to dig up the floor. "I have a feeling that if he's killed someone else the body's either in this sand here or out in the lake," she said. Several investigators took shovels and began to work, stooped over in the darkness and sweating like gravediggers. Two hours later they had nothing but sore backs and a moonscape of holes. If George had buried anybody, he hadn't done it here.

The search went on. Among the items located: How to

Host a Murder, a game found in the upstairs laundry cabinet. Sixty-five books and six videotapes, covering various aspects of bondage. Several tools, including a set of screwdrivers and pliers. And shelf after shelf of books, including *The Pale Horse* and a Stephen King thriller, *The Dark Half.*

As the searchers worked into the night, Susan headed home. She walked through the door at suppertime, wearing blue jeans and a black T-shirt with SHERIFF emblazoned on the back. The grime from George's house clung to her like a dusting of evil, and she wanted nothing more than to step under a hot shower and scrub it off. When she saw that some friends had stopped by unexpectedly, she apologized for her appearance and pulled Gary aside to ask him to show them the door politely.

"I'll take care of the guests," Gary said. "You go on and relax."

As the hot water washed over her, Susan replayed the day, each hour still vivid: the early-morning coffee, the stuttering conclusion of her phone call to George, the arrest watched from afar, the discovery of the secret room. Stepping out of the shower, she saw that TV was giving a big play to George's arrest. The phone rang; it was Gary's mother. For better than a year she had been helping take care of the kids while Susan was off on assignment. She had just seen George on the news. "That's George?" she said. "You've been working on *that*?"

Gary couldn't have been prouder of the job his wife had done. But when Susan told him the whole story, his pride gave way to anger. All these months he had thought Susan was meeting George only under constant surveillance by colleagues who could quickly rescue her. When she told him that her only protection was often a tiny and unreliable radio transmitter, he exploded. "What if the bug hadn't worked?" he demanded. "Even if it did, could they have gotten there in time? I can't believe you put yourself in that position. I can't believe the department did."

Susan put her hand on his arm. "It's over," she said softly. "You don't have to worry about it. It's over."

The telephone rang in Bill Hagmaier's office at the FBI Academy. It was Brad Brekke, calling to say they had arrested George. He told Hagmaier about the secret room, something right out of *The Silence of the Lambs.* Hagmaier knew that his worst fears about George had been confirmed, and then some. This guy could be capable of more than one murder, Hagmaier said. He asked Brad if they had searched the room for traces of semen or blood. Brad said they had but had found nothing. It looked as if George were just finishing the construction, getting ready to christen the room.

"If you're going to hide a room like that, you're doing it for a reason," Hagmaier later observed. "I think it goes well beyond renting a hotel somewhere and having a Mensa murder weekend. It's taking it beyond the normal little quirk."

Hagmaier, too, wondered if George had built the room for Susan. "George didn't appear to be the kind of guy that was going to go out and drag somebody in off the street by her hair. It had to be somebody whom he could use his wits to entice into his comfort zone."

Peggy Carr's son, Duane, heard the news on the TV. "An arrest today in the poisoning murder of a Polk County woman . . ." The words jolted him as he sat on a couch in his sister's apartment. On the screen Duane saw his old neighbor George Trepal, stepping out of a car and shuffling into jail, his hands cuffed behind his back, his legs shackled. Other images filtered through Duane's mind, forgotten bits of life before the poisoning: George peering out the upstairs window through binoculars. His wife marching over to chew out the boys for their loud radios. Duane and Allen joking about their eccentric neighbor, how strange he looked in black socks and sandals, how *creepy.* Sometimes,

Duane remembered, Allen pretended he was George, balancing a pair of glasses on the end of his nose, flaring his nostrils, and lunging at Duane with a rubber knife, yelling, *"I'm Trepal!"* The brothers had always gotten a good laugh out of that one.

Cissy couldn't believe the news. More than a year had passed since she had buried her mother. More than a year since she had heard more than a "We're working on it" from the police. After all that time, she remained convinced that Pye was the guilty one. When a reporter from the Tampa *Tribune* asked for her reaction to George Trepal's arrest, Cissy expressed disbelief. She said that George had pretty much kept to himself, and the only trouble she could recall was the spat over the radios. She remarked, "I can't believe somebody would kill you over loud music."

The article quoted Mensa members who doubted George's guilt. "He was a real great guy," said George's brainy friend Stewart Prince. "I can't believe it's true. He used to bring in people's cats and feed them."

Prince said that George couldn't be the killer; for one thing, he wouldn't have used a chemical as easy to trace as thallium. "I can't believe he would have used something with such a heavy, obvious chemical footprint," Prince said. "He would have used something that oxidizes or absorbs quickly." He added, "But I don't believe he'd do it."

Jay Gross, an old friend of George's, said that George was eccentric but no killer. "It's like accusing a sheep of attacking someone," Gross said. "George is not an aggressive person. He's a very fine man."

Susan's thirteen-year-old son, Greg, was thrilled to hear of the arrest. "Now I can finally tell my teachers what you've been doing," he said to his mother as he left for school. He came home that night, deflated and confused. "I told my teacher what you had been doing, and he said, 'If your

mom's been doing that, why isn't her name in the paper?'
He didn't believe me!''

Susan gave him a hug. "Greg, you just have to understand that my name can't be in there," she said. "I'm still
undercover."

"Can't it be in there *once*?" the boy pleaded. "So he'd
believe me?"

She told the boy her name would come out soon enough;
until then they all would have to be patient. The important
thing was to make sure George stayed in jail. After sending
Greg off to do his homework, Susan slipped into the back
room and planned her next phone call. Sherry, the concerned friend, was going to call Diana for the first time
since the arrest. The next morning she found Diana at her
office.

"Who is calling?" said the office manager.

"Sherry."

Diana came on the line. "I don't know what's going on
with George's arrest," she said. "It's all very bizarre. The
victim's family doesn't even believe that George did it. The
papers seem to know more than I do; I'm just trying to
cope with it all."

"Is there anything I can do?" Susan asked.

"Yes," Diana said. "Please write to him. He's pretty
depressed, and I know he'd love to hear from you." She
urged Sherry to be careful what she wrote. "Remember that
they read the prisoners' letters."

Susan had planned to stay in character as Sherry for as
long as possible. But when she arrived at work the next
day, she learned that her cover was blown. George's attorney had exercised his legal right to obtain copies of the
police reports that might be used against his client. The
reports laid out the undercover operation in detail.

In a way Susan was relieved. She was ready to say good-
bye to Sherry. She also wanted to see George, to introduce

herself by her real name. Although she had done her job, a vague guilt still tugged at her. In a way she wanted George to forgive her deceit. She wanted to tell him, "I lied to you, but there was a reason."

Chapter
TWENTY-FIVE

Upstairs at the Polk County Courthouse the man who was
to prosecute George Trepal built his case. Assistant State
Attorney John Aguero knew it wouldn't be easy. There was
no concrete evidence: no fingerprints on a Coke bottle, no
receipt showing a thallium purchase, certainly no confession. The evidence against George was purely circumstantial, making Aguero's role in persuading the jury that much
more important.

It would be months before the trial began, and Aguero
needed every minute. The stocky, mustachioed Aguero was
known as a pit bull inside the courtroom. But outside, the
thirty-seven-year-old prosecutor worked like a research li-
brarian, meticulously assembling and cataloging evidence
and preparing the arguments he hoped would sway the citizen jury. His scribbling filled page after yellow page, and
he quickly gathered enough information to fill 117 folders,
which climbed from the floor and threatened to obscure the
photographs hanging on the office wall, one depicting the
Florida electric chair, Old Sparky. In his five years as a
Polk County prosecutor, Aguero had sent six men to death
row. He planned to make George Trepal the seventh.

Six days after George's arrest, on April 13, 1990, Aguero
was summoned to court. George's lawyers were trying to
persuade a judge to free their client on bail. When Aguero

walked into the courtroom, he saw a young lawyer with a familiar face. He recognized Jonathan Stidham, the thirty-one-year-old son of a veteran Polk County lawyer, Wofford Stidham. Making no effort to hide his surprise, Aguero said, "What are *you* doing here?"

"I represent this guy," replied young Mr. Stidham.

"You've got to be joking!" Aguero said. Part of Aguero's bluster was the usual courthouse bravado, trying to intimidate his opponent. But part of his reaction was genuine shock; Stidham was just three years out of law school, and Aguero worried he might be getting in over his head. This was going to be a complicated and high-profile murder trial, a case to challenge the most experienced criminal lawyer. Aguero was afraid that Stidham might not only make a fool of himself but do such a bad job representing his client that Trepal could win an appeal on the basis of ineffective counsel.

"You don't want to cut your teeth on this," Aguero said. "Go out and get 'Joe shot Bob' and try a few of those and get your feet wet and you'll be fine—but don't start out with George Trepal."

Stidham didn't back down. He snapped, "I know how to practice criminal law."

Circuit Judge Dennis P. Maloney walked into the courtroom. A lawyer who had become a judge at the age of thirty-one, Maloney had a reputation as a courthouse heartthrob. But with his light-brown hair and square jaw, Maloney's style didn't come without substance. In the thirteen years since he had been named to the bench, he had forged a reputation as a thorough, thoughtful judge. He didn't have much patience for spats between lawyers.

Maloney addressed his first words to George Trepal, who was standing quietly by, dressed in his jail jump suit.

"Good afternoon, I'm Judge Maloney. How do you pronounce your name?"

"Tree-pal," George said. "The *E* is long."

Stidham spoke up. "Your Honor, my client will not be

testifying today, so you don't need to go through any rig-marole.''

"Okay, Mr. Stidham," Maloney said. "I have this down as a motion to set a bond."

Aguero told the judge that the State of Florida opposed the release of George Trepal, no matter how much money he put up as bond. He argued, "There's no way to protect the community from this man."

Aguero summoned Detective Ernie Mincey to the stand. He wanted to make sure the judge understood how rare thallium was and how deadly the man who knew how to use it.

"Have you sought to determine whether there have ever been any other cases of intentional thallium poisoning in the United States in the last two hundred years?" Aguero asked.

"I have," Ernie said, "and have found none."

"In your investigation of Mr. Trepal," Aguero said, "did you determine whether or not he had any background in chemistry such that he would be familiar with thallium?"

"I did," Ernie said, "and found that in fact he taught chemistry while serving prison time in the federal prison system for a drug conviction, where he was thought to be the chemist in a crank lab in North Carolina." And not just any crank lab, Ernie said. An official with the federal Drug Enforcement Administration had told him that "it was the biggest methamphetamine operation in the southeast United States at that time, and over seven million dollars would have been generated from it."

Ernie testified that police had found a bottle of thallium in George's garage, a homemade book outlining the way police officials investigate poisoning murders, and a hidden "torture-type room" and collection of bondage equipment. "It was a very bizarre situation," Ernie said. "This room didn't appear to be completely finished but would have been within days."

When he had finished, Ernie had painted just the picture

Aguero wanted: George as a mysterious, sinister man who could have killed his neighbors and might be preparing to make others suffer. Trepal's lawyer faced a daunting task in overcoming that impression.

Jonathan Stidham argued that much of the "evidence" against George could simply be a collection of coincidences. "The State, what they've come forward with is a bunch of, at best, circumstantial evidence," he told the judge. "They have someone who had the opportunity to do it, but they don't have any evidence that he did it.

"The evidence that they're trying to bring forward is that my client is a bit of a different person who happens also to be a chemist and lives next door," Stidham said. Noting that George had never before been convicted of a violent crime, the lawyer said there was no evidence that he would be a threat outside jail and therefore no reason for the judge to deny him bail.

"Judge, Mr. Trepal not only had the opportunity; he has the knowledge, had the motive, and he had the thallium in his garage." Aguero countered, "This man without any kind of conscience poisoned an entire family, including a two-year-old child, without thinking twice about it. The danger that he represents in the community is greater than any person that I have ever read about, seen—it's horrifying."

Maloney sided with the prosecution. "I'm denying the motion," he told Stidham. "There'll be no bond."

As he prepared for trial, Aguero was eager to question the accused killer's wife, Diana Carr. Everyone involved in the case, including Aguero, suspected that she had played some role in motivating George—even if she didn't know it. Like the detectives, Aguero suspected that Diana's fight with Peggy Carr had prompted George to act out his poisoning fantasy.

Although the law allowed Diana to refuse questions that incriminated her husband, Aguero hoped that he could shake her into letting something slip. He wanted to "rattle her cage, rattle it hard." To get her into his office, he issued a subpoena, a legal writ that compelled Diana to appear for questioning.

The meeting took place at Aguero's office in the Polk County Courthouse, just a few hundred feet from George's jail cell. Diana showed up angry. Aguero could see that subpoena or no subpoena she wasn't going to make his job easy. As she settled into a chair and looked around the room, Diana saw the five people building the case against her husband: Aguero; his investigator, Thomas Spate; FBI Special Agent Brad Brekke; Polk County Detective Ernie Mincey; and the woman she had known as Sherry Guin.

"This is Susan Goreck," Aguero said. "She's an investigator with the sheriff's department."

Diana glowered. As she began answering Aguero's questions, her responses came out in clipped, hostile tones.

The background questions were easy enough. Diana told Aguero that she was born on October 9, 1949, and grew up in Virginia as the daughter of a clergyman.

"What was your major in college?" Aguero asked.

"Chemistry," Diana said.

After getting a bachelor's degree in chemistry, Diana said, she went on to earn a master's degree in the same subject. Then it was off to the Medical College of Virginia, where she earned her M.D. in 1975.

"What kind of grades did you make there?" Aguero asked.

Diana muttered something, then spit out her response. "I passed!"

"Where did you meet Mr. Trepal?" Aguero said.

"Through Mensa," she said.

"When was that?" Aguero said.

"I have no idea," Diana said indignantly. "Do you know when you met your wife?"

"Sure do," Aguero said, his voice cool and bemused. Already he was getting to her.

"Well," Diana said, "I guess he didn't make enough of an impression on me. I don't know. We've been married about nine and a half years. It was probably about twelve or so years ago." Diana said that she and George met through a publication for Mensa members.

"Who wrote who?" Aguero asked.

"I wrote George," she replied. At the time, she said, George was living in Columbia, South Carolina, and she was in Augusta, Georgia. George was working in construction, while she was completing her medical residency. They began traveling back and forth to see each other.

"When did you first find out that he had been in prison?" Aguero asked.

"When I read it in the newspaper," she said.

"What was your reaction to that?"

Diana mumbled a reply. Aguero pushed harder, asking, "Are you aware that he was involved at a very high level in a rather large illegal drug laboratory?"

"All I know is what I read in the newspaper," Diana said. "So I don't know."

Irritation crept into Aguero's voice. "I'm going to tell you that that's what he did, and I'm going to ask you how you feel about that," he said.

"I don't know that I believe you," she retorted.

The conversation kept going downhill, as Aguero asked Diana to describe her relationship with George.

Her face reddening, Diana said, "That's none of your business."

Aguero moved on, trying some questions about Diana's work as an orthopedic surgeon. "What days do you operate?"

"Whenever people need operations."

"That's not something that you try to schedule like you do office hours on any kind of regular basis?"

"Yes," she replied, her voice dripping sarcasm. "I've tried to explain to the patients that they should break their things during office hours. But they haven't been able to cooperate.''

Sitting safely outside the line of fire, Susan stifled a chuckle. But the lawyer who had accompanied Diana to the interview, Richard McKinley, saw trouble coming. Holding his hand up, he asked Diana to step outside the room with him. When she returned, Diana showed a greater spirit of cooperation.

"When did you move to the house in Alturas?" Aguero asked.

"July of '82," Diana replied.

"Did the Carr family already live there?"

"I think they already lived there."

"Okay," Aguero said. "Describe for me your personal relationship with that family."

"Mostly just to say hello," Diana said.

Aguero pressed for more. "It's not a situation where you ever went over and had coffee in the afternoon or anything like that?"

"I've never been in that house."

"What problems have you personally had at any time with members of that family?"

"Had one disagreement about playing music."

"When was that?"

"I don't know," she said. "It wasn't that impressive."

"How did that happen?" Aguero said.

"The kids were out in the yard, boom boxes playing so loud that they were louder in my own house than I would have played them had it been my radio. Went over there and asked them to turn it down. They wouldn't. Went and knocked on the door, asked to speak to the mother. She came out; she yelled at me. I told her she didn't have any manners, and if she didn't turn it down that I would call the police as a public nuisance, that I didn't appreciate all this loud noise. So she had the kids turn it down."

"How about George?" Aguero said. "Did you ever observe George have any confrontations with the people next door? With the Carrs?''

"No," Diana said.

"The confrontation where you went over and knocked on the door," Aguero asked, "did you ever tell George about that?"

She replied, "I believe George was home when it happened."

To his frustration, Aguero couldn't pursue that line of questioning. Florida law allows criminal defendants to keep conversations between themselves and their spouses secret, a privilege George had asserted.

"Were you aware of any chemistry lab equipment being in either one of the houses that you were in?" Aguero asked.

"I believe George had some," Diana said. She added, "I wouldn't swear that I didn't have anything left over."

"Left over from what?"

"From when I used to be a chemist."

"You used to work in a lab?"

"Yeah."

"Have you ever seen any lab equipment set up in your house? In either one of those houses?"

"No."

Aguero moved on. "Was George sort of a stickler about not playing radios and not playing TVs?"

"He doesn't like television around him," she said. "I don't think he cared about radios."

"What's the reason he doesn't like TV?"

"It always bothers him."

After George's arrest the police had heard rumblings of violent arguments between him and his wife. Aguero wanted to see what Diana would say about that.

"Y'all ever fight?" he asked.

Any cool Diana had brought back into the room melted. She replied, "You know of any husband and wife that don't?"

"I've heard of some. I don't know if I believe them. Does that mean yes?"

"Means that we were normal, yes."

"Well, different people have different definitions."

Diana looked at her attorney, as if to say, "Do I have to put up with this?" She looked at Aguero and snapped, "I'm about tired of . . ."

Aguero pressed on. "Were any of the confrontations physical?"

"Might have been on an occasion or two," she said. "Was I scared of George? No. There hasn't really been any violence, I'd say, in three or four years. And most of our squabble was verbal."

"Did you ever have to call anybody to come get you because George ran you out of the house?"

"I think I might have left once or twice because I got tired arguing with him."

Aguero kept changing subjects, throwing out questions like change-up pitches, hoping to catch Diana off-balance. "Have you ever seen any illegal drugs in your house?"

"I'm not sure I'd know an illegal drug if I saw one," she replied.

Aware that police had filled several boxes with bottles of chemicals from the couple's houses, Aguero asked, "Are you familiar with George, at any time during your marriage, using chemicals to make anything? Anything at all?"

"No."

"Did you write a pamphlet for Mensa on voodoo that's got George's name on it?"

"No," Diana said. "George looked up that information and wrote it." However, Diana said she had written the scripts for the last two murder weekends. George had helped, she said, by doing research on the poisons used in the scripts. "When you're dealing with a genius-level group of people, you have to get the census and stuff right."

Aguero asked her about the secret room found in the

Sebring house basement. "Did you know about that room?"

"I knew that he was working on a room, yes."

"Were you aware that there was a platform of some sort built?"

"No," Diana said.

Aguero shifted the interview back to the subject of chemistry, and Diana acknowledged that George had some chemicals, although she had not seen him using them. Some were photography chemicals, she explained, while "some of them, I think, were pesticides."

"Did you ever see a brown bottle with a red cap that had thallium in it?" Aguero asked.

"I probably saw brown bottles with red caps," Diana replied. "Now whether they had big letters saying 'Thallium' on it, no. And I didn't—I don't go through my husband's things."

"Did you ever—yourself—buy, obtain in any way, receive, store, thallium in that house?"

"Not that I'm aware of," Diana said.

"Tell me about your interest in murder mysteries," Aguero said.

"I've been reading them since I was a little bitty kid," she said. "Started out with Nancy Drew."

"Did you ever read the book *The Pale Horse*?"

Diana's jaw tightened. She said, "I already told y'all I did."

"Are you aware of whether George has ever read that book?"

"I am not aware that he has ever read it."

Aguero asked her to think back to the time after her neighbors were poisoned, when she had told police she remembered reading about thallium in *The Pale Horse*. "Do you know what it was that stuck in your mind—that made you recall, when you were asked early on in this investigation, that thallium was the chemical in *The Pale Horse*?"

"I thought it was an odd metal to use. I mean, it's

not . . ." she answered. "You know, most murder myster-ies—do they not?—come up with arsenic or knives or guns. Thallium was a little bit odd."

"You ever use thallium in any of the Mensa murders?"

"No."

"When you first found out that the family next door had been poisoned, did you all take any particular precau-tions?" Aguero asked.

"Well, they told us not to drink the well water," Diana said. "We were using their well at that point."

"Okay," Aguero said. "But you all kept drinking it any-way, didn't you?"

"No. We had bottled water at the house."

Aguero told Diana he didn't have any more questions, but he did have a subpoena to take prints of her fingers and palms. As she and her lawyer left the office, she was told that Susan Goreck would be accompanying her across the street to the sheriff's office.

"I'm not going anywhere with that bitch," she bellowed. Diana's lawyer yanked her out of the room again, then re-turned a few minutes later. "All right, she's decided that she will walk across," McKinley told Aguero.

Susan led the way out of the courthouse and across to the sheriff's office, where she opened the door for Diana and her lawyer. They went upstairs, and Diana sat, jaw clenched, while an officer pressed her hands into ink and then onto a clean sheet of paper.

Meanwhile, back in his office, Aguero was walking around the room, uprighting the pictures of his family that he had hidden before Diana's arrival. He didn't want her to see what his wife and children looked like. He wouldn't take that risk.

Chapter
TWENTY-SIX

Now that she didn't have to hide her identity, Susan began working with Ernie to interview the people who knew George best. One of them was George Edward Trepal, George's seventy-eight-year-old father. A former New York City police officer, Mr. Trepal had been planning to move into an apartment George had been fixing up behind the Sebring house. Mr. Trepal had his things packed when Diana called to say that his only child had been charged with murder. Mr. Trepal came anyway.

When he arrived in Florida, Mr. Trepal visited George in jail. George told his father he was innocent, and Mr. Trepal says he never doubted him.

"I believe you," he told his son.

"Dad," George replied, "thank you for believing in me."

When Susan came to interview him, George's father did not lash out in anger. Perhaps he didn't yet fully understand the role Susan had played in locking his son away, or perhaps it wasn't his way to confront an enemy directly. Whatever the reason, he answered her questions with courtesy, while remaining firm in his belief that his son was wrongly accused. As Susan sat across from him, she was struck by the family resemblance. Mr. Trepal looked like an older, timeworn version of his son: on the short side, slightly stooped, with thick glasses and an eroding chin.

He didn't have much to tell Susan. He said he knew nothing about the murder of Peggy Carr. However, in this early meeting and a later interview, he was able to fill out the picture of George's early years.

Mr. Trepal recalled the difficult circumstances of George's birth that winter morning in 1949. Despite that rough start, his father recalled that "Georgie" had come home as a healthy baby weighing nearly nine pounds. "He was a fat little guy," Mr. Trepal said, stretching his arms and smiling wistfully. "He was about that wide, and he was about that high. You could roll him." The Trepals brought their son home to an apartment on East Forty-sixth Street, not far from the United Nations. Before long, though, Mabel had tired of lugging baby and gear up four flights of stairs, and she persuaded her husband to move nearer to her family in Florence, South Carolina. Mabel was a tall, vigorous woman. Back home, she left teaching and devoted herself to raising the son she had suffered to bring into the world.

As George grew, he didn't stray far from the family's two-story home on Pine Street. It had a big yard, with oak shade trees and his father's garden of flowers, cucumbers, and tomatoes. Inside Mabel used her schoolteacher's skill and discipline to make George a precocious student. But she apparently wasn't eager to share him with the world just yet. Her husband recalled that Mabel wouldn't let anyone else care for George—not a baby-sitter, not her mother, not even the boy's own father. "She just took over, and that's it," he said. "She wouldn't even trust him with anybody. It was her boy, and she was going to raise him."

Mr. Trepal also left his career behind in New York, quitting police work to open a radio and television repair business. Sometimes Mabel brought the boy to the shop. Young George didn't like to fish or hunt, but he loved electronics and spent hours wandering around his father's store, staring at the television sets with their rabbit ears and round picture tubes. At home he set up his own electronics shop. "When he was three years old, he was soldering already," Mr. Trepal said. "Anything that's electronic, we bought it for him. In fact, he even had one of those spheres that you touch and your hair goes up in the air. You couldn't go in his room. He had signs all over: DANGER! VOLTAGE! When you'd walk in there, you didn't know what you were going to touch and you'd get it."

Aside from going to the movies with his mother ("I'd say, 'You two go,' and I'd sit home," his father said), George didn't go out much. He had a few friends, but mostly he stayed home and read science books. As a teenager growing up in the turbulent sixties, George kept his hair short and never dated. "He never went with a girl," his father said. "Wouldn't go with a girl. He just didn't want to bother." While few boys make it to their eighteenth birthdays without a bloody nose, George walked away from conflicts; his mother saw to that. "She wouldn't let him fight," George's father recalled. "If he got into trouble, she took care of it."

George went off to college. He dropped out of one university but graduated from another. His parents paid for his education and, later, the bill for defending him against the drug charges brought by the U.S. government. Once George had left home, his father said, the Trepals lost track of their son. "I didn't even know his friends after he left," he said. "He'd just come home once in a while and stay overnight, and then he'd say 'So long' and go again."

In 1975 George ended up at Central Piedmont Community College in Charlotte, North Carolina, taking a class with a potter named Clara Rountree Couch. Susan found Ms. Couch at her studio in the mountains of North Carolina. The potter might have reminded George of his mother: She was roughly the same height, she was a teacher, and she spoke in the soft tones of the genteel South.

When George came into her classroom at the community college in Charlotte, Ms. Couch was wrestling with the problem of keeping bright colors—particularly reds and golds—from burning out of ceramic pottery. With his chemistry background, George was eager to help concoct a recipe for a colorfast glaze. Thallium can be used in some types of glazing, although Ms. Couch wasn't sure which chemicals George had used, only that many were dangerous.

While George was "very helpful" to Ms. Couch, she said that he seemed uneasy around the other students. In fact, he clung so tightly to her that she began to think she had become not only a teacher to George but also a mother figure. Despite his superior mind, George seemed desperately short on self-confidence. Ms. Couch observed, "He needed his bucket filled."

After leaving home, George began to keep journals, using them to record oddball ideas for making money ("Dildo with pressure sensors to check on quality of vaginal contractions . . . Torture cream for S&M people. Consists of no more than deep heating rub for the genitals . . . Expose-a-tit dress") as well as painful insights into his feelings of loneliness and isolation. Susan found the journals in a box of items taken from George's house, and she began to read. The handwriting, sloping and uneven, took her deeper into George's psyche.

In one undated journal George reflected on his upbringing.

As a child, you were very inquisitive, almost a pest at times. Often your parents couldn't answer your questions and this caused you to lose faith in their god-like ability to know things. This actually helped you to grow. This same inquisitiveness was what you were also disciplined for on many times.

As you grew you developed the ability for fantasy

and you lived in it quite a lot. During your early teen years you developed a form of hero worship and from this came the model stereotypes which shaped you as you are today. During these years, though you were with groups much of the time, you really felt isolated and not a real part of the group. You acted as part of the group but even this similar behavior didn't make you feel at ease.

Susan found that George's musings dwelt on the women in his life, women who seemed strong and often inaccessible. On more than one occasion he wrote about memories of his mother and his need for another.

You loved your mother as a child but felt at times that she was out of place as a woman.

WOMEN (no children)—You have a deep-seated fear that you are not suited to childbirth—You associate childbirth with death.

WOMEN, LARGE RURAL FAMILY—In your early teen years you fell in love with someone in your family though they may not have known this. . . .

Some thoughts on masochism in general: Fromm's view is right. The masochist lacks the ability to open himself and seeks help. Part of the ritual may relate to pleasing memories of his mother from infancy. This is seeking father love from the mother. If I please you then you will open me and I will be loved and able to love myself through you.

I notice that when I sleep I like to press against something with my face and chest and my legs assume a position as if I were climbing rock walls—or is that clinging to a big person? I will even go into spontaneous suckling behavior. Why do I carry this with me? Lack of breast feeding? Being weaned too soon?

I am like an infant looking for a warm tit to hang upon and suck.

Who was it who did the wire and cloth surrogate mother experiment with the monkeys? Marlow? Perhaps I should synthesize a mother. A large leather bag containing bladder of some dense liquid like silly putty? How about a tape loop of the heartbeat or a total electronic synthesis of it.

The journals show George drifting in and out of relationships, particularly during the drug-soaked 1970s. In his journal he chronicled the travails of love, addressing himself almost as if he were a psychologist dispensing advice to a patient.

July 5, 1972—Ginnie*
  Foreword: on July 3, 2 days ago, I did 250 mg MDA, 10 mg speed, and a lot of grass with Ginnie and we both tripped heavily. She said much and the trip was informative rather than pleasant. Since then I have slept a lot, eaten little, done no work, felt generally bad, and lacked concentration ability. I now see that this was a manifestation of subconscious analysis and problem solving. . . .
  "Need" and "love" are different in that "love" is a nebulous term and generally can't be defined even by one who loves. Ginnie's problem is that she needs to know she is needed. She tends to think of herself as apart from the human race due to some fault of her own making. . . . She disbelieves in her self worth (i.e. ability to inspire a need for her in others). . . . Her probable stereotype is a freak-folksinger (i.e. a misfit, an attempt to escape a world she feels she hasn't made it in). . . . The problem is how to raise her self-worth level so that she can begin

*Not her real name

to self-actualize. It is obvious that physical contact should be avoided in favor of mental and that any physical contact that should occur carry a basically non sexual note. . . .

I wish there were an easy way to solve the problem but the solution is that I must need her, which I do desperately, and my being away from her is painful. I hope that the stronger psychedelics, acid especially, can help for they lay bare the mind and fill the soul with love and a sense of being needed.

On my end of it, I find I have an ungodly bad case of love sickness. . . . Deep subconscious probe shows that the love I have for her is a true love and that her happiness is the most important thing in the world, even more important than I am. . . .

SHIT SHIT SHIT . . . Were she only not married . . .

July 19, 1973. It's been a full year now. She left Peter* for a week. We made love in many positions, planned toward our future, and spent four days naked in the sun on the Columbia farm. Then she left.

I'm rebuilding. I seem to be afraid of people and very afraid of love loss. I'm fighting this since it isn't objective. My intellect is fine, but my emotions are screwed up. This is the hardest educational experience I've had. . . .

For almost a year now I have been doing literature research on hallucinogenic drug manufacture. No one has really helped me or encouraged me. In fact, when they found I didn't plan to manufacture or deal they ignored me or ridiculed me. My project is now nearly through. I have done well and I have pride in it. The nature of the project is unimportant. What is important is that I can plan and carry out a long-term complex project on my own, internalizing

*Not his real name

my drives and needing no encouragement.

So, future self, internalize yourself. . . . You are very in need of a significant other, a girl to be exact, but don't be hasty in major life decisions. And always fight, if heaven came easy there would be no great demand for it.

By December 1974 George was apparently hoping to get involved with another unavailable woman, Carol.* But once again his hopes came to nothing.

I've been used and screwed over. Actually, I've screwed myself over by being so desperate for love that I thought a 3-marriage would work. I have been working on the basis that I can only love myself through others. I have to love myself through myself. . . .

C. needs a child, J. needs a mother. They're an inseparable team. I need a mother too.

March 17, 1975. I'm getting over C. . . . I've had times during the last months when I loved myself. I sat and the room filled with Georgeness and it was beautiful.

George, Susan learned, never felt more full of "Georgeness" than when he was sneaking drugs into other people's bodies, then sitting back to marvel at the effects. George's old drug partner David Warren provided the details.

David had met George in the early 1970s in North Carolina. Stopping by a relative's apartment, he saw George showing off a string of macaroni noodles soaked in a blend of amphetamines and green food coloring. George was boasting that because he knew the absorption rate of each noodle, he knew precisely what dose of drugs each would

*Not her real name

contain. George told David that he was working at a Charlotte hospital, delivering medications. Although he manufactured some amphetamines on the side, George said he preferred using hallucinogenics like LSD, mescaline, and peyote. He considered them "the path to enlightenment."

While George's encyclopedic knowledge and formidable memory impressed David, George also struck his new friend as terribly lonesome. George used drugs to try to buy companionship, David later recalled. The green macaroni, for instance, was George's ticket into one group. If he couldn't win people over, he could invade their minds and metabolisms.

David told investigators that when he and George returned from their trip to California in the early seventies, they opened a small shop in a Charlotte strip mall. Called Cotati East, it was like many of the head shops dotting the post-Woodstock landscape, selling herbs, oils, and substances they called legal psychedelics. It was also a front.

George told David he wanted to make some easy money, to retire early to a house in the country. Behind the scenes at Cotati East, George made methamphetamine, the drug known on the street by a variety of names: crank, speed, crystal. As long as things ran smoothly, David found George a pleasant friend and business partner. But if George got angry, David learned, he could be dangerous. With his knowledge of chemistry, George had a potent arsenal of weapons. He bragged to David about two times he had used those weapons to get rid of people who had become nuisances.

Once George wanted to help some friends get rid of freeloading roommates. He took a hallucinogenic drug he had been experimenting with—George called it WOW—and mixed it into dimethyl sulfoxide, a chemical that can carry drugs through the pores of the skin. George painted the drugs on the refrigerator handles and other objects the roommates would be touching. Before long the pesky roommates had vanished.

Another time, George bragged, he had used chemicals to get a neighbor to move out. George told David that he had synthesized a chemical similar to Mace and piped it into the apartment next door. George's complaint, according to David, was that the neighbor was playing the stereo too loud.

After getting out of prison, George met his future wife. In Diana, George found a woman who matched his intellect and, at last, returned his affection. After he and Diana had married, they bought the house next to Pye Carr. While George played with his computers, Diana established her practice as an orthopedic surgeon. Patricia Boatwright, a nurse and fellow Mensa member, worked in Diana's office for a time. In a sworn statement taken by George's lawyers, Boatwright reinforced the image of Diana as a difficult woman and demanding wife.

"She was a witch," Boatwright told Jonathan Stidham. "She would scream and throw things and make wild accusations in public."

"Was she always like this or just on occasion?" the lawyer asked. "Did it seem to be mood swings?"

"Wild mood swings," Boatwright said. "The next day she might blow a whole lot of money and throw us all a whale of a party and be sweet as pie." For a while, Boatwright said, she couldn't tell which was the real Diana. "This lovely person could not have been that witch that I'm still trembling from—but it was her all right."

"What about her and George's relationship?" Stidham asked. "What did you understand that to be?"

"Never did understand it."

"Did they get along?"

"As long as he said, 'Yes, dear,' " Boatwright replied. "Well, George helped me stay in Diana's employ. When it got so bad I couldn't stand it, I just knew I was quitting, I'd tell George about it. We'd have long conversations, and he'd finally somewhere along the line say, 'Hey, it's just as bad at home for me.'

"I was telling him, 'Hey, I cannot stand it anymore. I have to leave this witch lady, and I can't do it,' " she recalled. "It was kind of like we were a mini support group. He was making noises, and I was making noises, and together we'd stick it out a little better."

"Did you get along with George?"

"Yeah."

"Did you like him?"

"Yeah."

"Did you ever see George throw any temper tantrums like this?"

"No," she said. "I've never seen anybody throw tantrums like Diana's."

Boatwright said that both George and Diana had complained about the family living next door. "I thought their first name was 'goddamn,' " she joked. "They were just really rotten neighbors, noise-wise."

The neighbors seemed to bother George the most since he was often at home. Diana, she said, "mostly discussed how upset George was about them."

Boatwright's description of George fitted the FBI profile of a poisoner: a man who plays the passive role in a relationship, afraid to confront an overbearing mate. However, some of the other people who worked with Diana offered a different view: They said George did not shrink from confronting his wife. In fact, they said that Diana at times showed up at work with bruises, swollen eyes, and stories of battles with a strange and sometimes violent husband.

Beth Pitman told police she had worked for Diana Carr until 1986 and continued to socialize with her in the years that followed. Even as Peggy Carr and her children were being rushed to the hospital in 1988, Beth recalled attending a Halloween party George and Diana hosted at their Alturas home. She told police that Diana had dressed as a harem princess and George appeared as a head on a bloody platter.

Despite her busy professional and social life, Beth said, Diana was "a very unhappy person . . . very insecure." She said Diana talked constantly about her fights with George and sometimes showed up with bruises on her body. Yet for all her complaints about trouble at home, Beth said, Diana seemed eager to please her husband. She recalled Diana's telling her once, "I have to go home and entertain George."

At times Diana apparently did not entertain George well enough. Betty W. Smith, who worked with Diana and became her close friend, told police that George was "verbally and physically abusive to Dr. Carr." One Christmas, Betty told investigators, Diana called her on the phone. Crying hysterically, Diana said that George had gone wild and smashed the family Christmas tree. When Betty rushed over to Alturas, she saw the tree crushed against a wall, its branches and needles scattered across the floor. As she consoled Diana, George came walking down the stairs, saying, "I need love, Betty. I need love, Betty. George is horny. George is horny." When asked why he had smashed the tree, George said, "Diana told me I could get it anytime I wanted it. I told her I was horny, and she would not give me any."

Brian Palmer, who worked as a physician's assistant in Diana's office, told police that George was constantly complaining about his wife's hair or weight. He said his impression was that "Diana was afraid of George." But if George sometimes had little patience with Diana, he seemed to have even less for children—and not just the ones who lived next door. Brian told investigators that he and his wife wouldn't bring their children to the Alturas home because they knew George didn't like them. Once Brian and his wife accompanied Diana and George to a meeting in Boston. At George's suggestion, they ate in a Mexican restaurant. When a child began crying at another table, George stormed out of the restaurant. Brian observed, "George did not like confusion or noise."

Tammy Sue Dotson, who worked as Diana's medical assistant, echoed the view of George as a child hater. He had asked her if children would be going to Busch Gardens, a Tampa tourist attraction, in February. She told him that she didn't think so since children are normally in school that time of year. "Good," he told her. "I hate kids."

Some of the most damning information came from Patricia Ann Prince, who had worked as Diana's office manager. She became close friends with Diana but, she told police, "never hit it off with George." Prince said that George never worked. "George was too unstructured for work," she said. Diana, by contrast, worked long hours. When Prince would ask her why she was staying so late, Diana would say, "George is mad at me anyway."

One day Diana came to work and said that George had talked of having a vision. "God had told him to go and buy new underwear," Prince told police. "George really thought that he had talked to God." She recalled asking Diana, "Is he on something?"

Although George saved most of his strange behavior for home, Prince told police, he sometimes acted up in public and humiliated his wife. Once George and Diana attended a Christmas party at a country club. During one of the songs, she said, George stood up at the table, yelled, "Fuck Christmas!" and stormed out.

Another night Diana came over to Prince's home for dinner. After she left, she called Prince in tears. She asked if Prince could help her find a temporary home for her dog, saying that George had poisoned the pet with Valium to punish her for eating at Prince's house. "George had also threatened to poison all of Diana's cats when he would get mad at her," she told police. When Prince asked Diana why she didn't just rid the house of poisons, Diana told her that "George had poisons hidden all over the house. She'd never find all of them."

Prince also witnessed the aftermath of George's Christmas tree smashing and recalled that Diana briefly contemplated asking a judge to force George to undergo a psychiatric examination. But Diana decided against it, she said, for fear of what George would do when he got out of the hospital.

"I thought he looked like Charles Manson," Prince told police investigators. "I thought he would do something evil and spectacular someday."

Susan was fascinated by George's relationships with women, particularly Diana. Somewhere in that web of submission and abuse, love and loathing, would she find the forces that had turned George into a killer? When police were emptying the bookshelves at George and Diana's home, a letter fluttered out from one of the books and drifted to the floor. Later Susan pulled it from one of the evidence boxes and began to read. George had composed it on a typewriter, apparently for Diana.

November 9, 1980
HELLO LOVE,

I'm writing this in as specific a manner as possible to try to give you concrete examples. Please discuss this with me if you need to in case I don't make something clear.

Save this letter since it will be valuable in understanding me. I'll run a few photocopies and send them along so you can put them in different places which will cut down on the chances of losing this letter as the last one was lost.

I've told you I don't like the little girl talk you do. Specific things I object to are leaving out consonants as in "p'etty George" or "I got you ca'tured." Also you use first person when second person form is what is required. For example, "I ca'tured the George!" or "Where's the George?" You also ask utterly stupid questions or make statements that end in, "Do you know that?" Examples of stupid questions are:

When you get me worked up and real horny you ask, "Why should I play with you?" After we decide that we'll make love you ask, "Does anybody in here want to play?" Or you'll lie on me and ask, "I got you ca'tured. You know that?" All of this is done in a high squeaky voice.

I do not like children and I keep feeling like I'm raping a child. When six year old kids came into Mom's first grade class if they confused first and second person grammar they earned a special label: retarded. I have no wish to fuck a retarded child. However I do want to make love with an adult.

Also get yourself a new writer. I am overly tired of the lines:

P'etty George.

Are you stealing my underwear?

Does anybody in here want to play?

Are you my p'etty George?

I found your handle.

There must be uncounted good lines that you can think up or get from your books or TV or from Beth or Nancy or somebody. If in doubt use your mouth to kiss, bite, suck, lick, drool, or anything but talk.

Next subject: sure ways to get me pissed off.

You say that you need hugs to grow on. That's true. We both need attention. Giving me attention is sort of like filling a cup. When it's full I'm happy and until it's filled I'll go any lengths to get it filled.

You say you don't currently feel good about yourself. How do you think I feel about my self worth when you come in and HAVE to read and process the mail before you pay attention to me? Or how about when we get ready to make love and you say you have to use the bathroom and you go and sit and read comics? I get the deep down feeling that I really am not worth shit when finishing a comic book is a more desirable prospect than making love to me.

When the cats want attention you rub them until they have had enough and go to sleep. When I want more attention you bitch that I grab you and you don't like being grabbed. Why do the cats get better treatment than I do? Another ultimate insult is when you're not on call and we're making love and the phone rings and you answer it. I want to get the feeling that I'm loved and important at least some of the time and answering the phone means that whoever is at the other end NO MATTER WHO IT IS is more important than I am.

When you see someone you know in a restaurant or wherever you never ask if I want to meet them. You always drag me over to them without caring if I have any plans or whether I want to do anything else. Why doesn't my opinion matter? Of course if you don't stop and talk to everybody you see instead of just waving or saying something like, "Hi, we're just leaving. Hope you enjoy your meal," you might offend them. Here it comes down to who to offend, them or me. If I get offended I get pissed off, you catch hell from me later, and I become quite socially tactless with them. This is the very same thing that happened that night with Bill and Beth.

I hate being poked.

I hate being lied to. A lie is when you say you will do something and then not do it.

Now to sex. I keep saying I want you to be more spontaneous. Maybe I should restate that and ask you to surprise me. If you can't think up your own surprises I imagine your books must have some clever seduction scenes and TV is full of such stuff. Here is a list of possible surprises. It's not a complete list, just things that come to mind as I write.

Dress in something very sexy and meet me at the door when I come in.

Try to rape me. Do this in any room of the house

except the room we always make love in.

Ask "Would you want me to wear leather for you tonight?"

Wear something very sexy under your street clothes. Take me out shopping and then tell me what you've done and what will happen when we get home.

Get some very exotic makeup such as red or even black lipstick and see how outrageously you can make yourself up. For example how about long swept back eyebrows such as Mr. Spock would be proud of, lots of blue eye shadow underneath, and black or ruby red lips. Points are awarded for effort so the makeup job doesn't have to be all that neat or professional looking.

Wear your high heeled boots around the house just to get me <u>very</u> turned on.

Bring a small can of chocolate syrup (or whipped cream) to bed with you. Tell me I have to lick it off wherever you put it on yourself. Alternately let me put it where ever I want you to lick it off.

Make love to me in the running water of the shower.

Read the sections on bondage and slow masturbation in the Joy of Sex and follow the instructions given.

Ask me to give you a full massage. This is a massage on the floor (I prefer a table but the floor can be used), then lovemaking, then a whirlpool bath to get the massage oil off. Wine is optional.

I could go on but I hope you have the idea. Do things you don't normally do. Don't be a nice girl. I'm a very creative person. I guess that's pretty obvious from my varied interests, the way I play with words, the little humor fantasies I go off on, etc. I get bored easily. . . .

Susan put the letter down. In public Diana seemed the boss, George her meek servant. But in private that apparently wasn't always true. At first George's aggressiveness seemed to clash with the FBI profile of a passive poisoner. But as she reflected on it, Susan saw that much of George's behavior fitted. Except for the bruises reported by Diana's colleagues, George never attacked in a direct way. He shouted obscenities; he stomped on a Christmas tree; he poisoned his wife's pet. Even George's demeaning lecture on sex came indirectly, on paper instead of in person. Something else came through in that letter: George didn't like it when Diana abandoned her role as a strong partner, lapsing into games or little-girl talk. While clothed in intellectual arrogance and condescension, George's words came out in a whine: *Pay attention to me! Meet my needs!* George was like a spoiled child. When things didn't go his way, he stamped his feet and pounded his fists. He wanted Diana to be strong, to meet his needs, to be his mother.

Susan pushed the play button and settled into her chair. She had joined Brad, Ernie, and John Aguero to watch a collection of the videotapes found in George's house. Most of them had to do with sadomasochism: One showed bondage scenes taken from mainstream movies, another featured "Bizarre Erotic Fantasies," while still another offered practical tips on torturing a woman without killing her.

The film they were about to watch had been in George's VCR when the police arrested him. The title: *Ilsa, She Wolf of the SS*. The television screen brightened with images of SS officers, all fair-haired women, conducting the grim business of a concentration camp. A note from the producer explained that the film was based on actual atrocities committed in Hitler's camps during World War II. The film opens with the tinkling notes of a piano and a scene of a woman with blond hair and long black lashes writhing atop a man, full breasts swaying, long fingernails digging into her partner's flesh. Finally satisfied, the woman rises from the bed and dons a black uniform with a red armband. This apparently is Ilsa.

Ilsa's guards, all women, appear and grab the naked man, who protests that the commandant has promised he would not have to return to the camp. Her voice cold, Ilsa explains that he, a prisoner, must pay for having slept with a member of the superior race. The officers drag him into an operating room and strap him to a table, where he watches through saucer eyes as Ilsa lovingly cradles a large, shining blade. Her laughter mixes with his agonized cries, as the camera pans to show a river of blood streaming from his disfigured body. Ilsa has castrated her lover.

Susan felt revulsion rise in her throat. She had seen plenty of porn during her days in vice, but never anything as graphically violent as this. She watched in silence as the film unfolded in increasingly bloody scenes.

Ilsa orders in a group of women prisoners, who stand before her with bowed heads, naked. The commandant interviews each one, then takes a defiant prisoner aside, instructing her guards in thickly accented English, "Leave her for me. I will shave her so close the blood will run." The other prisoners are led into a torture room, where the guards, now topless, make them bend over and endure a brutal lashing. Ilsa takes an electrified cattle prod and shoves it inside the women prisoners, who scream in terror as their flesh burns. In the most grotesquely realistic scene, Ilsa rips the intestines out of a living prisoner, applying the electric cattle prod as the prisoner looks on helplessly.

Aguero broke the silence. "This is way beyond a normal porno film," he said. "This stuff looks real."

Susan shook her head, struggling for composure. She said, "I can't understand how somebody could watch this for pleasure."

As the film comes to a close, the prisoners stage a revolt, taking guns from their captors and killing them. Even Ilsa is not safe from revenge, as a man interrupts her bloody cavorting with another prisoner to put a gun to her head and pull the trigger. At last Ilsa, She Wolf of the SS, gets hers.

*   *   *

Susan didn't know what to make of the tapes. She knew George was into S&M, but she had him figured as the submissive partner. After seeing the torture room and this movie, she wondered. Did George enjoy submitting to punishment, dispensing it, or both? She called Bill Hagmaier for his opinion.

Hagmaier said he wasn't surprised to hear that George's psychological makeup was not as simple as it first seemed. George might fantasize about torturing women but lack the courage to do it himself; watching the video allowed him a vicarious thrill.

And what did the film say about George's view of women? In *Ilsa*, a woman was either submissive prisoner or bitch goddess. Perhaps George could see women only as one extreme or the other. It made sense. George's mother had given him life and shielded him from childhood's cruelties, but at the price of his independence. Diana could be seen as fitting the same mold; she paid the bills, ran the show in public. Even as he cherished the strength of these women, George might also resent it. Susan remembered how proud he had been of his ability to watch without feeling as his mother died, and he apparently also took pleasure in punishing his wife. In many ways George was like Ilsa's prisoners, submissive but ultimately murderous. Rather than contradicting each other, his passivity and his aggressiveness went hand in hand.

"The dominatrix is his best friend and worst enemy," Hagmaier said. "She inflicts the pain, but she also gives him pleasure."

Was it possible that George's murderous impulse came from a displaced hatred of the mother figures in his life? George would not want to kill Diana, Hagmaier said; he would fear and cherish her too much. But George might be willing to kill another woman, a mother who irritated but held no power over him. Someone like his neighbor Peggy Carr.

TWENTY-SEVEN

A month after the arrest Susan got her chance. The prosecutor had asked her about the scribblings found in George's notebooks and journals. Most held little evidentiary value; they were just random thoughts or zany ideas for making money. But Aguero was intrigued by one entry: "Exposure to ultrasonics makes a person irritable and I've heard rumors that it is used for riot control in France. Would it be good to get rid of neighbors?"

Aguero thought he might be able to use that passage as evidence in court. To do so, though, he would have to establish that George had written it. Aguero got a court order to force George to provide samples of his handwriting, and Susan volunteered to go with Ernie to the jail and take them. Wearing a sheriff's badge on her belt, she checked in at the booking desk and walked across a grassy courtyard to the visitors' area.

With each step toward the room where she would meet George, Susan felt the pressure build. She knew she shouldn't be nervous; she was just doing her job, wrapping up another case. But she knew that was a lie, and the questions echoed. How would George react when she walked in? Would he rage at her, accuse her of betrayal? She expected that and, in a way, hoped for it. If George showed anger, she could respond in kind. "How can you be angry at me?'' she could say. ''You poisoned an entire family over a loud radio.''

Rounding a corner, she saw George, dressed in the standard jail-issue orange jump suit, sitting with his lawyer in a tiny glass-walled cubicle. As she walked in, George looked up. His eyes warming with recognition, he smiled.

''Mr. Trepal,'' Susan said, ''I'm Special Agent Susan Goreck, Polk County Sheriff's Office. We're here to serve this court order on you to obtain handwriting samples.''

George's smile didn't fade, not for an instant. He picked up the pen and began to write: *''Exposure to ultrasonics makes a person irritable . . .''* Over and over, he wrote the words. His face remained blank, his feelings hidden. Looking down, though, Susan could see that his hand was quivering.

You can try to hide it, she thought. But it's there.

George finished the writing sample and handed over the pages with another smile. He pressed his fingers into an ink pad and then onto clean paper, yielding the fingerprints the judge had also ordered. As Susan gathered her things and turned to leave, George cheerfully called out, ''Bye!''

Susan had never seen anything like it. Most criminals explode when they discover they've been duped by an undercover cop. ''You lied to me,'' they say. ''Cops can't lie.'' But George didn't act like those other criminals; he treated Susan's visit like a social call, as if they were meeting for the first time and he wanted to make a good impression. Walking out of the jail, Susan turned to Ernie and said, ''How could he do that?''

Ernie laughed and lit a smoke. ''I sure as hell don't know,'' he said.

Then again, Susan reflected, George had never fitted the normal patterns. Why should he start now?

After Peggy Carr died, her children grieved in different ways. Allen, her older son, ran from his sorrow, jumping on his motorcycle and watching the speedometer climb: 80,

90, 120 miles per hour—so fast that a tiny patch of sand could easily have spun his motorcycle out of control and hurled his body into a tree or the path of an oncoming truck. The police wrote ticket after ticket, but Allen didn't pay them. The state suspended his driver's license, but that didn't stop him. Allen just kept on speeding. He just didn't care. Finally a judge got fed up and sentenced him to thirty-two days in the Polk County Jail.

This was in the summer of 1990, as the lawyers on both sides were preparing for George Trepal's murder trial. Allen knew about George's arrest, but for some reason he didn't think about where the authorities were holding the man accused of poisoning his family. If he had, he might not have been so surprised.

Allen passed the days in a cell with a handful of other prisoners. One day he heard a commotion. Gripping the bars, he peered through to see the correction officers leading handcuffed prisoners into a holding cell just across the hall, maybe ten feet away. Most of the guys were laughing it up, happy to be out of their cages, even if it was only for a quick trip to a holding cell and then to a court appearance.

One prisoner did not smile. A man with pale skin and a patchy beard, he sat against the wall with his legs crossed in the lotus position, penciling notes on a pad of paper. It was the glasses that triggered Allen's memory; they were thick and perched at the end of the man's nose. He stared at the silent prisoner, feeling a prickle of recognition and then the fire of anger. He called to one of his cell mates, a tall, skinny guy named Stretch. Allen said, "Come here for a second."

Allen pointed to the man scribbling notes. "I know that man," Allen said. "Get his attention. Ask him if his name is George."

Stretch didn't ask for any further explanation. "Hey!" he yelled.

The bespectacled prisoner looked up for a moment, his

face impassive, then back down at his notepad. He said nothing. Stretch hollered again, this time to the inmates surrounding George. "Hey, get that guy right there!"

Another inmate tapped Trepal on the shoulder. "I've seen you!" Stretch hollered. "Isn't your name George?"

George gave a slight nod but said nothing. He just looked back down at his notes. Stretch turned to Allen. "That's George," he said. "How do you know him?"

"He killed my mom," Allen said.

Stretch was incredulous. "Really?"

"Yeah," Allen said. "Haven't you seen him on the news? That's George Trepal."

Allen felt like a caged animal. The rage built up inside him, boiling to his face in a surge of blood. He gripped the cold steel separating him from the accused killer. What should he do? What *could* he do?

"Damn," Stretch said. "We're getting him."

"How?" Allen said. "I can't get to him."

Stretch called over a correction officer. Sometimes the officers would let inmates fight a little, he said, to break the monotony. Stretch asked him, "Can my boy get in that cell over there?"

"Why?" the officer asked.

"Because he wants to go see his lawyer."

No way, the officer said. He could see trouble coming, and he didn't want any part of it. But Stretch had another idea for Allen.

"Douche him!" Stretch said.

"Do *what*?" Allen said.

"Pee in a cup and throw it on him."

As George continued to ponder his notepad, Stretch signaled for the inmates around him to clear out. Meanwhile, Allen emerged from behind a curtain with a cupful of urine. He held it in his hand as the officers started moving the inmates out of the holding cell. En route to court, each had to walk right past Allen's cell. As George moved by, Allen heaved the piss at him. Golden and warm, the urine splashed against George's lips and washed through his beard, splashing onto the floor drop by humiliating drop.

The officers rushed over. Before they could whisk George away, though, Allen looked his former neighbor in the eye. George looked puzzled, as if he couldn't quite place his assailant. Through clenched teeth Allen whispered, "You know who I am!"

On September 8, 1990, George's wife visited the jail and submitted to the pat-down search required of all visitors. The idea was to make sure they weren't sneaking in knives, files, or anything else that would help prisoners break out. It was an unpleasant exercise for all concerned but a necessary one. Five months after George's arrest Diana knew the drill.

Nancy Chovan, a twenty-nine-year-old correction officer, began searching Diana at 7:15 A.M. "Let me see what's in your mouth," she began. After seeing nothing inside, Chovan followed the usual procedure, running the sides of her hands lightly down Diana's body to check for hidden items. The search included Diana's breasts, an ideal hiding place for small weapons.

Diana remained silent throughout the search, but the tension was building. As Chovan finished her work, Diana exploded.

"What's the matter with you?" Diana said, glaring at the woman officer. "Are you gay?"

Shocked by the outburst, Chovan hesitated for a second. "No!" she said.

"Well," Diana spit back, "how would you like it if somebody squeezed your titties?"

Another visitor, Jane Ann Johnson, had just been searched and was standing nearby when the angry words began. She looked over to see Diana shove the officer against a wall and grab her breasts. She heard Chovan cry in pain and tell Diana, "This is my job. I have to do this."

Collecting herself, Chovan told Diana that she would

have to leave the visitation area. Diana refused, saying she was going to visit George. She started walking toward the visitation gate.

"No, ma'am," Chovan said. "You need to leave the area now."

"I'm gonna go see my husband," Diana insisted.

"Okay," Chovan said. "Then you're gonna have to talk to my supervisor. We'll see what he says."

The supervisor arrived and told Diana that her actions constituted a crime. After she cooled off, Diana apologized and promised it would not happen again. Nevertheless, the same day Diana complained about the incident to lawyer Dabney L. Conner, who was Jonathan Stidham's law partner and a member of George's defense team. Conner addressed a letter to Sheriff Crow:

Dr. Carr's husband has been incarcerated at the Polk County Jail Annex for approximately five months. She has visited him every Saturday and many Sundays during this period. Dr. Carr has stated to me on prior occasions that she thought the searches of her body by a certain female guard (the one described below) were "too friendly." She drafted a letter to the Sheriff's Office concerning this but the letter was never sent.

Today a male guard (substituting for the regular guard), while examining a book Dr. Carr had brought for her husband, arrogantly stated something to the effect that "I make the rules. My word is law. I have on a green suit—I can say whatever I want." This guard then proceeded to make derogatory comments about the book (a book on chess).

The situation then deteriorated. Dr. Carr states that, a few minutes later, when her body was being searched by a female guard named Chauvon [sic], Ms. Chauvon squeezed Dr. Carr on the breast. Dr. Carr, who was offended by the squeeze, asked Ms.

Chauvon if she was gay. Ms. Chauvon laughed at Dr. Carr and Dr. Carr then squeezed Ms. Chauvon back on the breast.

Ms. Chauvon then summoned her supervisor who talked with Dr. Carr and her and eventually the matter calmed down. In the meantime, several female visitors in the area became incensed with Dr. Carr because a disturbance had been created and threatened to harm Dr. Carr when everyone returned to the parking lot. These threats were never carried out.

Dr. Carr is extremely upset about the searches of her body going beyond the point of reasonableness . . . May I please have your assurances that Dr. Carr will be treated with respect when she once again visits her husband at the jail annex this coming Saturday.

Conner had the letter hand-delivered three days after the confrontation. The sheriff replied the same day, in a terse letter informing Diana that she would not be allowed to visit the jail until further notice. Three weeks later Diana was charged with battery of a law enforcement officer, a third-degree felony.

Aguero got a letter from an inmate at the jail, Edwin S. Zarr. Zarr wrote to say that he had gotten to know George from playing chess with him and that George had talked a lot about what happened to his neighbors. Around the same time Detective Ernie Mincey got repeated phone calls from Zarr, who said he "had something important to discuss."

Ernie and Susan visited Zarr at the jail. He told them that George had complained about Peggy Carr and her family, blaming them not only for playing loud music but also for hosting loud parties, breaking windows, and throwing garbage all over the yard. Zarr said George told him "he could not communicate with the neighbors and felt they should

move out, not him. He tried every way he could to get them
to move out."

According to Zarr, George said the neighbors were poisoned "by putting a poison used to clean metal in Coke."
Zarr said he asked George "in a kidding way" who had
done it. George replied that police conducted a fifteen
month investigation before arresting him. George told Zarr
the police had no good evidence and that "he has this case
won."

While he and George generally got along, Zarr told the
investigators that he got on George's nerves one day. Zarr
had borrowed a dictionary from George, then returned it
with the cover folded back. That enraged George. Zarr recalled George's telling him that "people like me should be
put to death."

As George's trial date approached, the prosecution and defense teams fought to keep much of their opponents' best
ammunition out of the courtroom.

The skirmishing involved complex legal issues, but the
debate boiled down to this: George's lawyers wanted to
keep the jury from hearing about events from his life that
would discredit him but had no direct bearing on whether
he poisoned Peggy and her family. Aguero wanted to block
the defense team from raising issues that would discredit
the police and undermine their case against George.

With Judge Maloney presiding over the debate, each side
won some and lost some. In a major strategic victory, Trepal's lawyers succeeded in blocking testimony about many
chapters from George's past, including:

- The secret rooms he had built in the Alturas and
  Sebring houses and "all references to bondage and
  torture, masochism or sexual deviation."
- Most of David Warren's recollections about
  George's taking illegal drugs, giving drug-laced
  cookies to a stranger, pumping noxious fumes into

a neighbor's home, coating noodles with amphetamines, and painting hallucinogenic drugs on doorknobs.

- Many of the things George said to "Sherry" during the undercover investigation, including his saying that she could send her husband a "postcard bomb" or blackmail him, that she could sell drugs to make money, that he could help her change her identity and disappear, that he would like her to buy him some LSD, and that he enjoyed learning systems so he could abuse them. While all those exchanges shed light on George's character, Florida legal rules barred them from court because they did not directly address the issue of whether he had poisoned Peggy and her family.

The judge also ruled out:

- Allegations that George had abused his wife, poisoned her dog with Valium, forced her to flee from his temper, and stomped on the family Christmas tree.
- The mysterious death of Pye Carr's dog, which police suspected, but were unable to prove, came from thallium poisoning.
- Suspicions that George was a peeping Tom who had watched Peggy's house through binoculars and made obscene phone calls.
- A Mensa member's recollection that George had suggested using poison to get rid of an annoying cat.
- Insights gleaned from FBI behavioral scientist Bill Hagmaier. Although Hagmaier's profile had been chillingly accurate and his guidance had played a key role in helping Susan capture George, the judge ruled that such techniques were not scientific enough to bring before a jury.

- Testimony about the words "Help, We Are Being Killed," which police had found written on a bathroom shelf in the Sebring house. George's lawyers argued that the words were probably written before he and Diana moved in.
- George's interpretation of Buddhism.

An outsider might think that the judge had gutted the prosecution's case, but Aguero was not worried. He still had plenty of weapons to bring to court. Judge Maloney sided with Aguero in allowing him to:

- Show jurors a photograph of Peggy Carr's corpse.
- Tell them about how Trepal had spoken ill of Pye and his family and threatened to hurt the teenage boys.
- Introduce evidence of Trepal's previous drug conviction and how he might have used thallium to manufacture methamphetamines.

Finally, Aguero persuaded the judge to keep the trial in Polk County despite the defense's complaints about heavy press coverage jeopardizing a fair trial. At one point Trepal's lawyers asked the Florida Supreme Court to remove Maloney as judge, complaining that he had prejudiced himself by observing in a pretrial hearing that the evidence of George's guilt was "almost overwhelming." The court refused, concluding that Maloney would give Trepal a fair trial.

"Okay," Judge Maloney said at the final pretrial hearing. "We start at nine o'clock in Courtroom Number One downstairs."

Chapter
TWENTY-EIGHT

Allen arrived at the courthouse early, to make sure he got a good seat. There was already a crowd waiting outside, eager to witness opening arguments in the trial of a man accused of poisoning an entire family. Although he was a member of that family, Allen looked like any of the other citizens. He had dressed in blue jeans and a turtleneck sweater, nothing flashy. He didn't want to draw attention to himself. This was, after all, the moment he had been waiting for: a chance to be in the same room with George Trepal, without steel bars to keep them apart.

He walked through the lobby tiled with Italian marble, past bailiffs in polyester jackets, through the metal detector designed to catch anyone trying to sneak a gun or knife into court. The machine didn't make a sound as Allen walked through, but that didn't mean he had come unarmed. A black belt in kung fu, he needed only his hands to kill a man. For months he had been replaying the same scene in his head: As George looks over to see his victims, Allen dives over the rail, grabs him under the chin, and crushes George's windpipe. Before anyone can help, George has drawn his last breath.

Allen walked into the courtroom and familiarized himself with its layout: a cavernous ceiling supported by redwood-size columns; carpet the color of dried blood; the bailiffs stationed around the room, feet planted wide and hands folded together. His eyes traveled to the front of the room, where the defense and prosecution lawyers were spreading their notes across long tables, working under a light cast in the shape of the cross. Allen took a seat on the left side of the room, four rows back from where George would sit.

Spectators lined the courtroom's honey-colored benches and filled the room with anxious chatter. Then silence fell. Allen looked around to see two bailiffs leading George into the room. His hands were uncuffed, and he carried a pad and pencil. He sat down with his lawyers and leaned toward them to whisper something.

This is it, Allen thought. But he sat frozen, as Ernie Mincey's voice echoed in his head. Allen had told the detective about his dream of killing George, and Ernie had warned him to resist the urge, no matter how strong. Otherwise, Ernie told Allen, he would end up just like George. He would just take George's place in prison, and it would do nothing to bring Peggy back, Ernie said. "Let the system do what it's supposed to do."

So there Allen sat, quietly shaking. Cissy, who was sitting next to her brother, pressed her hand against his arm and whispered, "Don't look at him!"

"He isn't afraid to look at us," Allen said, nodding toward George. The defendant had turned around to look in their direction, his lips spreading into a tiny smile.

The jury, twelve citizens selected by the defense and prosecution from an initial pool of eighty-five Polk County residents, filed into the courtroom. The panel, four women and eight men, represented a variety of occupations: agriculture inspector, postal clerk, teacher, retired engineer, former clothing salesman, cosmetologist, electronics technician, physical therapist, mechanic, communications specialist, computer map maker, retired security officer, according to the Tampa *Tribune*. They had little in common, except a promise to consider the evidence with care and deliver an impartial judgment.

If the jury was the audience to the drama about to unfold in Courtroom 1, prosecutor John Aguero thought of himself as the director. He wanted the jurors to see him as the man who set the stage, directed the action, led them to the truth. For weeks Aguero had been crafting his opening lines. He had awakened in the middle of the night with sentences burning in his brain and had committed them to scraps of paper that now lay on the podium in front of him. When Judge Maloney nodded, Aguero pushed the podium over to the jury box, barely six feet away, and shoved his finger through the air at George Trepal. His voice filled the courtroom.

"This is a story about a man, Mr. George Trepal," Aguero said, "a man who thought himself so intelligent that he could commit first-degree murder and get away with it."

Aguero recounted the basic facts of the case: Peggy and Pye had married and moved their families together in a house on the Alturas hillside. The teenagers liked to play their truck radios loud, and the neighbors—George Trepal and Diana Carr—did not like it. One day in late October 1988 Diana angrily confronted Peggy about the racket. "The next day," Aguero recalled, "Mrs. Carr is complaining about chest pains."

Peggy was hospitalized, and doctors discovered that she had been poisoned by a rare chemical, thallium. After her son Duane and stepson, Travis, also fell critically ill, Aguero said, police traced the thallium to an eight-pack of Coke. "The FBI lab people will tell you that each of those bottles contained a potentially lethal dose of thallium. A half gram to a gram of thallium, sufficient to kill a one-hundred-fifty pound man. You will hear that Peggy Carr at the time of her death weighed approximately one hundred five pounds."

The police didn't have an easy time finding Peggy Carr's

killer, Aguero told the jury. The family had gotten a death threat months before the poisoning, but nobody knew who sent it. The killer had selected a poison that would not alter the taste or appearance of Coke and had planted it so carefully that investigators found no fingerprints or obvious signs of tampering. This was no amateur job, an angry relative trying to settle a fight with a spoonful of drain cleaner, Aguero suggested. This was the work of a serious criminal.

Police had investigated a variety of suspects, Aguero told the jury, but it wasn't until nearly two months after Peggy got sick that they interviewed her closest neighbor, George Trepal. The detectives immediately became suspicious, and an undercover agent was assigned to befriend George and build the case against him. It was this officer who had searched George's home and found the key evidence: a tiny bottle containing thallium powder. Another search, this one of George's new home, turned up other interesting items, including a "poisoning guide" assembled by George and *The Pale Horse*, an Agatha Christie mystery about thallium poisonings.

Aguero concluded, "When the evidence is presented to you, I'm sure that you will be convinced, convinced as you must be, convinced beyond a reasonable doubt that Mr. Trepal is the person who did poison that Coca-Cola."

Jonathan Stidham would not be defending George alone. The defense team also included Jonathan's sixty-one-year-old father, Wofford, and another veteran lawyer, Dabney Conner. All three were reared in Polk County, and each would play a unique role.

Jonathan Stidham referred to his father as "my old daddy," and the elder Stidham did his best to play the role of the courtly southern lawyer. Jonathan Stidham, by contrast, would play a more aggressive role. The thirty-one-year-old, who had joined his father's firm after graduating from law school, would cross-examine the prosecution's most damaging witnesses. Rounding out the team was Conner, a fifty-three-year-old with a chemistry background who would handle the technical issues.

Wofford Stidham had questioned prospective jurors in the weeklong selection process before trial, and it fell to his son to deliver the opening arguments.

"Good morning, ladies and gentlemen," Jonathan Stidham said, walking toward the jury box. "My old daddy has been talking to you for a few days, and now it's my turn." He said the police were wrong to think they had solved their case by focusing on George Trepal. The investigators would have done better, he suggested, to remain focused on an early suspect in the crime, Pye Carr.

Stidham said the trouble began after Pye married Peggy and they tried to merge two groups of teenage children. "The children were infighting all the time," he said. "Peggy's kids felt that Pye wasn't treating them fairly. Pye's kids felt that Peggy didn't treat them fairly. They thought it was a double standard. And as their marriage, which only lasted a short time, progressed, it also began to erode."

He asked the jurors to recall the week before Peggy fell ill. "Pye Carr was on vacation. He took the whole week off. On Thursday he left to go hunting, and he was gone until Sunday." The strangest thing happened while Pye was gone, Stidham said: Peggy became terribly ill. "Cissy came home on Sunday afternoon and begged her father, 'Please, Pye, take Mom to the hospital. Take her to the doctor.' He said, 'No, no, no. My sister is coming over. She will be okay.' " Finally Pye relented and took Peggy to the hospital, but there was nothing the doctors could do.

Health officials searched Pye's shed and found a Jack Daniel's bottle containing some sort of pesticide. But officials couldn't tell you what the pesticide was, Stidham said. "They never had it tested." When the officials asked Pye for permission to search the apartment behind the main house, Stidham said, Pye replied, " 'No, you can't go into the garage apartment because I don't have a key.' " When authorities did get inside the apartment, Stidham continued, they found a trace of thallium under a sink.

In the beginning, George's lawyer said, at least one investigator had taken Pye seriously as a suspect. "Detective Paul Schaill came on the case. His time on the case was limited to just a few weeks, but it was extremely thorough," Stidham said. "He uncovered some really super-interesting information. . . . Pye and Peggy's marriage had been, just before the poisoning, on the verge of a breakup."

Some of the troubles were predictable, the product of tensions between the kids. But that wasn't the only thing bothering Peggy, Stidham said. "She also, however, suspected that Pye had been cheating on her."

Before the case was a month old, Schaill was removed from the case and Ernie Mincey was running things, Stidham told the jury. Then authorities discovered the thallium had come from Coke bottles. Officials quickly concluded that the bottles had not been poisoned en route to a store in or near Alturas, Stidham said, without thoroughly investigating that possibility. "They couldn't tell which warehouse they had been sent to, they couldn't tell which stores they had been sent to, and they never have been able to tell us that."

While the detective was quick to cross Pye and the bottling company off the list of suspects, the younger Stidham said, he was eager to blame a man whose greatest crime may have been his eccentricity. On December 22, 1988, Ernie interviewed George Trepal. During the interview, Stidham said, George did some odd things: He carried a board inside the house, and he made some clucking sounds with his mouth. "Detective Mincey is going to tell you that on that date, when none of these other leads had been followed up, even with the place under the sink, with all the problems Pye was having with his wife and everything else . . . on that day, because George Trepal acted 'odd and irrational,' he became the prime suspect. And from that day on, they investigated no one else."

As the investigation went undercover, Stidham recalled, things began looking bad for George. He had organized murder mystery weekends. A bottle of thallium was found in his trash-filled shed. But even after arresting him, Stidham said, the authorities had trouble cementing the case against him. They tried to link George and the thallium bottle but found no fingerprints. They tried to prove George had purchased the poison but found no receipts. They seized stamps and envelopes and typewriters in hopes of linking him to the threatening note but found no connection. "All of the physical evidence that would have tied him to this case, they didn't find," Stidham said. "And never have."

Still, Stidham said, the police and prosecutor pressed on. But in the end, he concluded, they weren't the ones who would determine whether or not George was truly guilty. That power rested in the hands of a group of impartial citizens responsible for separating solid fact from flimsy suspicion. "One explanation does exist," he said, "and it should comfort you. Mr. Trepal didn't do it."

The next morning, when John Aguero walked outside his house to pick up the newspaper, he looked carefully up and down the street. He had prosecuted suspected killers before, but never one who frightened him as much as George Trepal. He seemed so cool, so calculating, so utterly free of conscience. Who was to say he couldn't arrange to have someone gun down the prosecutor or sneak some poison into his family's food? Aguero told his wife, "If you see anything in this house that you don't remember buying, throw it away."

Aguero had other things to worry about. The jurors had heard two very different stories in the previous day's opening arguments. This morning they would start hearing the evidence they would use to decide which version of events was credible. The prosecution would present its case first, and then Trepal's lawyers would have a chance to cross-examine Aguero's witnesses. Later the defense would have a chance to present evidence and testimony of its own. George himself might even take the stand.

Aguero's first witness, Rita Tacker, had worked with Peggy and become her close friend. If she had the chance, he knew, Rita would also become a star witness for the defense. Peggy had confided in her about the troubles with Pye, and Rita was convinced that Pye had killed her. Aguero didn't want to get into Rita's suspicions; he wanted to use her testimony for the narrow purpose of introducing jurors to Peggy and telling them how she had fallen ill. Still, he worried that Stidham would give Rita a chance to hammer Pye during cross-examination.

Before the morning's proceedings began, the jurors were sent from the courtroom, and the lawyers gathered at Judge Maloney's bench to debate how far Stidham would be allowed to take Rita's testimony. According to the rules of court, cross-examination was supposed to be limited to issues raised during the prosecutor's questioning; if Stidham wanted to raise other issues, Aguero thought, he should have to wait until the defense put on its case.

Jonathan Stidham asked the judge for leeway, saying Rita could tell jurors that shortly before the poisoning, Peggy had said "she was leaving Pye for good." Stidham said that Rita could detail Peggy's reasons: "He doesn't treat the children fairly, he works late hours, he's got a girlfriend, and he's drinking too much." Rita had told all this to the police, Stidham said, but investigators hadn't followed up. "The sufficiency of their investigation is absolutely relevant," he said. "It's crucial to the defense."

There was a big problem with what Stidham wanted to do, Aguero told the judge. Having one witness tell a jury what another person said would violate the rule against hearsay. Since Peggy Carr wasn't there to challenge Rita if she told a lie, that testimony might mislead jurors. Aguero argued, "You don't get to introduce something that a dead person said simply because you think it will help your defense.''

Maloney sided with the prosecutor. As Rita prepared to take the stand, the judge told Stidham, ''She may not be asked any questions regarding 'What did Peggy Carr say to you?' ''

Aguero went first, keeping his questions to a bare minimum. After Rita had identified a picture of Peggy and Pye in happier times for the jury, Aguero said, ''That's the only questions I have.''

Stidham stood up and walked toward Rita. ''Miss Tacker, you and Peggy had been friends for some time, is that correct?''

''Yes.''

''And were you familiar with her personal life as well?''

''Yes, I was.''

''Did the time ever come—close to the time that she became ill—that she came and stayed with you for a few days?''

''Yes, she did.''

''Why did she come and stay with you?''

''Because her and Pye were having marital problems.''

Aguero couldn't stand it any longer. ''Judge,'' he said, leaping to his feet, ''I object!''

Maloney stopped the questioning and sent jurors from the room. As soon as they were gone, Aguero protested that Stidham was trying to sneak in forbidden questions and to make it seem that the prosecution was avoiding damaging disclosures about Pye. Aguero pointed at Stidham, protesting, ''He knew the question was going to be objectionable, and he asked it anyway.''

Stidham, well aware that defying the judge could cripple his case, backed off. ''I apologize if I stepped out of bounds,'' he said. ''It was not intentional.''

In Aguero's opening remarks he had told jurors they would be hearing a ''story.'' As he began calling witnesses, it became clear that he was going to start from the beginning. First Peggy's restaurant friends told how she had fallen ill that weekend in October 1988. There was nothing to challenge in this recitation of events, so the defense table stayed mostly silent. That changed when Aguero began summoning Peggy's family.

Peggy's younger son, Duane, raised his right hand and swore to tell the truth. For the first time jurors saw for themselves the human cost of George's alleged crime. Here was a young man, a boy really, who had lost his mother and months of his own life to a poisoned Coke. His body was still withered from the thallium, and his voice came out in a whisper.

"Tell the jury the first thing that you can now recall," Aguero said.

"My feet started to hurt real bad," Duane said. "It was an incredible pain." All around him his family was getting sick, too. His stepbrother, Travis, lay in a bed beside him. And worst of all, his mother was nearly paralyzed.

Aguero suggested that it would have been easy for someone—especially a neighbor—to sneak an eight-pack of poisoned Cokes into the house. The week before the poisoning, he recalled, Duane and his brother had left the house unoccupied while they went out to buy paint. "Did you and Travis always lock the door every time you left, Duane?"

"No, sir."

Wofford Stidham rose to cross-examine Duane. The elder Stidham spoke softly, but he quickly showed that he, like his son, was here to put Pye on trial. "Did you ever observe any arguments between your mother and Pye Carr?"

"Objection!" Aguero thundered.

"Sustained," said the judge.

Stidham dropped the questioning but not before succeeding in planting a question in the jury box. *What is this about Peggy and Pye fighting, and why doesn't the prosecutor want us to hear it?*

*   *   *

Travis Carr, now eighteen, walked slowly to the stand. He was just a shadow of the carefree, robust boy who used to drink beers with his buddies and hurtle across the basketball court. The lingering effects of the poison showed mostly in Travis's face, which looked gaunt, even haunted.

"How long did you stay in the hospital, Travis?" Aguero asked.

"About six months," Travis said.

"When you first went into the hospital, could you walk?"

"Yeah," Travis said. But after that first week or so he became paralyzed, and it took months of therapy to regain his mobility. The damage wasn't just physical; Aguero knew that the thallium had also attacked Travis's mind, stripping away much of his memory.

"Were you conscious?" he asked Travis. "Did you wake up every day but you just couldn't talk?"

Travis looked up apologetically. "I can't remember too much about that time."

Wofford Stidham wasn't interested in Travis's medical condition. He wanted to use the youth to make jurors wonder if the police had tried to cover up important evidence.

"Shortly before you became ill, do you recall purchasing an eight-pack of Coca-Colas?" Stidham asked.

Yes, Travis said. He had bought some Cokes "a couple of days" before his family started getting ill.

That's what Stidham wanted to hear. He knew that if a family member had bought the Cokes, it would be harder to link George to the poisoned bottles. Instead of simply buying the Cokes, poisoning them, and planting them in the house, George would have had to steal them from the house and then put them back—a much trickier job.

"Did anybody ever try to convince you that you didn't purchase those Cokes?" Stidham asked.

"Well," Travis said, "yeah."

"Who tried to convince you that you didn't purchase those Cokes?"

"I don't really remember."

"They were police officers, weren't they?"

"Yes, sir."

Before the trial began, George had walked into the courtroom dressed in an orange jail suit. Judge Maloney ordered his lawyers to get him a less jarring outfit, and George reappeared in a brown blazer, a tie, and slacks. As the witnesses testified, he listened closely, scribbling notes on a pad and occasionally showing a small, puzzled smile. In the afternoon of that first day he looked up to see a big man with a crew cut walking toward the witness stand.

Pye Carr had heard the accusations, whispered in his hometown, now asserted boldly in court. It was his turn to help clear his name and put away his wife's true killer. Aguero began asking questions designed to portray Pye as the loving head of a tragic family. He also wanted Pye to come across as something of a "redneck," a man who lacked the sophistication to select a rare poison and put it in bottles without leaving any clues.

Pye himself had ingested some of the thallium, but he said that he ignored the pain in his feet while tending to his wife, son, and stepson. "I didn't really have any time to check my condition," he said. "I was too worried about my family."

Aguero dealt head-on with the suggestion that Pye had stopped authorities from going into the garage apartment where a trace of thallium was later found. "Did you ever prohibit any person, health official, environmental protection agency, police—anybody—from going in or around that house to take samples?"

"No, sir," Pye said. "I did not." (Later in the trial the health inspector who had found the trace of thallium confirmed Pye's statement.)

"Do you know how that thallium got in those bottles, Mr. Carr?" Aguero asked.

"No, I do not."

When Aguero finished, Judge Maloney turned to the jury. "Ladies and gentlemen," he said, "before we begin cross-examination, I need to speak with the attorneys. This should take me less than five minutes. If you would step into the jury room, please."

After the last juror had left the courtroom, Maloney turned to Wofford Stidham. "You want to talk about the marital difficulties?"

"Yes, Your Honor."

"I'm going to allow you to ask the question about the separation," Maloney said. " 'Were you and your wife having trouble?' 'Yes.' 'Did you separate?' 'Yes.' " But, Maloney said, nothing more than that. "I don't want any details about the separation."

Stidham wanted more. He told the judge, "I would also like to ask him questions about his former girlfriend."

"Tell me why," Maloney said.

"Because, Your Honor, the prosecution has painted a very nice picture of a very concerned and caring husband," Stidham said. "That was just not true."

As these men, these strangers, negotiated over the most intimate details of his life, Pye sat quietly in the witness chair. Meanwhile, the reporters scribbled in their notebooks, and the entire courtroom audience listened. Stidham gave the judge a preview of the questions he wanted to ask Pye.

"I would ask him if he told Laura Ervin that he had made a mistake by marrying Peggy, and that he wanted Miss Ervin back."

The judge turned to Pye and asked, "What would your answer to that be, sir?"

"My answer would be no," Pye said.

Maloney turned back to Stidham. "Do you have any evidence to the contrary?"

When Stidham acknowledged that he did not, Maloney said, "I'm not going to allow you to ask that question."

With the jurors back in their seats, Stidham began his cross-examination. After the earlier fire breathing, the questions proved surprisingly tame. Stidham did challenge Pye once. "You said you had never heard of thallium," he said. "Didn't you tell police where you could buy thallium?"

"Yes, I did," Pye said.

"You found out where you—"

"No," Pye said. "Let me correct that. I didn't tell them where you could buy it. I gave them listings." He explained that he had grown so frustrated by the lack of information from police that he asked a colleague to dig up a list of thallium suppliers from the mine's library. It was that list that he turned over to the detective.

That was it. Stidham announced that he had no further questions. Peggy Carr's widower—the man the defense had suggested was the true villain—strode out of the courtroom. In a conference with the lawyers afterward Judge Maloney remarked that the defense had failed to take the opportunity it had sought: to ask Pye about his troubles with Peggy.

"I thought you said we couldn't go into it," Jonathan Stidham said.

Maloney replied, "I said that you could."

That night, January 16, 1991, war broke out in the Persian Gulf. The next morning Judge Maloney asked the jurors to stay focused. "In view of what happened last night, I know it is going to be difficult to pay absolute attention to what goes on in this courtroom, but I'm going to ask you to do that." Referring to the American soldiers fighting half a world away, he said, "They have a duty, and you have a duty."

"Mr. Aguero," Maloney said, turning to the prosecutor, "are you ready?"

"Yes, sir."

Aguero called a series of witnesses to fill out his portrait of Pye as a caring man who would never poison his own wife and children. Dr. John Miller, one of the first physicians to examine Peggy, described how Pye tenderly carried his wife in. "She was literally draped in his arms," Miller recalled.

The most poignant defense of Pye came from a surprising source, Peggy's sister. Dressed in black slacks and a black sweater, Shirley walked into the cavernous courtroom. She was nervous but tried to keep her composure. She looked at the judge, at the jury, at Aguero. Finally she gazed to her left and saw, for the first time, the man accused of taking her sister's life. George didn't blink; he just sat there and stared, as if she weren't there. He acts like he doesn't have a care in the world, Shirley thought, like it didn't bother him to take Peggy's life.

Aguero asked her to recall the day Peggy went into a coma. "Did you ever see Pye Carr that day?" Aguero asked. Once again the prosecutor knew he was taking a risk; Shirley had made no secret of her dislike for Pye.

"Yes, sir, I did," Shirley said. "I was in there when he came into the room. He walked over to her, and he was rubbing her cheek, and tears started running down his face."

Now it was Jonathan Stidham's turn to object. "Relevance, Your Honor."

Maloney sustained the objection, but the damage was done. Court was about to adjourn for the weekend, and Aguero had given the jury a powerful image to take home with them: a husband standing beside his new wife, grief-stricken and powerless to bring her back.

Looking back on the first days of the trial, Aguero saw that he had spent more time defending Pye than prosecuting George. On one level that frustrated him. But on another, he was relieved; he would have been in "a hell of a lot worse situation" if the defense team tried to pin the murder on George's wife. Aguero was certain he could clear Pye's

name. Diana, on the other hand, was a much better suspect:
She was a doctor who might have access to thallium, had
reason to hate the neighbors, and possessed the chemistry
skills to do them in. There wasn't enough evidence to
charge her, but there was more than enough to raise a reasonable doubt about her husband's culpability.

As the trial moved into its second week, Aguero knew
he needed to dispense with the issue of Pye and get on with
the case against George. He summoned Ernie to the stand.
The detective recalled investigating Pye but dismissing him
after coming across George. Ernie told jurors how nervous
George seemed as he answered routine questions and how
George echoed the death threat when asked why he thought
someone wanted to poison Peggy and her kin.

"To get them to move," he'd said. "Like they did."

Having established why the police first suspected
George, Aguero decided to dispense with the defense's suggestion that authorities had pushed Travis Carr to lie about
buying the tainted Cokes.

"Did Travis Carr tell you that he bought the Coca-
Colas?" Aguero asked.

"Yes, he told me that he bought them," Ernie said.
"And he also told me he didn't buy them. I could never
get a consistent response."

"Did you ever find out who bought the Cokes, Detective?"

"I did not."

When cross-examination began the next morning, Jonathan
Stidham wasted no time in attacking Ernie's investigation
of Pye Carr. He suggested that the detective ignored evidence that Pye had taken out two hundred thousand dollars
in life insurance on Peggy, Travis, and Duane. He also in-
timated that Ernie had overlooked Pye's contact with an
old girl friend. The picture Stidham tried to create was
clear: Pye as a man who had wanted to kill his family,
pocket the insurance, and run off with another woman.

Ernie flatly rejected Stidham's argument. He said that a thorough search found no proof of any insurance policies. He explained that Pye's "girlfriend" was actually a former fiancée, and Pye had made no plans to run off with her.

"I did not find, after interviews with family members, people who knew Peggy and Pye Carr, them to be any different from most people's problems," Ernie said. By the time of the poisoning, he said, those tensions had been worked out. "As a matter of fact, all the interviews and reports I received were that they were a loving couple again and getting along extremely well."

Aguero had done a good job dismantling the defense's attack on Pye. But one question lingered: Why was there a trace of thallium in the apartment behind his house? Had Pye poisoned the Cokes there, unwittingly spilling some thallium in the sink and planting the rest in George's garage?

Aguero summoned George Coppenger, the chemist in charge of the state lab that identified thallium in the Cokes and the apartment. Because it takes only a tiny amount of thallium to kill someone, Coppenger said his lab measured the concentrations in parts per million. Each empty Coke bottle contained anywhere from 25 to 185 parts per million thallium, he said. By contrast, the lab only found 16 parts per *billion* under Pye's sink. In other words, there was at least a thousand times more thallium in the empty Coke bottles than under the sink.

Another witness, FBI chemist Donald G. Havekost, testified later that more sophisticated testing found no evidence of thallium under the sink. Considering the small amount found the first time, he said, it could have simply been a false reading.

Even if the tests had confirmed a trace amount, the chemist said, it would have been insignificant. Havekost reminded the jurors that thallium is an element that occurs in nature. "Sixteen parts per billion?" he said. "You can find that in some tap water."

Chapter
TWENTY-NINE

Like the other witnesses, Susan was barred from sitting inside the courtroom while the others testified. But she kept busy, working at a table outside the courtroom doors, making sure all the prosecution's witnesses appeared when they were supposed to. Finally, as the trial moved through its second week, it was her turn to take the stand.

The night before, Susan had stayed up late writing out basic facts—her job title, length of employment, daily duties—that she knew would be part of the questioning. She was so nervous that she was afraid she would stumble over something so simple that jurors would doubt the rest of her testimony. She walked gingerly into the courtroom, fearing that her trembling knees would fail her. Sitting in the witness chair, Susan knew that George was right in front of her, but she didn't look at him. She focused on Aguero and the jurors.

"Tell the court your name, please, ma'am," Aguero said.

"Susan Goreck."

"How are you employed?"

"With the Polk County Sheriff's Office."

After five minutes Susan felt better. She had made it through the first questions without incident. Her voice was strong, her mind clear. She stole a glance at George and was amazed at what she saw. He was sitting there, listening to her with great interest, as if she were unfolding an intriguing murder mystery story. He was staring at her, but his eyes held no anger.

Susan recalled going undercover at the Mensa Murder Mystery weekend staged by George and Diana shortly after Peggy Carr's death. There were some striking parallels between the weekend's make-believe murders and the real one next door, she told the jury. For one, the murder weapon was poison. For another, the victims received threatening notes, something that Susan knew was uncommon in real-life homicides.

"Detective," Aguero said, "I want to show you a document that's been marked for identification as State's Exhibit Number One Hundred Eighty-one and ask you if you recognize what that document is."

"Yes, I do," Susan said. She identified it as a manual written by George for the weekend, entitled "Voodoo for Fun and Profit."

Aguero handed the manual to Susan. "Now, detective, would you read for the jury the portion of the document which you felt had some significance to this case?"

Wofford Stidham rose to his feet. "Your Honor," he protested, "I object to self-serving speculation."

"I overrule the objection," said Maloney.

Susan began reading George's words. "Few voodooists believe they can be killed by psychic means but not one doubts that he can be poisoned. When a death threat appears on the doorstep prudent people throw out all their food and watch what they eat. Hardly anyone dies from magic. Most items on the doorstep are just a neighbor's way of saying, 'I don't like you. Move or else!' "

George had been silent throughout the trial, sitting beside his lawyers with that strange smile on his face. But as Susan read his words, the smile faded.

Susan described the way she had tricked George by turning herself into a character named Sherry. After she had expressed an interest in buying George's house, Susan recalled, he gave her a full tour but failed to mention that his only neighbors had been poisoned. "He said the last crime took place about nine years ago," she told the jurors. "A break-in."

She recalled how George fitted the profile of a poisoner, fleeing from direct conflicts while quietly plotting revenge against "Sherry's" estranged husband. She told the jury about George's showing her the poison berries and the picnic to which she brought a selection of soft drinks for George to choose.

"What did he select?" Aguero asked.

"Coca-Cola," Susan said. "On every occasion that we ate out or ordered something to drink, he always drank Coca-Cola."

All those episodes shed light on George's personality, but Aguero knew that he needed something more to carry jurors beyond a reasonable doubt. He asked Susan to recall the night that she had "moved into" George's home to search for poison.

Susan recalled rummaging through closets, swabbing drainpipes, even digging through a rat's nest of trash inside a drawer in George's workshop. It was in that drawer, she recalled, that FBI agent Brad Brekke had found a small bottle with a red cap and some sort of powder inside. Lab tests showed the powder to be thallium nitrate.

As expected, Susan's testimony was long and damning. When it came time for George's lawyers to challenge it, Wofford Stidham quickly ran out of questions.

Stidham argued that Susan had tricked George into letting her rent the house, rendering the search illegal. The problem was, the defense had made that argument to a judge before the trial and lost. And it was not the kind of complaint that wins over a citizen jury; most people would dismiss it as a "technicality." Even if a juror was inclined to agree with Stidham's legal point, it didn't change the fact that George had the poison stashed in his garage.

The lawyer did better when he tried to put a different

spin on George's poison berry lesson. "The time that you stopped on the road and Mr. Trepal showed you some red berries that he said were poisonous," Stidham said. "He expressed concern for the children in the area at that time, didn't he?"

"Yes," Susan said. George had said that the berries could make children sick. For Stidham, it was an important point: George could have been speaking from worry, rather than a killer's fascination.

And what about that thallium bottle, Stidham said, the evidence used to tie George to this horrible crime? "Were there any fingerprints on the bottle?"

"There were no fingerprints," Susan replied.

Aguero told Susan she could step down; he planned to recall her later, to fill in elements of the story he was unfolding. The prosecutor then called a rapid-fire series of technical witnesses. Industry experts pointed out that thallium nitrate is rare and hard to come by. Although thallium occurs in nature, a scientist explained, Peggy Carr had twenty thousand times the normal level in her system.

As the weekend neared, Aguero had one last mission.

"At this time," he said, "the state would offer into evidence the item marked for identification as State's Exhibit Number Forty-eight."

George's lawyers had been dreading this moment. Exhibit No. 48, they knew, was the autopsy photo of Peggy Carr. Jonathan Stidham asked for a bench conference, and the lawyers huddled near Judge Maloney, talking in low tones.

"The picture is awful," Stidham said. "We will stipulate to that. The jury doesn't have to be put through looking at this, and it's inflammatory. The whole purpose is to send them home for the weekend thinking of this."

"I overrule the objection," Maloney said.

Aguero handed the color eight-by-ten to the first juror. On the trial's first day the jurors had seen a picture of Peggy in happy times, smiling in the sunlight with her new hus-

band. This picture showed the tragic end of Peggy's life:
She had become just another corpse on an autopsy table,
bathed in cold light, a few strands of hair left on the pale
skin of her head, her eyes forever closed. Aguero watched
the first juror stare at the picture, then pass it on. There
were no gasps or cries, as Aguero often heard when the
autopsy picture showed a bullet hole or the jagged tear of
a knife. But he could see that the picture was doing its job.
A hard silence settled on the courtroom.

Aguero said, "No more questions."

Under Florida law, Aguero had to show George's lawyers
every piece of his evidence before the trial began, to allow
them to map out a defense. During that pretrial process,
called discovery, George's lawyers had learned about David
Warren and Richard Broughton. They knew that Warren,
George's friend from his drug days, was a man who could
testify about George's selling some drugs and using others
to poison people he did not like. And they knew about
Broughton, the federal drug agent who had shut down
George's illicit lab.

The defense team wanted Judge Maloney to block most,
if not all, of Warren's testimony. They cited a rule of the
Florida evidence code that strictly limits prosecutors' ability
to introduce evidence of other crimes. The rule says that
evidence can be used to establish "motive, opportunity,
intent, preparation, plan, knowledge, identity or absence of
mistake or accident" in the crime at issue. But it cannot be
used "to prove bad character or propensity" to commit a
crime.

In a bench conference Aguero made his intentions clear.
He wanted the witnesses to make two points: that George
had a history of using poison on his enemies rather than
directly confronting them. Furthermore, Aguero said, DEA
Agent Broughton would explain that George didn't have
just the inclination to poison but also the tools. The type
of thallium used to kill Peggy can be used as an ingredient

in illegal crank labs, such as the one George had run.

In the end Maloney handed each side a partial victory. He sided with the defense and forbade David Warren's testimony about George's using chemicals as weapons. But he sided with Aguero in clearing the way for jurors to hear about George's 1970s drug enterprise.

Broughton, a broad-shouldered man with graying hair and a Carolina accent, testified that he had been a federal drug agent for two decades. He said he remembered very well a group of criminals producing illegal drugs during the 1970s.

"Are you familiar with the role which Mr. Trepal played in that group?" Aguero asked.

"He was the chemist and mastermind of it," Broughton said.

"Are you familiar, Agent Broughton, with whether thallium is used in the production of methamphetamine?"

Yes, Broughton said. Thallium can be an ingredient and a by-product of that process. Under questioning by Jonathan Stidham, he acknowledged that Trepal also could have made the drugs without thallium.

"Thallium is not required," Stidham said. "Correct?"

"That's correct," Broughton said.

The next morning the news reporters made sure they got to court in time. This was the day George Trepal's wife was scheduled to testify, and they were expecting fireworks. Diana did not disappoint.

When Diana walked through the metal detectors, she saw Susan just a few feet away, sitting at her table outside the courtroom. Diana marched toward her, shouting, "I hope you know just what a bitch you are!"

Susan leaped up, planting her left foot and holding an arm up in a defensive posture. Tom Spate, the prosecutor's investigator, grabbed her arm. "Sit down, Susan," he said. "I'll take care of this."

After Diana had cooled off, Aguero told Maloney about

the confrontation. "Judge," he said, "I don't want to turn this into a circus act." He asked the judge to instruct Diana to hold her temper. Richard McKinley, Diana's lawyer, stood by. Maloney flashed the lawyers a look of disgust and told them to settle it among themselves. "I'd like for you all to go and speak with the doctor, and I'd like you to let me know just as soon as you're ready to go."

Aguero and McKinley took Diana to the balcony overlooking the courthouse lobby, where Aguero asked her to cooperate. "I'm going to ask you very limited questions," he said, "and I just want short, direct answers. I know you don't like this, but you don't have any choice. Why don't we just go get it done?"

Diana agreed. Once she took the stand, however, it was clear she was still burning.

"Ms. Carr," Aguero said, "do you know an individual named George Trepal?"

"Excuse me," Diana snapped. "It's *Doctor* Carr."

"Dr. Carr," Aguero said. "Was there an occasion in which you got into an argument with Peggy with regard to some music being played?"

"I think argument is too strong a word for it," Diana replied. "Yes, I did have a discussion with her about some loud music."

"What was her reaction to your request?"

"Well, she said she didn't have to. But she did actually ask them to turn it down."

"Was Mr. Trepal home that day?"

"I believe he had gotten home shortly before I did."

Because Aguero could not ask Diana to incriminate her husband, he moved on. He said, "At any time when you lived either in the Alturas home or in the Sebring home, did you yourself have any thallium?"

"No," Diana said.

"Are you familiar, ma'am, with a book entitled *The Pale Horse*?"

"Yes, I am."

"Have you ever read that book?"

"Yes, I have."

"Did you own that book at the time Mr. Trepal was arrested?"

"I believe so."

Aguero didn't push any further. Diana was in court this day against her will; he had issued a subpoena to force her there. Her testimony could help him, but it also carried a risk. Because she was testifying against her will, she enjoyed a measure of immunity; Aguero could not use any of her answers against her in the future—even if she had incriminated herself.

The prosecutor had a nagging fear that Diana would stand up, tell the jury she had poisoned Peggy Carr, and leave them no choice but to acquit her husband. Then Aguero would be stuck with one acquitted defendant and a confession he could not use against another.

Jonathan Stidham walked toward the witness. For reasons that became clear only in the trial's final hours, he began asking Diana questions not about George but about herself.

"Dr. Carr, you've told us that you were a doctor," he said. "Would you give us briefly what your educational background and your degrees are?"

Diana explained that in addition to her medical school training, she had earned three other degrees: a bachelor's in chemistry, a master's in chemistry, and a master's in clinical pathology.

"You mentioned earlier that you read murder mysteries, is that correct?"

"Since I was about eight years old, yes."

"How many murder mystery books would you say that you have in your house?"

"Several thousand."

"As far as you know, does Mr. Trepal read murder mysteries?"

"No," Diana said. "He mostly reads science fiction."

Stidham stopped his questioning to make a request. He asked the judge to send the jury from the courtroom for what lawyers call a proffer. He wanted to put some testimony on the record that the judge had earlier forbidden. That way, if George was convicted, his lawyers could ask an appeals court to decide if the jury should have heard it. Maloney agreed.

"Dr. Carr," Stidham said, "I believe that you testified that you were the one who wrote the plots to the murder mystery weekends. Is that correct?"

"That's correct," Diana said.

At that point Diana's lawyer stood up. For the record, McKinley said that his client would expect immunity from prosecution for any answers she gave to Stidham's questions.

"No, sir," Aguero said, rising to his feet. "No, sir!" He said that Diana enjoyed immunity only as long as she was answering questions under the prosecutor's subpoena. If she volunteered new information to the defense, he said, he could use it against her. "She answered all the state's questions," Aguero said. "The state is the only agency that can confer immunity."

In other words, *be careful what you say, Dr. Carr, because I'm listening.* Diana must have gotten the message because she didn't say another word. Now it was Stidham's turn to protest.

"The defense strenuously objects to Mr. Aguero's intimidating the witness by taking away their immunity," he griped. "It's blackmail!"

With the jury's gaze firmly fixed on George Trepal, Aguero called a series of witnesses to talk about his clashes with the family next door. Ronnie Chester, Cissy's ex-husband, recalled the day George had come over to demand that he turn down the radio. "He acted like he was upset. He was shaking," Chester said. "So I turned the radio down. And it wasn't like two minutes later he was standing behind me

again asking me to turn it down.'' Alan C. Adams, who
had done some remodeling and lawn care work for George
and Diana, recalled hearing George shout obscenities at the
neighbor kids. ''One time I recall, he said, 'I will get
them,' '' Adams testified. ''And one other time he got
highly upset when they rode some motorcycles through the
yard and said, 'I'm going to kill you.' ''

George watched the parade of witnesses impassively, the
agitation he had shown during Susan's testimony lost under
a mask of cool detachment. But when the prosecutor called
Patricia Boatwright to the stand, his eyes lit with recognition. A fellow Mensa member, Boatwright had become
good friends with George. She recalled a day when George
had stopped by his wife's office while the poisoning was
topping the headlines.

''We were all agog, saying 'Gee, tell us all about it,' ''
she recalled.

''Okay,'' Aguero said. ''What was Mr. Trepal's response
to that?''

''For the first time that I remember, George didn't meet
my eyes,'' she said. ''The subject was then dropped.''

''Did you have occasion to see Mr. Trepal after that?''

''Yes.''

''Did you ever discuss or did he ever discuss with you
this poisoning?''

''Not really. It always just fell like a thud, and the subject
was changed.''

Peggy Carr's daughter didn't expect much from the trial.
Cissy realized that a conviction would do nothing to remove the pain of her mother's death. But she hoped the
trial would help her understand a crime that seemed so random, so senseless. She had so many questions: What made
George angry enough to kill? How did he poison the bottles
and sneak them inside? How did Susan capture him? As
the trial went on, she hoped, she would finally hear the
truth—''the whole truth.''

What Cissy didn't understand was that courts don't try to help victims learn the facts. In fact, to ensure a fair trial, judges do just the opposite. Like other witnesses, Cissy and her family were barred from entering the courtroom while other people testified. The idea was to keep one witness from influencing—even unintentionally—another's recollection of events. It was an important legal rule, but it only added to the victims' feeling that they had been forgotten. Cissy and her aunt Shirley went to Aguero and asked if, once they had finished testifying, they could sit in.

He agreed. As the trial moved through its third week, the prosecutor knew he would not be calling any more family members. He asked the judge if they could come into the courtroom, but George's lawyers objected. They said they wanted to reserve the right to summon family members during the defense portion of the trial.

Aguero scoffed at that argument, saying he doubted the defense was serious about calling the family. "They have never been contacted by the defense about any possibility that they would testify," he told the judge. "I think they're just being punished for being family members."

Maloney listened to Aguero's argument but sided with the defense. For Cissy and the other victims, the courtroom doors would remain locked.

Susan Goreck took the stand again, this time to recall the day when two business cards stunned the normally talkative George into a guilty silence. As the jurors listened, she recalled the winter day when she asked George to meet her at McDonald's. "I wanted to tell him," she explained, "that I had found out that some of the neighbors were poisoned in Alturas."

Susan had arrived at the meeting with a microphone hidden in her purse and a video camera rolling inside a nearby car. Aguero plugged in the tape and let the jurors see for themselves. George appeared on the screen, greeting his friend "Sherry" and sitting down across from her.

"How's your world going?" George asked.

"Well, not real good. That's why I need to talk to you," the undercover agent replied. "I . . . think you neglected to tell me something."

George's voice came out of the television and drifted across the courtroom, sounding airy and unconcerned. "Oh, what's that?"

"That something had happened in the neighborhood."

"Oh, yeah," George replied. "Somebody got poisoned next door. . . . "

The jury saw George's nonchalance fade when his friend handed him the business cards of Detective Mincey and FBI Special Agent Brekke. For the first time George struggled for words.

"I hope I'm not a prime suspect," the jurors heard him say. "That could be messy."

Chapter
THIRTY

On February 4 Aguero rested his case. Now George's lawyers would have a chance to make their best argument for their client's innocence. They could now call Rita Tacker to describe the trouble between Peggy and Pye. They could call Mensa members to criticize police for misconstruing their suspect's intelligence and eccentricity. They could call George himself to say that while he disliked his neighbors, he would never, *ever* plot to murder them.

Instead the lawyers did nothing.

"The defense rests," said Wofford Stidham.

George's lawyers gave themselves at least one advantage in not putting on a case of their own: They got to have the first and last word in closing arguments. Wofford Stidham stood, walked toward the jury, and gently argued for his client's life. The case against George Trepal was like a puzzle, he said, a jumble of circumstances that must fit neatly together to prove guilt.

"I submit to you that a lot of the pieces of the puzzle are missing," Stidham said. "And a lot of them don't fit."

The first missing piece, the lawyer said, was the answer to the question of who had purchased the Cokes. "There is not one tiny smidgen of evidence presented to you about George Trepal buying these Coca-Colas to put thallium in,'' he said. He urged them to dismiss Susan Goreck's testimony about Coke being George's favorite drink. "That's really incriminating, isn't it?" he said. "It's laughable. Half the world drinks Coca-Cola."

He suggested the jurors would do better to cast a suspicious eye toward Pye Carr. After all, he said, Pye and Peggy had been having marital problems. Pye had been in touch with an old girlfriend. And he owned the apartment where officials found a trace of thallium.

"Why was that thallium underneath the sink in the Pye Carr apartment?" he said, his voice echoing through the courtroom. "Surely I don't think that you would believe it was put there by a man from outer space," he said. "It was there."

And what of the case against his client? Stidham argued that the police had felt obliged to identify someone, *anyone*, as the killer. He suggested that Detective Ernie Mincey, for one, had bowed to pressure from Coca-Cola, a company so eager to avoid a public relations disaster that it flew him across the country in its corporate jet. "Taking a trip to Washington on a corporate jet that costs hundreds, if not thousands of dollars an hour to keep airborne instead of going on a two-hundred-and-fifty-dollar ticket. That's pretty heady stuff for somebody like Detective Mincey," Stidham said. "I'm not saying he's bad in any way. I'm just saying . . . that created a problem of sorts, an obligation. A public official wants to satisfy those people who have been so nice to him. And that obligation puts pressure on someone like Detective Mincey and his colleagues to find a culprit."

In trying to establish the culprit as George Trepal, his lawyer contended, police used the flimsiest evidence. They did not produce solid proof that George had sent the death threat, purchased thallium, or sneaked the poisoned Cokes into the neighbors' home. And while several weeks passed between the crime and his emergence as a suspect, George did not take his chance to dispose of the items now introduced as evidence, including the poisoning guide and the tainted Coke bottles.

"One must wonder why a perfect crime genius would leave those Coca-Cola bottles sitting in an unoccupied house for twenty days," Stidham said.

Stidham tried to diminish the importance of George's having written a voodoo manual with a passage that mirrored the death threat sent to Peggy's house. In fact, he said, George might have gotten the idea from the thallium poisoning that had occurred next door. "It was not so remarkable that Mr. Trepal wrote this pamphlet."

He scoffed at the prosecution's trying to hold George's knowledge of chemistry against him. "The main thrust of this big cloud of suspicion the state has tried to cast over Mr. Trepal is that he had a chemistry background and he had a bunch of chemistry books in his house. From this they want you to conclude virtually he's the only person who could have committed this crime," Stidham said. Recalling earlier testimony on technical elements of the case, he said, "Virtually every chemist that was called to this stand had heard of thallium. And they should have, because thallium is an element. It's one of the basic structures of things."

Stidham asked the jury not to make too much of the bottle of thallium found inside George's garage workshop. "The garage, we know from the testimony, was unlocked all the time that Dr. Carr and Mr. Trepal lived there, and it was unlocked when they left," he said. "The possibility is very real that somebody else could have planted the bottle there.

"The state wants you to speculate that the bottle belonged to Mr. Trepal," Stidham concluded. "The state has created this great cloud of suspicion. I'm sure it's going to be argued that this couldn't be a coincidence, who else could have done it? The fact is, we don't take away people's freedom, their life, because of suspicion and innuendo."

*   *   *

Aguero had expected the defense to attack the circumstantial nature of his case. As he rose to his feet, he knew he must show that this was not coincidence: It was evidence, damning evidence.

Walking to the jury box, Aguero pointed to George. He invited the jurors to behold "very likely the most dangerous, diabolical man you will ever come face-to-face with in your entire life. Very dangerous. That's what the evidence showed."

He reminded jurors that George was on trial not just for murdering one person but for trying to exterminate an entire family: mother, father, teenagers, even Kacy, "a child only two years of age who would have had to have ingested very little out of one of those Coca-Cola bottles to die."

"Mr. Trepal didn't bother," Aguero said. "He just put the Coke in the house and whoever died, died. But he intended to kill them all."

Recalling the defense argument that police had not identified George's fingerprints on the poisoned Cokes, Aguero reminded jurors that police hadn't identified *anyone's* fingerprints on the bottles. "Somebody wiped them clean," he said. "Mr. Trepal's prints are not on anything, because he was trying to outsmart the police—and he was trying very hard."

And what about all those "coincidences"? His voice sarcastic, Aguero began stacking them up: Peggy and her family got sick right after a fight with George's wife. George was the only neighbor in a position to watch the house and see when it was empty. He was a chemist who had a bottle of thallium in his garage. And when Susan confronted him for the first time with the fact of police suspicion, the normally talkative George fell into stunned silence.

Aguero reminded the jurors of the McDonald's videotape. "This is a coincidence that boggles the mind," he said. "The defendant tells Inspector Goreck that if he is being sought by the police, it must have to do with the poisonings—and that he must be the 'prime suspect.'

"If somebody told you that the police were looking for you," Aguero continued, "is the first thing that comes to your mind, 'I must be a prime suspect in a murder'? Why didn't Mr. Trepal just figure that, 'Well, if the police are looking for me, bring them on. Give them my number. They can call me up. Give me that and I will call them right now from this fast-food restaurant and find out what the heck they want.' Did he do any of these things? This man has a bizarre sense of what he imagines must be going on with the police. Why? Because he is the only one that knows he's guilty."

Aguero veered away from George for a moment, to confront any lingering questions about Pye Carr. "The defense seemed to be trying to tell you that Pye Carr killed his family," he said. "Ludicrous!" He ticked off the reasons why: Pye knew little about thallium, he took his family to the hospital and stayed by their side day and night, he himself accidentally drank some of the poisoned Coke, and finally police found no evidence that he had taken out any rumored insurance policies.

"So where are we?" Aguero said. "It's somebody that knows where this family is on a regular basis." Somebody who happened to have thallium nitrate in his garage. Who preferred Coke, while Peggy Carr had always drunk Pepsi. Who had experience running an illegal drug lab. Who had boxes full of dangerous chemicals and sophisticated chemistry equipment. Whose wife was a doctor and could tell him that routine hospital tests wouldn't reveal the presence of thallium.

Aguero chuckled at the suggestion that George would have sneaked back inside Pye's house after the poisoning to remove the remaining bottles of Coke. "The defense says, 'Well, if Mr. Trepal could have got in there the first time, he could have got in there again,'" Aguero said. "Well, there's a big difference between the first time and going in again, and that is that the health department, the agriculture department, the FDA, the Environmental Protection Agency, and Polk County sheriff's department, and the FBI are all looking at that house. Now it ain't so easy to go next door.''

If jurors needed any more to convince them, Aguero suggested, they need only look at the poisoning guide George had carefully compiled—a guide that included detailed information on thallium poisoning.

''Just a coincidence that Mr. Trepal had this guide in his house?'' Aguero said, picking up the book. ''Maybe it is. Then again, maybe Mr. Trepal had been planning the perfect murder for quite some time. Maybe he was practicing when he was at Mensa murder weekends, when he was doing his research. And just maybe the Pye Carr family gave him a reason to give it a shot—and he did.''

Aguero asked the jurors to consider one final ''coincidence'': the fact that George, a highly intelligent man who had studied police procedure and orchestrated murder mystery parties, showed *absolutely no interest* in discussing the real-life mystery unfolding right outside his door.

''Right next door he's got the most complex murder case in this area, ever,'' Aguero said. ''And what happens? He doesn't ever talk about it, ever. Isn't that bizarre? This man who wants to solve these things doesn't care?'' Aguero recalled the testimony of George's Mensa friend Pat Boatwright. ''Now Pat Boatwright comes in here and says, 'Well, not only that, not only did he not talk about it, I was his confidante. I was the person who he confided in, who he talked to. I was his friend. And the minute I asked him the question, he averted his eyes and he never looked me in the eye again for months.' Why?''

These are not coincidences, Aguero told the jurors; these are facts. ''Ladies and gentlemen, that man poisoned the Pye Carr family, and I ask you to find him guilty.''

Since they would not be testifying after all, Peggy's family and friends had been allowed into the courtroom for closing arguments. They sat near the front, in full view of the jurors. Cissy saw their eyes turn to her when Aguero reminded them that her daughter, Kacy, was one of the people poisoned. As Aguero took apart the ''coincidence'' defense, Cissy silently cheered him on. ''Wow, he's great!'' she whispered to her new husband, Gary Shiver. ''If I was a juror, I'd convict him.''

But the trial wasn't over yet. Wofford Stidham had one last chance to make his case. He used it to drop a bombshell.

''There's another point I want to raise,'' he said solemnly. ''I don't want to raise it, but I have to. I'm sure some of you thought about it during the trial, and there were some allusions to support it during the testimony. There's just as much evidence, just as much reason to suspect Dr. Diana Carr as there is George Trepal.''

The courtroom fell silent except for the rapid scratch of pens on reporters' notepads. So George's lawyers were going to trot this argument out after all, Aguero thought, and at the end of the trial, when he would have no chance to counter it. Sitting on a bench nearby, Susan shook her head. She wondered: Had George approved of this tactic?

Stidham went on. ''I'm not suggesting that there is enough evidence to establish that Dr. Carr put the thallium in the Coca-Colas. I'm not suggesting that she did it, because I don't know. But I'm suggesting there are just as many reasons: Dr. Carr testified that she has two degrees in chemistry. Having two degrees in chemistry, she, too, would know about thallium. As counsel pointed out during his argument, being a medical doctor, she would know that thallium was not part of a routine screen for heavy metals.

''She was an avid reader of murder mysteries. She testified she had a thousand or two thousand murder mystery books at her house. She was the author of the mysteries that were presented to the Mensa members to be solved,'' Stidham said. ''She's the one who wrote the four mysteries for the weekend Ms. Goreck attended, all of which involved poisoning. Living in the house with George Trepal, she obviously had access to his books. Thallium is used in certain medical procedures, thallium stress tests, and some medical instruments around hospitals.'' (What Stidham did not mention here was that police found none of Diana's fingerprints on George's poisoning manual and that her orthopedic practice did not involve the use of thallium.)

Stidham reminded the jurors that Diana had access to the workshop where the bottle of thallium was discovered. ''How can you say that it belongs to him?'' he asked. ''It could have just as easily belonged to her.'' There was one other thing, he said. ''Who was it that had the only confrontation with the Pye Carr family that's been described by some of the witnesses as being somewhat violent? I'm talking about screaming, hollering, cussing, and pushing,'' Stidham concluded. ''That was Dr. Carr, not George Trepal.''

The twelve jurors began their deliberations at 10:10 A.M. on February 5, 1991. A month earlier they had pledged to listen carefully to the lawyers' arguments, to weigh the testimony of dozens of witnesses, to reserve judgment until they had considered all the evidence. Now it was time to make their choice.

At 11:50 A.M. the jury returned to the courtroom. They didn't yet have a verdict; they wanted to watch the videotape of the McDonald's meeting one last time. When the tape ended, they filed back to the jury room and closed the door.

At 4:25 P.M. the door opened.

Cissy was sitting in the courthouse lobby anxiously passing the time with Gary, her aunt Shirley, uncle Johnny, and uncle Raymond. Allen was standing nearby, talking in sign language to some deaf people he had met. Duane wasn't there; he didn't want to be. Tom Spate, the investigator in Aguero's office, walked out to the couch where the family had gathered. He said, ''The jurors are back.''

Cissy looked at her husband, and Gary gave her hand a squeeze. In the courtroom Cissy settled into her seat and looked at one of the jurors, a petite young blond woman. Cissy saw the sorrow in her eyes. The juror looked from Cissy to George and then at her own hands, folded in her lap. They found him innocent, Cissy thought. Remembering the judge's admonition not to show emotion when the verdict came back, Cissy stared down and began to cry softly.

Susan Goreck was sitting on another bench not far away. Some of her colleagues from the sheriff's office sat behind her, patting her on the back and offering words of encouragement. A reporter from the Lakeland *Ledger* sat beside her. Susan smiled politely but said little. For more than a year she had been working toward this moment, putting her life on hold and at risk. And yet it wasn't until this moment that she had reflected on the potential consequences. What if they find him not guilty? she thought. What would George do to me, to my family? She remembered Hagmaier's insight. "George doesn't get mad," the FBI murderer profiler said. "He gets even."

George sat beside his lawyers in jacket and tie, his left arm resting on the defense table. His beard had gone mostly gray over the past months, and the smile had vanished from his face. The light glinted off his glasses as the jury foreman handed the verdict over. Judge Maloney read the document out loud.

"State of Florida, Plaintiff, versus George J. Trepal, Defendant. We, the jury, find the defendant, George J. Trepal, guilty of first degree murder.

"We, the jury . . ." Maloney went on, reciting each of the counts against George: one count of first-degree murder, six counts of attempted first-degree murder, seven counts of poisoning food or water with intent to kill or injure, one count of tampering with a consumer product. Fifteen counts in all, and fifteen times the word rang out like a hammer on cold steel, *Guilty. Guilty. Guilty . . .*

Susan felt someone squeeze her arm. It was the reporter

Suzie Schottelkotte. She was saying, "Susan, you can breathe now."

As Susan smiled for the first time, George's lawyers slumped in disappointment. Susan, Ernie, and Aguero grinned, shaking one another's hands and accepting the congratulations of their colleagues. Sitting with her family, Cissy had the strangest reaction. She didn't feel like doing any of those things the judge had warned against: hollering or clapping or jumping up and down. She looked at George Trepal, the man who had murdered her mother, and felt not triumph but pity. A man that intelligent, he could have done something worthwhile with his life, Cissy thought. And now he's probably going to the electric chair.

Cissy felt Gary grab her hand. She realized she was crying again, about to burst with a riot of conflicting feelings. Suddenly she just wanted to be somewhere else, anywhere but in that courtroom. God, she thought, I can't wait to get outside.

As she was walking out, Cissy took one more look at George. As she saw him walking across the room flanked by bailiffs, the pity she had felt a moment earlier disappeared. George was smiling. She whispered, "How can I feel sorry for you?"

Cissy walked through the big doors and into a crush of cameras, lights, and questions. The balconies overlooking the lobby were packed with lawyers, courthouse workers, members of the curious public. As she walked out into the soft light of late afternoon, she heard people cheering and clapping. A television reporter thrust a microphone at her.

"What do you think about the verdict?" someone asked.

Cissy said, "I'm just glad it's over."

EPILOGUE

___

When you become fairly liberated, you become aware of your old karma coming back to you. Yes, you do suffer, but you understand the process and don't resent it. Don't suffer melodramatically.

—George Trepal,
Writing in a journal

George's new home has three concrete walls, a skinny mattress, and a stainless steel toilet and sink. The doors are made of cold roll steel, five eighths of an inch thick; for George they will probably never open again. He lives on Florida's death row.

On March 6, 1991, following the jury's recommendation, Judge Maloney sentenced George Trepal to die. Two years later the Florida Supreme Court rejected what will most likely be the first of a series of appeals by George and his legal representatives. The appellate process is long and highly technical, an important exercise conducted by lawyers and judges who work in air-conditioned offices far from George's cell at the Union Correctional Institution.

As they deliberate, George waits. Union Correctional was Florida's original state prison, a complex of beige buildings squatting in the pine scrub and hard sun of northern Florida. A mile-long border of fence and razor wire rims the prison, bolstered by eight towers, where guards keep watch with shotguns and high-powered rifles. To reach this perimeter, an escaping prisoner would have to get past thick concrete walls, door after locked door, and dozens of television cameras monitored around the clock.

Union Correctional is no rehab unit for men who made a mistake and are headed back toward productive lives; it is a place whose sole mission is to keep some of Florida's most dangerous criminals locked away. The bulk of Union's inmates have a chilling history of violence, both outside prison and inside. "Most people at UCI get here having worn out their welcome somewhere else," said the superintendent, Dennis O'Neill.

George and his three hundred neighbors on death row live in rows of beige cages, each six-by-nine-foot cell with bare walls, a small black-and-white TV, and a mattress unfolded on a steel platform. They follow a numbing routine: wake before dawn for breakfast shoved through the bars, breathe air thick with sweat, watch *Jeopardy!* or the soaps on the black-and-white TV, yell out chess moves to a neighbor, write a letter, read a book, try to get some sleep—and wait for the day when the man takes a $125 funeral suit off the rack.

As of late 1994, George's wife had not visited him in prison, but an old Mensa friend had. One spring day Stewart Prince drove a Yamaha scooter to a Polk County restaurant to talk about George. Prince arrived wearing an off-white jacket with a Mensa patch, his brown hair tangled by the wind, his blue-gray eyes framed by thick glasses. He ordered a cup of hot tea and spoke in a voice that was soft but certain. To Prince there was no question; George was wrongly accused.

Prince said George and he have a lot in common: Both are "quiet and shy," happiest when working on computers, writing articles for small publications, or socializing with their high-IQ friends. He vividly recalls the Sunday when the newspaper on his doorstep carried the picture of George being taken into jail in handcuffs. "Boy, George really knows somebody in the newspaper that's willing to make a fake page for him," Prince said that morning. "This is really going to great lengths for George for a practical joke."

It was no joke. Prince said the police mistook George's eccentricity and intelligence for a guilty conscience. "I think this is what got George in trouble," Prince said. "You know, he's a vital, freethinking person. And the bureaucratic mind sees things he's published and written, and 'Uh-oh, he's psychotic.' " In truth, Prince said, George is a gentle man who would stop at the mall and buy oatmeal cookies for his wife, who never turned away a stray cat, and who used chemicals only to develop photographs, identify minerals, and clean the big fish tank he kept on the porch.

When Prince goes to visit George in prison, he brings some cash for the canteen. He said that George likes egg rolls, potato chips, and chocolate milk. Besides the occasional visit, George only gets out of his cell twice a week for exercise, and he has to wear handcuffs to walk to the shower.

George did not respond to requests seeking his comment for this book, nor did the three lawyers who represented him at trial. But Prince said George did ask him to pass along some alternate theories about who might be the true culprit in the murder of Peggy Carr. One theory is that an irrational patient or another doctor was trying to do in George's wife, Diana Carr. This person obtained thallium, poisoned the Cokes, and planted them in the wrong Carr household, according to the theory.

One hot September day prison officials unlocked the doors and allowed a brief tour of death row. As a visitor walked through, the condemned men did their best to pass the time, reading under the hard light of a fluorescent panel, smoking in the darkness, or watching TV, their faces lit by a dull blue glow. Because there is no air conditioning, many had stripped to boxer shorts in the heat. Most appeared sullen, bored, or simply numb.

George, by contrast, seemed the picture of contentment. In his cell at the far end of a row, he could be seen tucking a bed sheet under his mattress. He had arranged piles of papers—most likely letters and legal correspondence—in neat, symmetrical stacks. When a guard delivered a bundle of mail and the day's newspaper, George smiled and called out a smart ''Thank you, sir!''

Bill Hagmaier at the FBI had predicted that George would be a model prisoner, and he was right. It makes sense, really: Although it takes away his freedom of movement, prison gives George almost everything else he needs for a life of pure thought. He has a clean and well-lit room, plenty of time to read, and somebody who takes care of paying the bills and cooking the meals. Florida's death row offers another important feature: The inmates are forbidden to play their radios or TVs out loud. Instead they have to listen through individual headsets. The result is George's idea of heaven—constant quiet.

Diana Carr also declined to discuss the case. After her husband entered the Florida prison system, Diana still had to deal with the charges that she had roughed up a correction officer inside the Polk County Jail. On August 23, 1991, she pleaded no contest to a reduced charge of assault on a law enforcement officer, a misdemeanor. The judge withheld a formal adjudication of guilt and placed her on six months' probation. She returned to her medical practice in Sebring.

George's father went ahead with his plans to move to Florida, moving into the apartment George had prepared behind the Sebring home.

In George's first years of imprisonment, Diana wanted little to do with her husband. ''I asked her to go with me,'' the elder Mr. Trepal said. ''She wouldn't go. I think she wrote to him and said that she didn't love him anymore, and she didn't want any part of him." By late 1994, however, relations had warmed. "She's been writing to him and she's been sending him money," George's father reported. "She's taking care of him."

George told his father he had been playing chess with the other inmates and winning. "He looks good. He says, 'Well, you just have to wait it out now, that's all.' " So Mr. Trepal waits, convinced of his son's innocence, making plans for the day when George walks out of prison and father and son rent a house together. In the meantime, Mr. Trepal spends his day doing crossword puzzles, fishing with his pals, and tending to his garden. He reported a healthy crop of tomatoes, although the neighbor kid had just swiped a few.

A few plants sat outside the window of Mr. Trepal's apartment. They were Christmas cacti, which are green and prickly for most of the year, but bloom with lovely flowers during the season of hope and good cheer. A visitor asked if they were part of Mr. Trepal's garden. "No, those are his," he said. "I'm taking care of them for him."

The people who put George in prison have moved on. Brad Brekke left the FBI and became the head of security for a large corporation. Ernie Mincey left the homicide unit and returned to the road as a deputy. John Aguero went on to prosecute other high-profile murders. Bill Hagmaier expanded his duties at the FBI, coaching undercover officers around the world and directing the Child Abduction and Serial Killers Unit. Susan Goreck earned the rank of lieutenant and took over as head of the department's internal affairs division. On her walls hang the awards she won for her work in solving the Alturas murder, and on her bookshelf are some of the files she has kept from her days as Sherry Guin. George is never far from her mind.

Susan is happy to have put George in prison, but her memories cloud with regrets. She has never forgiven herself the time she lost with her family while pursuing George.

And she is still not sure people understand how a part of her—she calls it "Sherry"—came to see a killer as a friend. She has come to terms with that ambivalence, though. If she hadn't opened up to George in at least some genuine way, she knows, he would have gotten wise and fled to freedom.

She still wonders if George was responsible for other murders. Clearly he had experience in picking a chemical that could escape detection even as it slowly poisoned its victim. Had some of his other enemies succumbed to mysterious illnesses over the years? Only George could say—and he's not talking.

George did communicate with Susan once. It was in court, on the day the judge sentenced him to die. During a break in the proceedings George swiveled around, looked at her, and began mouthing some words. This is it, Susan thought. This is what I've been waiting for: the anger. He's trying to tell me, "I'm going to get you." When she couldn't make out precisely what George was saying, she sent a bailiff to ask what he wanted.

The bailiff returned and said, "He was trying to give you a smile, say hello, and tell you to have a nice day."

After George's conviction Susan received some threatening phone calls. Local police and the FBI traced the calls and built a thick file on the people associated with George. They stand ready to move if there are any further signs of trouble.

Although his name had been cleared at the trial, Pye Carr decided he would no longer live in the town where so many people had suspected him. Pye and his son, Travis, moved down the hill and across a busy road, into a house with a swimming pool and an exercise machine that helped Travis regain control of his muscles. Pye, his children, and his sister Carolyn Dixon declined to comment for this book. However, after George was sentenced, Pye told a newspaper reporter: "I think the electric chair is too good for him.

Peggy died a horrible death, and she was too good a person for that.''

With Peggy gone, the glue that had held her new family together cracked and crumbled away. These days Pye's and Peggy's children rarely talk. As Pye and his children move in one direction, Peggy's children move in another.

Cissy married a gentle man named Gary Shiver, and together they are raising a family that includes Kacy, now a schoolgirl, and their son, Ethan, who was born nearly three years after Peggy's death. Sometimes Cissy worries that she will forget her mother's face and the soothing sound of her voice. To summon her memory, Cissy speaks her name. "Mama," she says to the empty room, "I love you."

Allen and Duane remember in their own ways. Allen thinks of his mother when he sees a waitress with dimes and quarters jingling in an apron pocket. Allen is the father of a young boy, Brendon, and works interpreting for deaf schoolchildren.

Duane has had a rougher time. After violating his probation on minor charges of criminal mischief and petty theft, he was sent to jail. One day he sat in the dayroom, where prisoners can use the phone, watch television, and play cards. He took a pen and yellow notepad and began to write:

DEAR MOM:
This is your baby boy. How you been? What are you doing? I hope you're having more fun than I am. I'd like to tell you that I love you and I'm sorry for all the bad things I've ever done to you. Hopefully, you're in a better place now. I often think about you and wish you were here. I haven't been so good, and I know you're not proud of me. I'm sorry. I'll try to get my life straight when I get out.

Duane made good on his promise, winning early release and going to work in the electrical business run by Cissy's husband. With the thallium finally flushed from his body, he's gained weight, feels good, and has made plans to marry his sweetheart, Shannon.

On the third anniversary of Peggy's death, her sister, Shirley, filled a thermos with black coffee, threw a box of brownies on the front seat, and drove through the night to Florida. The next morning she and Peggy's children went to the cemetery. The family walked slowly to the mausoleum where, high on a marble wall, a bronze plaque bore the name PEGGY A. CARR.

The family stood in silence, gazing up and holding one another close. For the first time since Peggy's death, Cissy saw her brother Allen yield to his sorrow and begin to cry. The silence broke when baby Ethan awoke and began to wail. Shirley and Peggy used to promise they would care for each other's kids if anything happened. Shirley put her sorrow aside to gather Ethan into her arms. She will have so much to tell him.